Maritime Issues in the South China Sea

South China Sea (SCS) issues are complex and dynamic, ranging from historic claims to present day military occupation, from military security to regional stability, from rhetorical appeasements to hand-line national interests, from intraregional competition to extraregional involvement. The submissions made in 2009 by several Southeast Asian states to the United Nations Commission on the Limits of the Continental Shelf (CLCS) respecting outer limits of extended continental shelves beyond 200 nautical miles in the South China Sea resulted in renewed attention to the maritime disputes over the insular features and the waters of the South China Sea among several claimant States. Questions have resurfaced about the future of cooperation in the region. Furthermore, the improvement of cross-Strait relations between Taiwan and China after 2008 has added a new element to the evolution of South China Sea issues. This book describes these recent developments in depth and provides an examination of possible future developments in the South China Sea.

All articles but one in this book were originally published as a Special Issue in *Ocean Development & International Law*.

Nien-Tsu Alfred Hu, Director and Professor, The Center for Marine Policy Studies, National Sun Yat-sen University, Taiwan, Republic of China.

Ted L. McDorman, Professor, Faculty of Law, University of Victoria, Canada.

Maritime Issues in the South China Sea

Troubled Waters or A Sea of Opportunity

Edited by
Nien-Tsu Alfred Hu and Ted L. McDorman

LONDON AND NEW YORK

First published 2013
by Routledge
2 Park Square, Milton Park, Abingdon, Oxfordshire OX14 4RN

Simultaneously published in the USA and Canada
by Routledge
711 Third Avenue, New York, NY 10017

First issued in paperback 2014

Routledge is an imprint of the Taylor and Francis Group, an informa business

© 2013 Taylor & Francis

This book is a reproduction of articles from vol. 41, issues 3 and 4 of *Ocean Development & International Law*. The Publisher requests to those authors who may be citing this book to state, also, the bibliographical details of the special issue on which the book was based.

All rights reserved. No part of this book may be reprinted or reproduced or utilised in any form or by any electronic, mechanical, or other means, now known or hereafter invented, including photocopying and recording, or in any information storage or retrieval system, without permission in writing from the publishers.

Trademark notice: Product or corporate names may be trademarks or registered trademarks, and are used only for identification and explanation without intent to infringe.

British Library Cataloguing in Publication Data
A catalogue record for this book is available from the British Library

ISBN 978-0-415-50636-6 (hbk)
ISBN 978-1-138-85044-6 (pbk)

Typeset in Times New Roman
by Taylor & Francis Books

Publisher's Note
The publisher would like to make readers aware that the chapters in this book may be referred to as articles as they are identical to the articles published in the special issue. The publisher accepts responsibility for any inconsistencies that may have arisen in the course of preparing this volume for print.

Contents

	Citation Information	vii
	Co-editor's Preface *Nien-Tsu Alfred Hu and Ted L. McDorman*	ix
1	Introduction: South China Sea: Troubled Waters or a Sea of Opportunity? *Nien-Tsu Alfred Hu*	1
2	Maritime Delimitation in the South China Sea: Potentiality and Challenges *Robert W. Smith*	12
3	A Strategic Perspective on Security and Naval Issues in the South China Sea *Chris Rahman and Martin Tsamenyi*	35
4	The ROC's Maritime Claims and Practices with Special Reference to the South China Sea *Kuan-Hsiung Wang*	54
5	The South China Sea Workshop Process and Taiwan's Participation *Yann-Huei Song*	70
6	Regional Cooperation in Marine Environmental Protection in the South China Sea: A Reflection on New Directions for Marine Conservation *Aldo Chircop*	87
7	Towards Establishing a Spratly Islands International Marine Peace Park: Ecological Importance and Supportive Collaborative Activities with an Emphasis on the Role of Taiwan *John W. McManus, Kwang-Tsao Shao and Szu-Yin Lin*	110
8	Semi-enclosed Troubled Waters: A New Thinking on the Application of the 1982 UNCLOS Article 123 to the South China Sea *Nien-Tsu Alfred Hu*	121
9	Post-2009: An Overview of Recent Developments Concerning the South China Sea *Nien-Tsu Alfred Hu and Ted L. McDorman*	155
	Index	174

Citation Information

The following chapters were originally published in *Ocean Development and International Law*, volume 41, issue 3–4 (July–September and October–December 2010). When citing this material, please use the original page numbering for each article, as follows:

Chapter 1
Introduction: South China Sea: Troubled Waters or a Sea of Opportunity?
Nien-Tsu Alfred Hu
Ocean Development and International Law, volume 41, issue 3 (July 2010)
pp. 203–213

Chapter 2
Maritime Delimitation in the South China Sea: Potentiality and Challenges
Robert W. Smith
Ocean Development and International Law, volume 41, issue 3 (July 2010)
pp. 214–236

Chapter 3
A Strategic Perspective on Security and Naval Issues in the South China Sea
Chris Rahman and Martin Tsamenyi
Ocean Development and International Law, volume 41, issue 4 (October 2010)
pp. 315–333

Chapter 4
The ROC's Maritime Claims and Practices with Special Reference to the South China Sea
Kuan-Hsiung Wang
Ocean Development and International Law, volume 41, issue 3 (July 2010)
pp. 237–252

Chapter 5
The South China Sea Workshop Process and Taiwan's Participation
Yann-Huei Song
Ocean Development and International Law, volume 41, issue 3 (July 2010)
pp. 253–269

CITATION INFORMATION

Chapter 6
Regional Cooperation in Marine Environmental Protection in the South China Sea: A Reflection on New Directions for Marine Conservation
Aldo Chircop
Ocean Development and International Law, volume 41, issue 4 (October 2010)
pp. 334–356

Chapter 7
Toward Establishing a Spratly Islands International Marine Peace Park: Ecological Importance and Supportive Collaborative Activities with an Emphasis on the Role of Taiwan
John W. McManus, Kwang-Tsao Shao, and Szu-Yin Lin
Ocean Development and International Law, volume 41, issue 3 (July 2010)
pp. 270–280

Chapter 8
Semi-enclosed Troubled Waters: A New Thinking on the Application of the 1982 UNCLOS Article 123 to the South China Sea
Nien-Tsu Alfred Hu
Ocean Development and International Law, volume 41, issue 3 (July 2010)
pp. 281–314

Co-editor's Preface

The South China Sea, while referred to differently by different groups, is the South Sea to the Chinese people and in the Chinese language. It is a semi-enclosed sea, as defined in Article 122 of the 1982 United Nations Convention on the Law of the Sea (LOS Convention), which because of its strategic location has become a testing ground for the utility of contemporary international regimes and the eventuality of regional cooperation.

The scattered insular features of islands, islets, reefs, rocks, banks, shoals and submerged reefs along with the long-standing Chinese "U-shaped dotted lines" map and the competing claims made by littoral States have created a difficult situation for maritime zones delimitation. This situation is further complicated by the known and/or potential of rich natural resources, living and non-living, within the area. So tempting are such resources and so intense the "sovereignty" issues that the littoral States of the South China Sea have invested significantly in military and law enforcement forces to support their claims over all or a part of the insular features and surrounding waters in the region.

There are also vital sea lines of communication through the waters of the South China Sea for the movement of goods and fossil fuels to Northeast Asian nations and strategic maneuvering and the deployment of armed forces by extra-regional powers to the region. Some littoral States are aligned with extra-regional powers in order to balance the emerging regional, if not global, reality of the People's Republic of China (PRC).

There is also a changing "cross-strait relationship" between the Republic of China (ROC or Taiwan) and the PRC. On South China Sea issues, the "two Chinas" essentially hold the same position in terms of their common claims over the South Sea. ROC/Taiwan has significant interests in the South China Sea and has occupied and continuously controlled the largest island in the Spratly Islands (Tai-Ping Island, 太平島 in Chinese or Itu Aba Island in English) for more than 60 years.

All the aforementioned issues are reflected in the book's subtitle "Troubled Waters or A Sea of Opportunity," a classic case of the glass half empty/half full perspective.

The genesis of this collection was the International Conference on Issues in the South China Sea (南海問題國際研討會), held in Taipei, Taiwan, 19–20 August 2009, organized by The Center for Marine Policy Studies (CMPS, 海洋政策研究中心) of the National Sun Yat-sen University (國立中山大學) and chaired by one of the co-editors. Selected papers presented at the Conference were published in *Ocean Development & International Law* (*ODIL*) in 2010 as a Special Issue entitled "Issues in the South China Sea" (Vol. 41, Numbers 3 and 4, pp. 203–356), under the guest editorship of one of the co-editors. The publisher of *ODIL*, Routledge, identified the Special Issue as fitting within their "Journal Special Issues as Books" (SPIBS) program to be published in book form to extend the readership for the material.

CO-EDITOR'S PREFACE

A feature of the "Journal Special Issues as Books" program is that the articles from the *ODIL* Special Issue are republished unaltered. To this the co-editors have added this brief preface as well as an epilogue chapter which provides updates of recent legal and political developments and analyses of such developments respecting the South China Sea region.

Each of the co-editors has come to this work following different paths. Both have been involved in academic work respecting South China Sea matters for decades. Both have government experience, albeit for one of the co-editors that experience did not involve Asia in any direct way. And, of most importance, both have worked together on conferences, editing and brainstorming, which for each, has been a career highlight.

We thank the authors of the various chapters for sharing their expertise and insights at the 2009 Conference in Taipei and for their further work in preparing and finalizing their papers for publication in *ODIL*. We also thank the staff of The Center for Marine Policy Studies, especially the Executive Secretary of the CMPS, Ms. Yu-Ling Emma Lin, for their dedication in ensuring a well-organized and enjoyable Conference and for their assistance in the preparation of this book. Rosemary Garton, the editorial assistant for *ODIL*, deserves a special note of thanks for her work on the papers published in *ODIL*.

We hope that this book will contribute to a fuller understanding of the issues at play in the South China Sea region. It is our view that the South China Sea area is one of opportunity and hope that globalization, regionalization and bilateralism, each in different ways, will lead to the situation where the label "dangerous waters" often found on nautical charts comes to refer only to navigational risks.

Prof. Nien-Tsu Alfred Hu, Kaohsiung
Prof. Ted L. McDorman, Ottawa
October 2012

Introduction

South China Sea: Troubled Waters or a Sea of Opportunity?

NIEN-TSU ALFRED HU

The Center for Marine Policy Studies
and College of Social Sciences
National Sun Yat-sen University
Kaohsiung City, Taiwan, Republic of China
and
National Cheng Kung University
Tainan City, Taiwan, Republic of China

> *As a semi-enclosed sea, the South China Sea is the location of conflicts and disputes arisen from intra-regional claims by bordering States over various insular features and the surrounding waters and from extra-regional interests projected in the region. Regional cooperation is an approach called for by the 1982 United Nations Convention on the Law of the Sea (UNCLOS) to address potential conflicts and disputes in semi-enclosed seas. The submissions to the Commission on the Limits of the Continental Shelf (CLCS) by two bordering States and the improved cross-Strait relations between Taiwan and China are two recent developments that have implications for stability and cooperation in the region. This article provides a background to these developments and highlights the assessments on the situation and prospects of the South China Sea presented by articles in this and the next Special Issue.*

Introduction

South China Sea has long been labeled as "troubled waters" or "a flash point," whether viewed from regional security,[1] or in terms of living[2] and nonliving marine resources.[3] Although the signing of the Declaration on the Conduct of Parties in the South China Sea in Phnom Penh, Cambodia, on 4 November 2002 by China and the Association of Southeast Asian Nations (ASEAN) countries[4] was seen as an encouraging sign for stability in the South China Sea,[5] the submissions made in 2009 to the Commission on the Limits of the Continental Shelf (CLCS)[6] by Malaysia and Vietnam[7] have resulted in a resurfacing of questions about the future of cooperation in the region.

The submissions to the CLCS, the responses these generated, and the improvement of cross-strait relations between Taiwan and China provided the background for The Center for Marine Policy Studies (CMPS) of the National Sun Yat-sen University in Kaohsiung City, Taiwan, a leading marine policy think-tank in Taiwan, hosting of the International Conference on Issues in the South China Sea in Taipei on 19–20 August 2009. Papers from the Conference make up the articles in this Special Issue I and the next Special Issue II.

This article provides an introduction to the recent actions by the South China Sea States that have raised questions and concerns about cooperation within the region. Special attention is given to the Republic of China (ROC) and the People's Republic of China (PRC) dotted line maps and cross-Strait relations. This article also provides an overview of the articles in these Special Issues and their contribution on the current situation with respect to cooperation in the South China Sea.

Submissions to the CLCS and the Philippine Legislation

While it is understood that the CLCS is not a forum for the settling of maritime disputes involving maritime claims and delimitation between or among States, the CLCS can be used as a policy tool to highlight, accentuate, or assert a State's maritime claims. This is exactly what has happened in the South China Sea region.

The joint submission by Malaysia and Vietnam with respect to the southern part of the South China Sea and the submission by Vietnam in the North Area (also in the southern part of the South China Sea) encountered protests from the PRC[8] and the ROC.[9] In addition, in view of its lack of access to the United Nations system, including the CLCS, the ROC Foreign Ministry issued a comprehensive declaration on 12 May 2009 outlining its position with respect to the CLCS and its right to make claims on the extended continental shelf beyond 200 nautical miles in the East China Sea, in the waters to the east of Taiwan Island proper, and in the South China Sea.[10]

The PRC stated in its Note Verbale dated 7 May 2009 that:

> China has indisputable sovereignty over the islands in the South China Sea and the adjacent waters, and enjoys sovereign rights and jurisdiction over the relevant waters as well as the seabed and subsoil thereof (see attached map). The above position is consistently held by the Chinese Government, and is widely known by the international community.
>
> The continental shelf beyond 200 nautical miles as contained in the Joint Submission by Malaysia and the Socialist Republic of Viet Nam has seriously infringed China's sovereignty, sovereign rights and jurisdiction in the South China Sea.[11]

The reading of the above PRC's statement can lead to the following observations: The PRC asserts sovereignty over the islands in the South China Sea and the adjacent waters of such islands (i.e., Xisha Qundao, Nansha Qundao, Zhongsha Qundao, and Donsha Qundao). Second, the PRC asserts sovereign rights and jurisdiction over the "relevant waters" as well as the seabed and subsoil thereof. The "relevant waters" are the waters encompassed by the nine discontinuous U-shaped lines shown in the map in Figure 1, although the PRC has not specified the legal nature of the "relevant waters." Third, the PRC's position concerning the islands and their adjacent waters, the relevant waters and the seabed and subsoil thereof, as well as the map itself, has been held by the PRC consistently and is widely known by the international community. This implies long usage or historical title. Fourth, the PRC

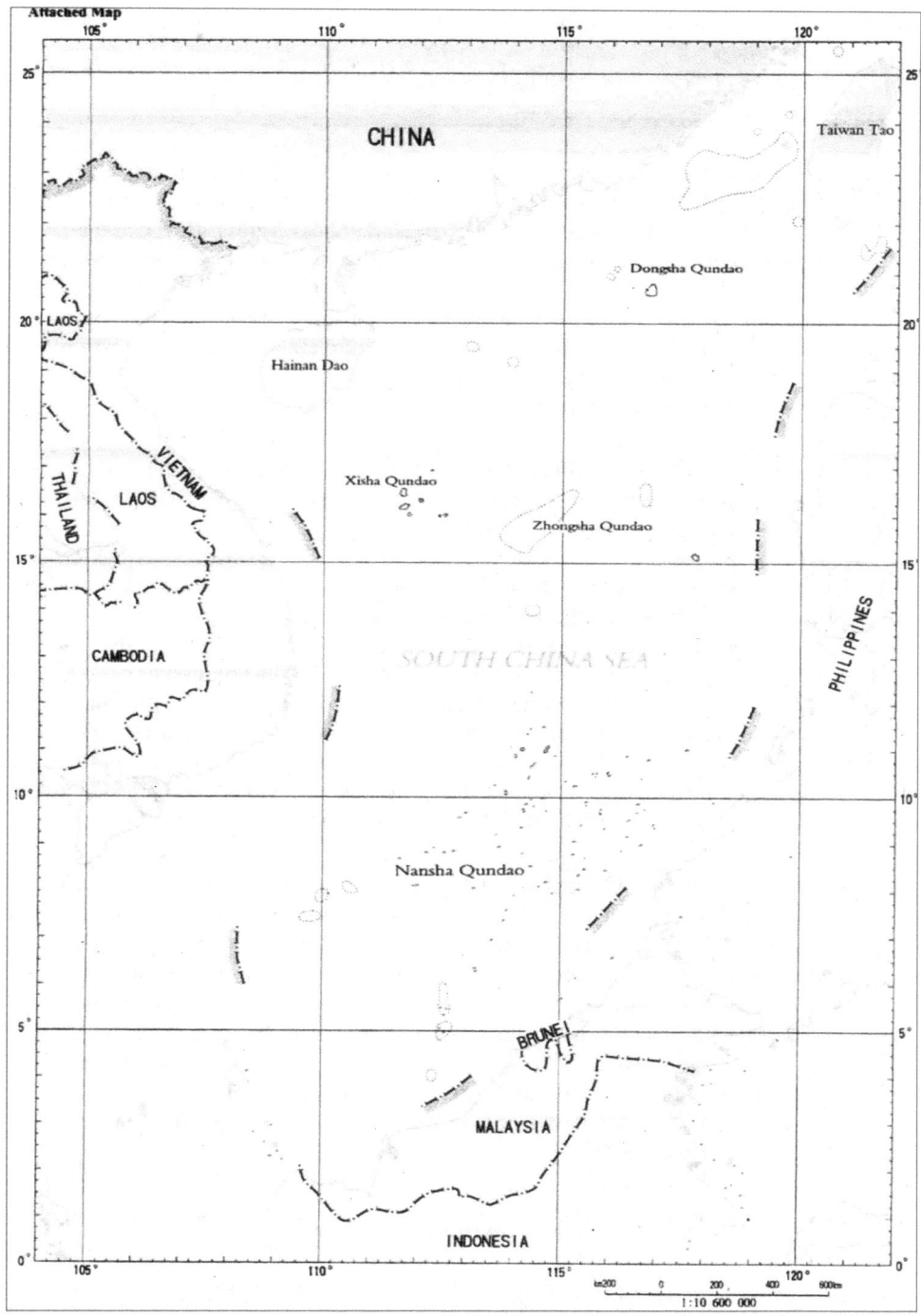

Figure 1. Map attached to China's Note CML/17/2009, submitted to the United Nations 7 May 2009.

asserts sovereignty, sovereign rights, and jurisdiction in the South China Sea delineated by the U-shaped lines.

In the above noted ROC's statement concerning the joint submission of Malaysia and Vietnam and the submission of Vietnam, it states:

> In terms of either historical, geographical or international legal perspective, the Nansha Islands (Spratly Islands), Shisha Islands (Paracel Islands), Chungsha Islands (Macclesfield Islands), Tungsha Islands (Pratas Islands), as well as their surrounding waters, their respective sea bed and subsoil belong to the existent territories of the Republic of China. The sovereignty of these archipelagoes belongs to our Government is an undeniable fact, Taiwan therefore enjoys and deserves all rights accordingly. Any sovereignty claims over, or occupation of, these islands and their surrounding waters will not be recognized by the Government of the Republic of China.[12]

Apparently, the ROC also takes a historical perspective and characterizes the four groups of islands and their surrounding waters, seabed, and subsoil as a part of its existent territories and that it has sovereignty over these archipelagoes.

Reference also needs to be made to the new legislation in the Philippines, the Republic Act No. 9522 (An Act to define the archipelagic baselines of the Philippines) enacted on 10 March 2009,[13] in which the Philippines defined its archipelagic baselines. Article 2 declares that the Philippines exercises "sovereignty and jurisdiction" over the Kalayaan Island Group and the Bajo de Masinloc/Scarborough Shoal.[14] The Philippines has deposited with the United Nations a list of geographical coordinates of the points contained in the Act.[15] The ROC, the PRC, and Vietnam have all communicated their nonacceptance of the Philippines legislation. The ROC declared that all the four groups of islands in the South China Sea and the surrounding waters are the territories of the ROC.[16] The PRC lodged a protest note dated 13 April 2009 to the UN Secretary-General in which it is stated:

> The above-mentioned Philippine Act illegally claims Huangyan Island (referred as "Bajo de Masinloc" in the Act) and some islands and reefs of Nansha Islands (referred as "The Kalayaan Island Group" in the Act) of China as "areas over which the Philippines likewise exercises sovereignty and jurisdiction." The Chinese Government hereby reiterates that Huangyan Island and Nansha Islands have been part of the territory of China since ancient time. The People's Republic of China has indisputable sovereignty over Huangyan Island and Nansha Islands and their surrounding maritime areas. Any claim to territorial sovereignty over Huangyan Island and Nansha Islands by any other State is, therefore, null and void.[17]

Vietnam made a similar communication.[18]

The U-shaped Lines and the Improved Cross-Strait Relations

While there are problems and difficulties between the two sides of Taiwan Strait, the territorial claims over the insular features within the U-shaped lines and claims over the waters within the lines constitutes a common ground for the both sides of the Taiwan Strait vis-à-vis other claimants of the South China Sea. The assertion of the U-shaped lines claims and the improved cross-Strait relations since mid-2008 have significant implications for the situation in the South China Sea.

In a chronological sense, it was the ROC Government that first made territorial claims on all the islands, islets, reefs, rocks, banks, and shoals and claimed all the waters as "historic waters" in the South China Sea (to the Chinese people and in the Chinese language, it is called "South Sea," or "Nan-Hai," rather than South China Sea)[19] within the 11 discontinuous U-shaped lines presented in a map issued by the Department of the Territories and Boundaries of the Ministry of the Interior in December 1946 while the ROC still ruled mainland China (see the map in Figure 2).[20] The ROC conducted surveys and named a number of the insular features following the World War II. In September 1947, the Ministry of the Interior of the ROC Government ordered the annexation of the four island groups in the Nan-Hai under the administrative jurisdiction of the Kuangtung Provincial Government and formally approved and publicized the names of the insular features of the four island groups to all the countries of the world. This met with no opposition from other countries.[21]

Since 1949, after its establishment on the mainland, the PRC Government has succeeded the ROC's claims in the South Sea with a set of revised, but similar, nine discontinuous U-shaped lines. The ROC Government in Taiwan has continuously held to its original claims. Thus, the "two Chinas" have possessed the same position in the South China Sea over the past 6 decades.

Since Ma Ying-Jeou took office as President of the ROC on 20 May 2008, the cross-Strait relations between Taiwan and China have undergone a substantive change.[22] Both sides have taken a more positive and friendlier attitude toward each other. This change exists on many fronts.[23] The development of recent cross-Strait relations, combined with the long-standing and common positions of both sides toward the territorial claims over insular features in the South China Sea and the claims of sovereign rights and jurisdiction over the waters encompassed by the U-shaped lines, have facilitated the collaboration of Taiwan and China for the first time in a second-track regional forum specifically dealing with the issues of South China Sea.[24]

Assessments of the Current Situation and Perspectives on the South China Sea

With their strategic location and potential surrounding waters and associated resources therein, the insular features in the South China Sea are the "blocking stones" for any peaceful settlement and development in the region. Hope for the region is based on politically acceptable, legally sound, and practically feasible maritime delimitation solutions.

In his article "Maritime Delimitation in the South China Sea: Potentiality and Challenges," Robert W. Smith, after briefly examining the existing bordering States' claims in the South China Sea, suggests a long-term solution scenario of maritime delimitation that starts from identifying areas of the South China Sea in which only two countries dispute the area, then moving into the more tricky central part of the South China Sea where multiple claimants exist. His proposal is to have an outside entity (an organization, government, group of experts) offer nonbinding advice and recommendations on how to allocate the area to the respective States or to create joint development schemes. Smith is of the view that the opportunities are endless for the countries to work together and to enjoy the fruits of what the waters and seabed have to offer.

As already noted, it is the ROC Government that made the earliest claim to all of the insular features and waters of the South China Sea within the U-shaped lines, which was

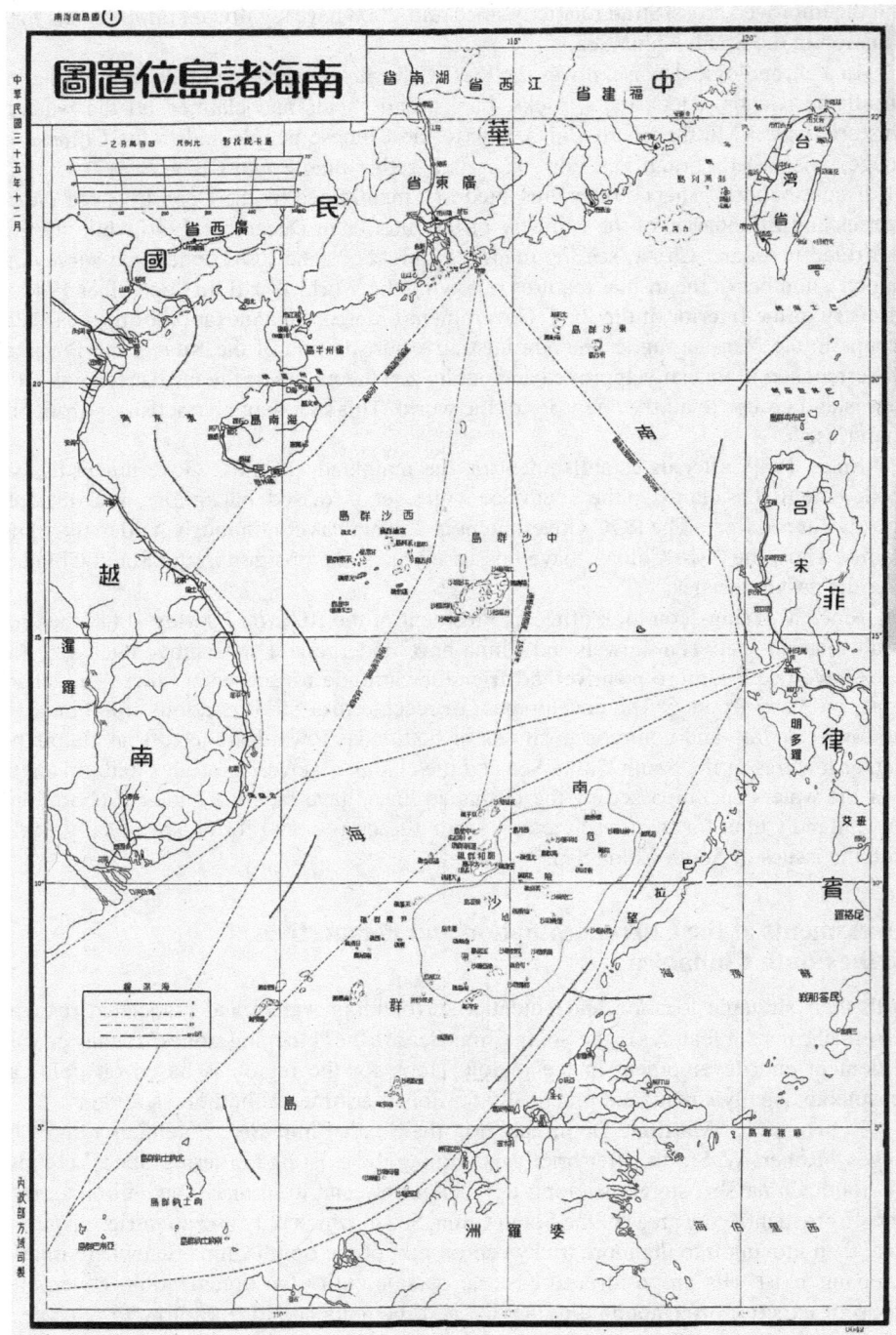

Figure 2. A reproduction of the official map issued by the Republic of China Government on December 1946 with U-shaped 11 discontinuous lines. [*Source:* Chang Wei-I (張維一), *Nan-Hai Tsu-Yuan K'ai-Fa yu Chu-Ch'uan Wei-Hu* (南海資源開發與主權維護 *The Resources Exploitation and Sovereignty Protection of the South Sea*) (Taipei County, Taiwan: P'an Shih Library, December 1994), map presented on a folded page at the end of the book.]

followed by the PRC Government. The position, practice, and interpretation on the ROC and PRC claims, especially the nature of the discontinued U-shaped lines, needs to be examined if one intends to grasp the common position of the two Chinese Governments in the South China Sea. Kuan-Hsiung Wang offers his observation and analysis on this issue in the article "The ROC's Maritime Claims and Practices with Special Reference to the South China Sea." Wang first presents the maritime zone claims and related legislation of the ROC, and then moves to the ROC claims and practices in the South China Sea. Wang argues that: (1) the method of constructing the discontinuous U-shaped lines is through the median line principle by which the lines fall in the middle of the insular features that the ROC Government claimed and the opposite land masses of other bordering States of the South China Sea; (2) the legal status of the U-shaped lines is not baselines separating the territorial sea and the internal waters, rather the lines indicate all the insular features that are under the ROC or PRC sovereignty; and (3) based on existing practices in the waters enclosed by the U-shaped lines, it would be difficult for either the ROC or the PRC to claim such waters as territorial waters, let alone internal waters, and whether the insular features possess maritime zones such as an EEZ and continental shelf is contingent on the ambiguous legal distinction between islands and rocks that cannot sustain human habitation or an economic life of their own.

Taiwan has been handicapped in dealing with other claimant States through normal diplomatic channels,[25] and yet Taiwan is in control of the largest island in the Spratly Islands. One international mechanism that has sought to overcome this situation has been the second-tract forum, the Workshops on Managing Potential Conflicts in the South China Sea (the SCS Workshops) initiated and sponsored by the Indonesia Government. Yann-Huei Song offers a historical account of this dialogue process with special reference to the interactions between Taiwan and China in his article "The South China Sea Workshop Process and Taiwan's Participation." Song takes the adoption of a joint project proposal submitted jointly by Taiwan and China at the 2009 SCS Workshops as a major step regarding Taiwan's participation in the Workshop process. He raises issues about the implications of this for future interactions or maneuvering perceived or taken by different actors, both intra- and extraregional.

Establishing MPAs within undisputed marine areas needs no bilateral or multilateral cooperation. It is cooperation within disputed waters that requires political will and policy input. "The Spratly Islands constitute one of the most ecologically significant areas of the Earth, hosting a high diversity of marine species, providing critical habitats for endangered species, and providing marine larvae to reestablish depleted stocks among the heavily overfished and degraded coastal ecosystems of the South China Sea," and Taiwan has a strong capacity for biodiversity research. Because of this, John W. McManus, Kwang-Tsao Shao, and Szu-yin Lin, in their article "Toward Establishing a Spratly Islands International Marine Peace Park: Ecological Importance and Supportive Collaborative Activities with an Emphasis on the Role of Taiwan," suggest that Taiwan should promote the Spratly Islands as an international Marine Peace Park. Their view is that the protection of the natural resources of the Spratly Islands is vital to maintaining the fisheries and economically important ecosystems throughout the coastal areas of the entire South China Sea, and this should outweigh the socially and economically costly and environmentally destructive military maintenance in the region. They argue that the recent developments in the cross-Strait relationship between Taiwan and China has improved since 2008 and this will give Taiwan a better chance to promote the Spratly Islands as an international Marine Peace Park.

Is it possible that the bordering States of the South China Sea could come together to take the South China Sea as a common heritage and give themselves the opportunity of joint development through regional cooperation in the spheres of management and conservation of marine living resources, protection of marine environment, and joint scientific research programs? Nien-Tsu Alfred Hu, the organizer of the 2009 International Conference and the Guest Editor of this Special Issue, looks at this issue based on existing practices and precedents in two other semi-enclosed seas (i.e., the Mediterranean Sea and the Caribbean Sea) and draws certain lessons for the bordering States of South China Sea to consider. In his article "Semi-enclosed Troubled Waters: A New Thinking on the Application of the 1982 UNCLOS Article 123 to the South China Sea," Hu first notes the treaty obligations provided for in Article 123 of the UNCLOS on the bordering States of an enclosed or semi-enclosed sea to cooperate in three substantive spheres directly or through an appropriate regional organization or other interested States. He then examines the practices in the Mediterranean region and the Caribbean region on the protection of marine environment and management of marine living resources. After putting the lessons learned from two semi-enclosed sea regions into the context of South China Sea, Hu puts forward his thinking on future cooperation in the South China Sea. He argues that: (1) the involvement of the UN system will not guarantee the success of regional cooperation; (2) a cooperative program with a large geographical coverage, a great number of participating States, and a high degree of diversity among participating States can result in difficulties; (3) inviting or allowing the involvement of other extraregional interested States or international organizations may not be helpful; (4) a complicated cooperative mechanism with too many agenda items and too high expectations can overwhelm the capacities and political will of participating States; and (5) the bordering States of the South China Sea must have the political will to incorporate Taiwan as an equal partner in bilateral or multilateral engagement in the region.

The South China Sea is important not simply because of its numerous insular features, but also because of its strategic geography of choke points of sea lines of communication (SLOC). Chris Rahman and Martin Tsamenyi first describe this strategic geography in their article "A Strategic Perspective on Security and Naval Issues in the South China Sea" (This particular article will appear in the Special Issue II). These authors then analyze recent naval and strategic developments, especially naval modernization, in the region. They argue that "the small size of even the largest islands in the Spratly group, their isolation and need for infrastructure and constant replenishment, mean that they would have minimal strategic value in any significant conflict;" nevertheless, "any strategic value they may hold pertains mostly during peacetime, as surveillance or staging outposts, and as political indicators of intent with respect to territorial and maritime claims." Their article also analyzes and predicts certain types of military operations in the exclusive economic zone (EEZ) in the region, including those operations undertaken by extraregional powers and responses from littoral states, especially the contention between the PRC and the United States. They conclude with an observation that "China is increasing its pressure on other claimant States in the South China Sea and 'unwelcome' forces such as those of the United States in a concerted fashion;" while "[o]ther South China Sea States are also asserting their own claims and developing their own naval capacity, albeit to a lesser degree than China." This observation leads to their conclusion that "[a]ny thoughts that the South China Sea can become a zone of peace and cooperation may have to be placed on hold for some time yet."

If regional cooperation is one of the solutions to the tensions and conflicts in the South China Sea region, what will the road map look like? Aldo Chircop, in his article "Regional Cooperation in Marine Environmental Protection in the South China Sea: A Reflection on New Directions for Marine Conservation," (this particular article will appear in the Special Issue II) indicates that "[d]espite ongoing conflict management and confidence-building efforts in the South China Sea, there is still no clear path to the resolution of complex multilateral sovereignty and maritime boundary disputes." Chircop observes that "[o]ver the past two decades, however, there has been a growing sense of urgency in the need to take action in marine environmental cooperation at global and regional levels" and that there are numerous globally or regionally accepted international instruments that apply to all the littoral players, but Taiwan, of the South China Sea. Thus, there is no lack of legal commitments for the South China Sea States to cooperate on the marine environmental protection. Chircop notes that "[a]t this time most of the marine areas [within the South China Sea] under current protection fall within undisputed waters and what is missing is networking of existing [marine protected areas] MPAs as well as cooperation to pursue the common conservation interest in disputed waters." He suggests that the littoral States should pursue the creation of MPA networks under the concepts of "Large Marine Ecosystem" (LME) and "ecosystem-based management," along with another layering of protection through the designation of "special areas" or "Particularly Sensitive Sea Areas" (PSSAs) under the International Convention for the Prevention of Pollution from Ships 1973/78 (MARPOL)[26] regime and through the International Maritime Organization (IMO) ship routing measures. Accordingly, Chircop suggests that

> [t]he region should take greater ownership of initiatives to protect its common ecosystemic heritage and commit financial and administrative resources. International organizations may play important facilitative roles, but those roles will necessarily be catalytic and the ultimate responsibility to make marine conservation work rests on the regional States.

Conclusion

Is the South China Sea troubled waters or a sea of opportunities? The answer is contingent on the political will of the bordering States. There are numerous international legal instruments that provide for rights and obligations for policy formulation on the part of the bordering States. These legal instruments, however, point in two different directions: one is to take them as legal bases or tools to augment each individual bordering State's interests, like the recent contention in the CLCS forum; the other is to take them as legal bases or tools to reduce the tensions and conflicts through regional cooperation by means of the formulation of regional mechanisms for marine environmental protection and management and conservation of marine living resources. The bordering States should have the collective wisdom to solve their common problems within the region, but this is based on political will.

Notes

1. BBC News, 14 February 1999, "World: Asia-Pacific Analysis: Flashpoint Spratly," available at news.bbc.co.uk/2/hi/asia-pacific/279170.stm (accessed 7 April 2010); Peter Brookes, "Flashpoint: The Great Wall Goes to Sea," 8 July 2009, The Heritage Foundation, available at www.heritage.org/Research/Commentary/2009/07/Flashpoint-The-Great-Wall-goes-to-sea (accessed 7 April 2010).

2. AFP, 13 April 2008, "South China Sea Headed for Troubled Waters: Marine Experts," available at www.illegal-fishing.info/item_single.php?item=news&item_id=2816&approach_id=29 (accessed 7 April 2010).

3. "Oil on Troubled Waters; Vietnam's Conoco Deal Draws Fire from China," *Far Eastern Economic Review* (1996), available at www.faqs.org/abstracts/Business-international/Oil-on-troubled-waters-Vietnams-Conoco-deal-draws-fire-from-China.html (accessed 7 April 2010); Monica Feria,

"South China Sea Flashpoint: Oil Finds Raising Stakes in the Spratlys," *Philippine Daily Inquirer*, 19 April 2008, available at khmerkromngo.org/articles/philippineInquirer041908.htm (accessed 7 April 2010).

4. The text of the Declaration is available at the Web site of ASEAN at www.aseansec.org/13163.htm (accessed on 7 April 2010).

5. See Nguyen Hong Thao, "The 2002 Declaration on the Conduct of Parties in the South China Sea: A Note," *Ocean Development and International Law* 34 (2003): 279–285.

6. The Commission of the Limits of the Continental Shelf was established by Annex II of the 1982 UN Convention on the Law of the Sea, done at Montego Bay, Jamaica, 10 December 1982, entered into force 16 November 1994, 1833 *U.N.T.S.* 397. Regarding the work of the Commission, see its Web site at www.un.org/Depts/los/clcs_new/clcs_home.htm.

7. Malaysia-Viet Nam Joint Submission to the Commission on the Limits of the Continental Shelf Pursuant to Article 76, paragraph 8 of the United Nations Convention on the Law of the Sea 1982 in Respect of the Southern Part of the South China Sea, Executive Summary, May 2009, available at the Web site of the Commission, supra note 6. Viet Nam Submission to the Commission on the Limits of the Continental Shelf Pursuant to Article 76, paragraph 8 of the United Nations Convention on the Law of the Sea 1982, Partial Submission in Respect of Vietnam's Extended Continental Shelf: North Area (VNM-N), Executive Summary, April 2009, available at the Web site of the Commission, supra note 6.

8. People's Republic of China, Letter to Secretary-General of the United Nations, Doc. CML/17/2009, New York, 7 May 2009; and Letter to Secretary-General of the United Nations, Doc. CML/18/2009, New York, 7 May 2009, available at the Web site of the Commission, supra note 6.

9. ROC Foreign Ministry reacted to the two submissions with a statement in Chinese issued on 8 May 2009, available at www.mofa.gov.tw/webapp/ct.asp?xItem=38031&ctNode=1548&mp=1; and with a statement in English on 11 May 2009, available at www.mofa.gov.tw/webapp/ct.asp?xItem=38046&ctNode=1548&mp=1 (accessed 10 May 2010).

10. See this Declaration at the ROC Foreign Ministry Web site at www.mofa.gov.tw/webapp/fp.asp?xItem=38073&ctnode=1548 for Chinese version; and at www.mofa.gov.tw/webapp/ct.asp?xItem=38077&ctNode=1901&mp=6 for English version (accessed 17 May 2010). In the English version, there are minor translation errors and imprecision from the original Chinese version.

11. PRC Letters, supra note 8.

12. See the English version of the ROC Foreign Ministry Statement, supra note 9.

13. See the text of the Act at www.lawphil.net/statutes/repacts/ra2009/ra_9522_2009.html (accessed 7 April 2010).

14. To both Taiwan and China, the Kalayaan Island Group is just a set of islets of the Nansha Qundao/Islands (or Spratly Islands, 南沙群島) while the Scarborough Shoal is "Huangyan Dao" (or 黃岩島) belonging to the Macclesfield Islands/Bank (or Zhongsha Qundao/Islands, 中沙群島).

15. See the maritime zone notification made by the United Nations concerning the Philippines' deposit of its geographical coordinates of basepoints, available at www.un.org/Depts/los/LEGISLATIONANDTREATIES/PDFFILES/mzn_s/mzn69.pdf (accessed 7 April 2010).

16. See the Chinese version of statement issued on 4 February 2009 at the Web site of the ROC Foreign Ministry at www.mofa.gov.tw/webapp/ct.asp?xItem=36869&ctNode=1548&mp=1; and the English version statement issued on 6 February 2009, available at www.mofa.gov.tw/webapp/fp.asp?xItem=36914&ctnode=1902 (accessed 16 May 2010).

17. See People's Republic of China, Letter to Secretary-General of the United Nations, Doc. CML/12/2009, New York, 13 April 2009, available at the Web site of the UN Division on the Law of the Sea at www.un.org/Depts/los/LEGISLATIONANDTREATIES/PDFFILES/DEPOSIT/communicationsredeposit/mzn69_2009_chn.pdf (accessed 16 May 2010).

18. Vietnam, Permanent Mission to the United Nations, "Vietnam's Response to Philippine President's Signing of Baseline Act," 13 March 2009, available at www.vietnam-un.org/en/news.php?id=77&act=print (accessed 7 April 2010).

19. See ROC Ministry of the Interior, *The Claim of the Sovereignty of Nan-Hai, Including the Historic Waters, Belonging to This Country* (南海主權(含歷史性水域)屬我之主張), in Chinese,

September 1992, on file with the author. This pamphlet-like government publication describes the geographic extend of the Nan-Han as "starting from the North Verker Bank (北衛灘) at 21°4′N to the north to the James Shoal (曾母暗沙) at 3°5′N to the south, and starting from the Vanguard Bank (萬安灘) at 109°36′E to the west to the Seahorse (or Routh) Bank (海馬灘) at 117°50′E to the east." Three out of the four figures of longitude and latitude are slightly different from the ones cited in Nien-Tsu Alfred Hu's article in this Special Issue from Chang Wei-I (張維一), Nan-Hai Tsu-Yuan K'ai-Fa yu Chu-Ch'uan Wei-Hu (南海資源開發與主權維護 *The Resources Exploitation and Sovereignty Protection of the South Sea*) (Taipei County, Taiwan: P'an Shih Library, December 1994).

20. A reproduction of the map can be seen at Chang Wei-I, *ibid.*, folded page at the end of the book.

21. See ROC Ministry of the Interior, *The Claim of the Sovereignty of Nan-Hai, Including the Historic Waters, Belonging to This Country*, supra note 19, at 14.

22. For a description and analysis of China versus Southeast Asia in general, and the situation of South China Sea in particular, before 2006, see Michael A. Glosny, "Heading Toward a Win-Win Future? Recent Developments in China's Policy Toward Southeast Asia," *Asian Security* 2, no. 1 (2006): 24–57.

23. The change includes the admission of Taiwan as an observer in the United Nations World Health Assembly, the submission of a joint project proposal by Taiwan and China at the 2009 nineteenth Workshops on Managing Potential Conflicts in the South China Sea (the SCS Workshops), and the mutual efforts in concluding an Economic Cooperation Framework Agreement (ECFA) by June 2010.

24. Regardless the amicable surface, there is still a strong undercurrent in the international context in which China exerts its diplomatic pressure to control Taiwan's status. For example, in the International Consultations for the establishment of a regional fisheries management organization in the South Pacific, Taiwan was treated as a "Special Observer," rather than an equal negotiating partner as in other similar negotiations and was designated as "Chinese Taipei Fishing Entity," rather than "Chinese Taipei," in the Final Act of the International Consultations on the Establishment of the Proposed South Pacific Regional Fisheries Management Organization signed on 14 November 2009. This implies that the South China Sea situation may well be a special case where China is willing to collaborate with Taiwan due to their common position on their claims in the South China Sea.

25. For a historical account of the evolution of the "One-China policy" with special reference to the key statements from Washington, Beijing, and Taipei, see Shirley A. Kan, "China/Taiwan: Evolution of the 'One China' Policy—Key Statements from Washington, Beijing, and Taipei," Congressional Research Service (CRS) Report for Congress, 17 August 2009, available at www.fas.org/sgp/crs/row/RL30341.pdf (accessed 5 May 2010).

26. Convention on Prevention of Pollution from Ships (1973/1978), 1340 *U.N.T.S.* 61.

Maritime Delimitation in the South China Sea: Potentiality and Challenges

ROBERT W. SMITH

Oakland, Maryland, USA

The South China Sea potentially is rich in hydrocarbon resources, but until such time that there is certainty of which country has exclusive maritime jurisdiction over what part of the seabed little or no exploitation will occur. Maritime boundary delimitation or some form of joint resource development is hampered by a legacy of sovereignty disputes over miniscule pieces of territory that are scattered throughout this water body. Unfortunately, the UN Convention on the Law of the Sea does not address how to resolve sovereignty disputes. The small disputed islands have no intrinsic value other than possibly providing the territorial basis from which to make the maritime claims. Given the nationalism associated with the territorial claims, any viable long-term solution will have to address how to discount these features and the States will have to have the political will to push their sovereignty claims aside in order to move forward towards some sort of joint development arrangements.

Introduction

Among the many headlines pertaining to the South China Sea during the spring and summer of 2009 were: "New Philippine Border Law Re-ignites Territorial Disputes in South China Sea,"[1] "Taiwan Reaffirms Sovereignty over South China Sea Islands,"[2] "China Tells Neighbours to Keep Off Disputed Islands,"[3] "South Korea, Vietnam: A Deal to Explore Contested Waters,"[4] and "US Reaffirms Its Rights to Operate in South China Sea."[5] So, what has happened to reignite the long-standing disputes in the South China Sea?

Pursuant to the provisions of the United Nations Convention on the Law of the Sea (LOS Convention)[6] all States that were party to the LOS Convention prior to 1999 were to make their continental shelf submission to the Commission on the Limits of the Continental Shelf (CLCS) by 13 May 2009. This pertained to all the States surrounding the South China Sea: Brunei, China, Malaysia, the Philippines, and Vietnam.[7]

An assertion to exclusive jurisdiction over the continental shelf must originate from territory, be it from a continental mainland or from an island over which a country has clear ownership. In its decision in the *North Sea Continental Shelf Cases* in 1969, the International Court of Justice (ICJ) stated that

> the rights of the coastal State in respect of the area of the continental shelf that constitutes a natural prolongation of its land territory into and under the sea exist ipso facto and ab initio, by virtue of its sovereignty over the land.[8]

Surrounding the South China Sea are the undisputed land territories of Brunei, China, Malaysia, the Philippines, Taiwan, and Vietnam. But, scattered throughout the region are approximately 160 features—small islands, cays, and drying reefs. According to one analyst, these small features are found in a marine area covering approximately 900 kilometers by 360 kilometers (an area of 240,000 square kilometers).[9] And, in the northern part of the South China Sea, there are the Paracel Islands (or Xisha Qundao, Haoang Sa in Vietnamese) and the Pratas Islands (or Dongsha Qundao). In order to enjoy exclusive rights to the continental shelf in this area, the claimant countries believed it was important to reiterate their sovereignty claims to many, or all, of these small features that speckle the South China Sea. Jurisdiction over the water column would be affected as well.

The intent of this article is not to discuss in detail the history of the sovereignty claims or the respective legal merits of these claims. Rather, a brief overview will be provided as to the current state of affairs. Then, some thoughts will be given as to possible actions that could be taken by the countries, or even by the international community, to prevent these disputes from escalating into something more serious and to find a meaningful long-term solution(s) to the situation. In the short term, the recent public attention being given to the statements by the countries likely will prevent any meaningful discussions to occur to resolve these disputes. Possible solutions, however, may be possible in the long term when the parties realize that creative compromises will be needed to exploit the living and nonliving resources throughout much of the region.

Geographical Scope

The insular territorial features, for the purposes of analysis, can be grouped into two general areas: the Paracel Islands, in the northern South China Sea; and the many small islands and cays in the south that generically have been labeled over the years as the Spratly Islands (or Nansha Qundao), even though Spratly Island (or Nanwei Dao) is but one island.[10] It should be noted that many of these small islands, reefs, and atolls are not well surveyed and, over the years, issues have arisen as to whether or not a given feature is even above water at high tide. Knowledge of the tidal datum is important since a claim to offshore maritime jurisdiction must originate from terra firma, a piece of land that is above water at all times.

The sovereignty over the Paracel Islands is disputed between the two Chinas and Vietnam, whereas the numerous islands in the central part of the South China Sea are disputed, at least in part, among the following political entities: China, Malaysia, the Philippines, Taiwan, and Vietnam. As shown on a map produced by the U.S. Department of State, these small pieces of territory are occupied, in no particular geographic pattern, by the People's Republic of China (PRC), Malaysia, the Philippines, the Republic of China (ROC), and Vietnam. (See Figure 1.)[11] Brunei's claim to a continental shelf, based on an extension of the inshore limits created by the British in 1958, incorporates Louisa Reef (or Nantung Chiao), a feature that has a couple of rocks that are above high tide and "a navigational

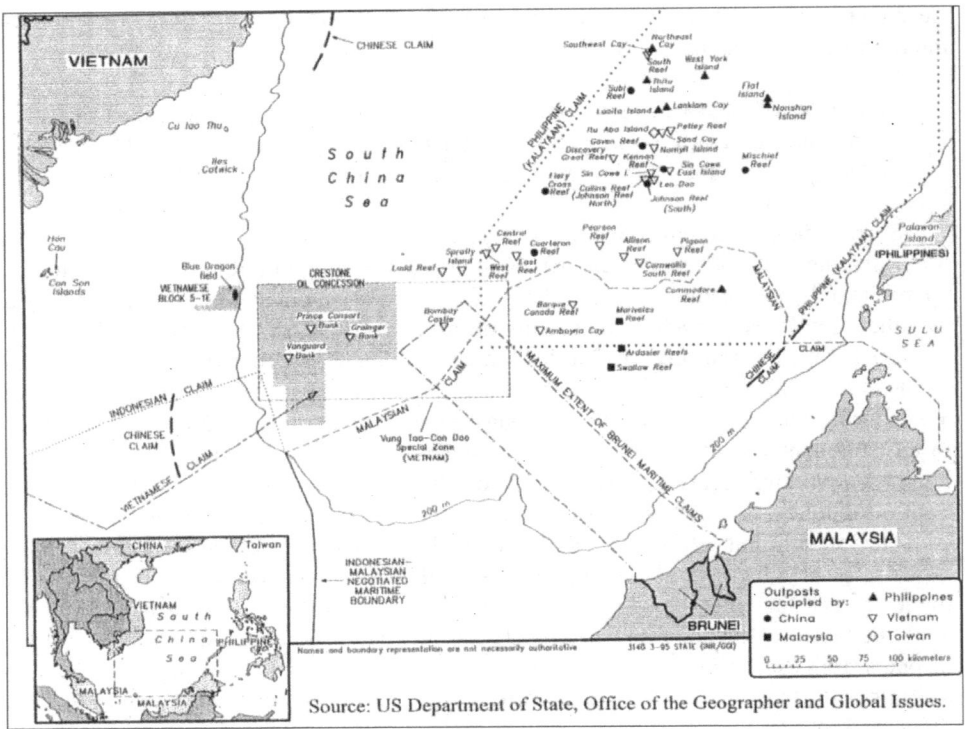

Figure 1. Claims in the South China Sea.

light maintained by Malaysia."[12] There are no communities, in the traditional sense, on these features. Several of these small pieces of territory support some people representing a particular claimant country for which food and water must be brought in. Several features have been enlarged to accommodate an airstrip for small planes to bring in supplies and people. The islands themselves essentially have no intrinsic value. It is the maritime area that possibly could be generated from them that creates the potential value. The word "possibly" is used because, under the international law of the sea (LOS Convention, Article 121(3)), it is questionable whether or not a country would have entitlement to an exclusive economic zone (EEZ) or continental shelf from these small islands, cays, rocks, and atolls.

A recent article in the *Los Angeles Times*, for example, reported on the Philippines' attempts to populate its Pagasa Island (a name in Tagalog, or Zhongye Dao, Thi Tu Island in English).[13] According to the article, in 2002 "the Philippines decided to establish a small colony of hardy civilian settlers on the island augmenting the two dozen military workers who earn special 'loneliness pay' to live on the far-off spot and bolstering its claim that possession is nine-tenths of the law." These inhabitants spend 3 months at a time on this 75-acre property. This is the only Philippine claimed possession in the South China Sea that has a year-round population. As an example of life on this island, the article states that "telephones and satellite TV are powered by generators that run only part time. Air conditioning is nonexistent, and on the hottest days many wonder why they ever came in the first place."

Geologists speculate that the South China Sea seabed could offer commercially viable oil and gas deposits. In addition to possible hydrocarbon resources, the region has productive fishing grounds. The region also provides vital shipping routes for trade to and from East Asia to all parts of the world. It is the resource potential that is the root of most, if not all, the current interest in claiming exclusive national jurisdiction over the waters and seabed of the South China Sea. This jurisdiction must emanate from undisputed territory.

For any of these countries to exploit the natural resources of the South China Sea, there is a need for certainty over jurisdiction of the maritime space. For example, oil companies will not spend large amounts of money to explore an area to determine the likelihood of oil and gas deposits if they are not certain that they will enjoy the right to exploit the resource if any are found. Oil and gas exploitation is a complicated process involving several steps, including: research and development, bidding, and securing a license for a particular location and a set time frame during which to set up the infrastructure to drill and to transport the oil either to a tanker or a land-based terminal. This process just will not happen in a disputed area.

This certainty could be brought about in one of two ways. First, there could be a clearly defined maritime boundary established by treaty, which is not contested by a third party, that delimits the national maritime jurisdiction for each State. Following the entry into force of such a treaty, the counties could proceed with exploration and exploitation on their side of the boundary in a manner in which they choose. Included in such a boundary agreement could be provisions for joint development or unitization over the resources in the boundary area, particularly for resources that may straddle the boundary. There could also be an international agreement involving the affected parties that clearly sets forth the duties, responsibilities, and rights for each State in a defined area.

Until there is an element of certainty, there will be little, if any, exploratory work conducted in the core region of the South China Sea where there are multiple overlapping claims. There appears to be some activity by the countries to enter into joint exploration agreements, for example, among China, the Philippines, and Vietnam (an agreement signed on 14 March 2005).[14] If there is work done in the disputed area, it likely will be done under the protest of the other countries.

In the South China Sea, from the Spratly Islands north, there is only one maritime treaty that has been concluded. By a treaty signed 25 December 2000 (which entered into force on 30 June 2004), China (PRC) and Vietnam delimited the territorial sea, EEZ, and continental shelf in the Gulf of Tonkin.[15] (See Figure 2.) The boundary terminates before entering into the South China Sea. The treaty contains provisions on fishing activities in the boundary area. This treaty represents China's first maritime boundary agreement concluded with any of its neighbors. Although each side had put forth historic arguments to support its respective boundary position, it appears that both sides based the agreement on the LOS Convention, which emphasizes achieving an equitable solution.[16] The treaty did not address their sovereignty disputes over the Paracel Islands or the Spratly Islands.

There may be another boundary agreement. In its Preliminary Information submission to the CLCS Brunei made the following statement:

> The maritime boundaries between Brunei and Malaysia out to 200 nautical miles have been delimited by two series of agreements.
>
> First, the territorial sea and continental shelf between Brunei and Malaysia were delimited as far as the 100 fathom isobath by two 1958 British Orders in Council.

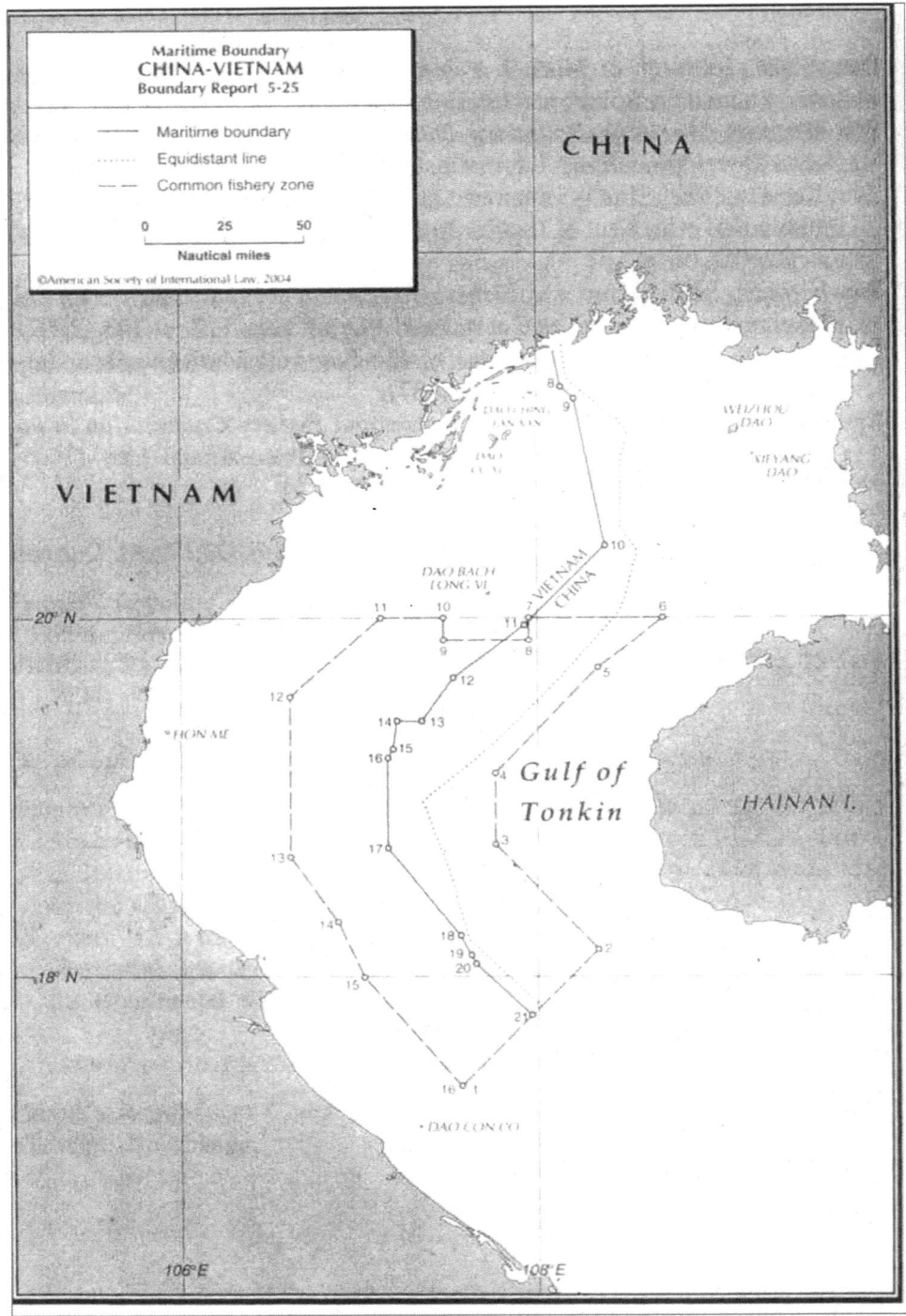

Figure 2. China-Vietnam maritime boundary. (*Source:* David Colson and Robert Smith (eds), International Maritime Boundaries, Volume V, American Society of International Law, 2005, p. 3754. Reprinted with permission.)

Second, the territorial sea, the Exclusive Economic Zone and the continental shelf out to a distance of 200 nautical miles were delimited by an Exchange of Letters dated 16 March 2009.[17]

The substance and legal validity of the 16 March Exchange of Letters between Brunei and Malaysia are unclear at this point. Does the exchange of letters constitute a maritime boundary agreement with specific lines delimiting, or merely an agreement on intent to reach an agreement? In its joint submission with Vietnam to the CLCS, Malaysia, for instance, did not show boundaries with Brunei beyond the 100-fathom depth contour (e.g., what was established by the British in 1958).[18] Brunei, on the other hand, in 1988 legislation published what it unilaterally believed to be its maritime boundaries with Malaysia.[19]

The LOS Convention

The South China Sea coastal States that are members of the United Nations are all party to the LOS Convention. Table 1 lists the dates on which each State became party.

The LOS Convention provides the bases by which States have entitlement to offshore areas. It addresses all aspects associated with national maritime claims: baselines, territorial sea, contiguous zone, EEZ, continental shelf, and bilateral boundaries (territorial sea, EEZ, and continental shelf). With the exception of baseline claims, of which several States in this region have enacted laws that exceed the provisions of the LOS Convention, the laws implemented by these coastal States, for the most part, have been made in accordance with the Convention. It is not the place here to review in detail all the national maritime claims. It should be pointed out, however, that should any of the States enter into boundary talks, then certain straight baseline claims could complicate negotiations.

One piece of national legislation worth citing is the 2009 Philippine law that established its archipelagic straight baselines.[20] Prior to this law, in 1961, the Philippines claimed straight baselines around its islands, a claim that clearly exceeded the provisions of international law.[21] The 1961 claim was based on the limits set forth in Article III of the Treaty of Paris Between the United States and Spain of 10 December 1898.[22] The 2009 law that the Philippines enacted is in accordance with the LOS Convention provisions on archipelagic straight baselines. It meets the water:land ratio and the length of the baselines are within the guidelines set forth in the LOS Convention.[23]

Knowing the political sensitivities surrounding the multiple claims to the Spratly Islands, the Philippines Government purposely did not include any of those contested

Table 1

Dates the South China Sea States became party to the 1982 United Nations Convention on the Law of the Sea

State	Date
Brunei	5 November 1996
China	7 June 1996
Malaysia	14 October 1996
Philippines	8 May 1984
Vietnam	25 July 1994

islands within its archipelagic claim. Even so, prior to passing the archipelagic straight baseline bill into law, it took the Philippines Congress months of debate over whether or not the law would adversely affect the Philippines position with regard to its neighbors on the ongoing sovereignty dispute over the South China Sea islands. As the clock was ticked toward 13 May, the Philippines wanted to use the archipelagic straight baselines as part of its continental shelf submission to the CLCS.[24] The final law did state that the islands of Kalayaan and Scarborough Shoal were "a regime of islands under the Republic of the Philippines."[25]

The Philippine law met with protests from China, Taiwan, and Vietnam, which added to the 2009 turmoil of reiteration of claims, counterclaims.[26]

The LOS Convention and Island Sovereignty Disputes

As discussed in one study, disputes involving islands fall under two major categories:[27]

- a dispute over the sovereignty of the island(s) itself; and,
- a dispute over the affect the island(s) may have on the delimitation of adjacent maritime space.

There are important distinctions to be made between these two categories in the relationship between the particular type of dispute and the role the LOS Convention may, or may not, have on bringing about resolution. Whereas the LOS Convention addresses boundary delimitation situations where there are overlaps between respective territorial seas (Article 15), the EEZ (Article 74), and the continental shelf (Article 83), there are no provisions that address how to resolve sovereignty disputes. While the LOS Convention provides for several international bodies to adjudicate disputes, and for the CLCS to give recommendations for national limits to continental shelves beyond 200 nautical miles, there is nothing in the body of the Convention that deals with sovereignty issues. States have turned to various forms of dispute settlement to resolve sovereignty disputes, but these have been bilateral agreements between the claimants and not necessarily tied to the LOS Convention.

As noted above, the application of the LOS Convention is premised on the assumption that a particular State has undisputed title over the territory from which the maritime zone is claimed. Any attempt to conduct activities in a disputed offshore marine area, or to enforce against a country having a competing claim, likely will be met with diplomatic protests and perhaps even confrontation.

Article 121 of the LOS Convention

An article in the LOS Convention that could affect a possible solution to the Spratly Islands sovereignty disputes is Article 121, on the regime of islands, and specifically Article 121, paragraph 3 which addresses "rocks." First, Article 121, paragraph 1 states that an island "is a naturally formed area of land, surrounded by water, which is above water at high tide." Paragraph 2 of this article states that, with the exception of the paragraph 3 provision, an island is entitled to a territorial sea, contiguous zone, EEZ, and continental shelf. Paragraph 3 of Article 121 states:

> Rocks which cannot sustain human habitation or economic life of their own shall have no exclusive economic zone or continental shelf.

The intent of the negotiators of this provision was to prevent a country from claiming a large area of ocean space and seafloor based on a very small feature located off its coast in a mid-oceanic location. For example, a mere point of a feature above water at high tide could generate a 200-nautical-mile zone of 125,600 square nautical miles (430,796 square kilometers) if there were no overlap with a neighboring State. The drafters of the LOS Convention believed this to be unfair as that very small piece of territory would receive a disproportionate amount of ocean space and seafloor, given its miniscule size. Thus, Article 121, paragraph 3 was drafted and accepted.

However, what does this paragraph mean and how can its terms be applied in the real world? When this language first appeared, as Article 132 of Working Paper 8, in the Informal Single Negotiating Text in May 1975[28] (the first text produced during the Third United Nations Conference on the Law of the Sea), the following basic problems of interpretation and definition were immediately identified:

(1) what constitutes a "rock" as a form of an island? And (2) what is meant by "cannot sustain human habitation or economic life of their own"?[29]

Various authors and organizations have attempted to place an area measurement to the various terms. Hodgson (a former geographer of the U.S. Department of State), for example, when analyzing rocks on the question of "special circumstances" in relation to maritime boundary delimitation, characterized islands as follows:

1. Rocks, less than .001 square miles in area;
2. Islets, between .001 and 1 square mile;
3. Isles, greater than 1 square mile but not more than 1,000 square miles; and
4. Islands, larger than 1,000 square miles.[30]

In the Hodgson system, those features with an area of .001 square miles or less, or 2,590 square meters or less, would be a "rock." If this size is what the negotiators had in mind, then this type of island would measure about 51 meters on a side or, if circular, have a radius of approximately 28.7 meters.[31] Unfortunately, the LOS Convention is silent on size. There is no objective means by which to measure a given geographical feature to determine that it is an Article 121, paragraph 3 rock.

The question of what is meant by "cannot sustain human habitation or economic life of their own" is equally void of any objective test in the LOS Convention. There is no guidance given to clearly and unequivocally say a certain feature meets that statement. The definition, for example, does not refer to uninhabited rocks, but rather to uninhabitable rocks. What is now uninhabited could possibly sustain human habitation should people care to live there, and if people or countries are willing to import potable water and food.[32]

On the idea of having an economic life of its own, does having a lighthouse (manned or not manned) give the feature an economic life since it has value to shipping? If a feature is an important nesting ground for marine life or birds, is that an economic life? If the feature has a natural beauty that attracts tourists in boats (thus generating income) to view it from the sea, is that an economic life? It is possible that the drafters of the LOS Convention may have had in mind the idea that if potable water did not exist on the feature or if there was no soil to grow anything, then that was an Article 121, paragraph 3 rock. But, this clarification or objective standard is not written in the Convention.

Hodgson and Smith conducted an analysis of where Article 121, paragraph 3 rocks may possibly exist worldwide.[33] If the Hodgson size criterion were accepted, then most of these small features would be located immediately offshore coastal States. As an example, thousands exist along the coasts of Alaska, Chile, Australia, China, Korea, and Cuba. Few, if any, of these features if discounted with respect to delimiting the State's EEZ or continental shelf would adversely impact that State's entitlement to those zones. Other non-Article 121, paragraph 3 features nearby would be influential. In reality, most of these coastal States would opt to enclose these small features within a straight baseline system and the overall issue would be moot.

A few noncoastal, mid-oceanic rocks do exist that would have a significant impact on adding ocean area to a country's marine jurisdiction. Perhaps the most famous rock and one in which the negotiators had in mind when crafting Article 121, paragraph 3 is Rockall. This is a small (approximately 624 square meters; 0.000241 square miles) feature owned by the United Kingdom that is situated about 162 nautical miles northwest of Scotland. The United Kingdom is the only State that has made a public statement that a feature belonging to them, Rockall, is an Article 121, paragraph 3 rock and therefore does not enjoy an EEZ or continental shelf.[34] Moreover, the United Kingdom does claim a 12-mile territorial sea from Rockall's baseline.

Other possible rocks cited by Hodgson and Smith are Maro Reef, in the Hawaiian island chain of the United States, although larger islands and reefs are nearby thereby minimizing the adverse impact on the U.S. EEZ area if Maro Reef was not used; and Brazil's St. Peter and St. Paul's Rocks (approximately 0.0016 square miles) and New Zealand's L'Esperance Rock (about 0.01875 square miles), which are a bit larger than the Hodgson size criterion. Those authors' recommendation that, due to the difficulty in interpreting and applying this provision,[35] it could be deleted from the negotiating text was ignored and Article 121, paragraph 3 exists today.

The difficulties associated with applying this provision continue. One feature receiving recent attention is Japan's Okinotorishima Atoll. This feature is but a seamount breaking the ocean's surface. The Japanese Government has built a wall around this natural feature, and enclosed it as a tomb, in order to preserve it from disappearing from natural forces.[36] This is a good example of a singular feature generating a 125,600-square-mile EEZ. The PRC has protested Japan's right to claim a 200-mile EEZ and continental shelf from Okinotorishima.[37] South Korea also has submitted a letter to the CLCS objecting to Japan's use of the feature in its continental shelf submission.[38] At the 2009 Meeting of States Parties to the LOS Convention, China attempted to get the issue of Article 121, paragraph 3 on the agenda, but it was unsuccessful.[39]

Article 121, Paragraph 3 and the South China Sea

How may an application of Article 121, paragraph 3 impact national maritime claims in the South China Sea and, subsequently, maritime boundary delimitations? One analyst has noted that, while there may be more than 170 features in the South China Sea, most are submerged banks and shoals and perhaps only about 36 tiny islands are above water at high tide.[40] The largest of these islands is Itu Aba (or Tai-Ping, occupied by Taiwan), which is approximately 1.4 kilometers long and 400 meters wide (0.56 square kilometers or 0.163 square nautical miles). This size would fall into the "islet" category under the Hodgson tabulation. Thitu Island (or Zhongye Dao, Pagasa Island in Tagalog), occupied by the Philippines, is the second largest island with an area of approximately 0.27 square kilometers. It is likely that most of these atolls, while small in comparison to most islands in the world, would be larger than a "rock" using most definitions.

One could certainly question whether these small features, which are scattered throughout the south central part of the South China Sea, can "sustain human habitation or economic life of their own." Granted, even if some of the 36 features (be they named islands, atolls, islets, etc.) have people on them, food and water must be transported in from the claimant country. For many of these islands, it has become difficult to distinguish what is the natural feature and what is man-made. Several of the countries have built up an island by importing sand, gravel, and cement to create airstrips, harbors, and other installations. Under the LOS Convention man-made structures, unless a part of harbor works, cannot be used as a baseline from which to determine offshore limits.[41]

An interesting situation is developing with regard to China's position toward Article 121, paragraph 3 rocks. It has protested Japan's use of Okinotorshima as a basepoint from which to claim an EEZ and continental shelf. In a note dated 9 February 2009, China stated that it "wishes to draw the attention of the members of the Commission, the States Parties to the Convention as well as Members of the United Nations to the inconformity with the Convention with regard to the inclusion of the rock of Oki-no-tori in the Japanese Submission."[42] Yet, if China claims all the islands in the Spratly group with a view to claiming EEZs and continental shelves from them, then there must be some inconsistency in its position on Article 121, paragraph 3.

Continental Shelf Submissions and the South China Sea

Table 2 shows the dates when countries either made their submission or preliminary information to the CLCS with respect to their proposed outer limit of the continental shelf beyond 200 nautical miles. Malaysia,[43] the Philippines,[44] and Vietnam[45] all have made partial submissions, while Brunei[46] and China[47] have provided the CLCS with preliminary information. With their preliminary information submissions, neither Brunei nor China provided any maps or geographic coordinates for their continental shelf limits in the South China Sea. The Philippines' partial submission, concerned its continental shelf limits for the Benham Rise region, to the east of the Philippine islands. No limits were put forward for its South China Sea continental shelf.

Malaysia and Vietnam have made a joint submission for their respective continental shelves in the southern part of the South China Sea. As expected, this action generated several diplomatic notes to the United Nations from China,[48] Malaysia,[49] and Vietnam.[50] China protested the joint submission and reasserted its sovereignty over all the islands in the South China Sea. The PRC letter included a map that showed the dashed lines around the perimeter of the South China Sea indicating it claimed all the islands. In its note, China stated that it

Table 2
Continental shelf actions by the South China Sea States

State	Date of submission	Date of preliminary information	Comments
Brunei		12 May 2009	
China		11 May 2009	
Malaysia	6 May 2009		South China Sea; joint with Vietnam
Philippines	8 April 2009		Benham Rise region
Vietnam	6 May 2009		South China Sea; joint with Malaysia
	7 May 2009		In "North Area"

has indisputable sovereignty over the islands of the South China Sea and the adjacent waters, and enjoys sovereign rights and jurisdiction over the relevant waters as well as the seabed and subsoil thereof. ... The above position is widely known by the international community.[51]

On 8 May 2009, Vietnam submitted to the Secretary-General a note rejecting China's claims as having no "legal, historical, or factual basis."[52] Vietnam reiterated its "indisputable sovereignty" over the Hoang Sa (Paracels) and Truong Sa (Spratly) archipelagoes. On 20 May 2009, Malaysia submitted a note to the United Nations in which it acknowledged that the "Joint Submission is made without prejudice to the question of delimitation of the continental shelf between States with opposite or adjacent coasts."[53] Malaysia stated that it had informed China of the joint submission prior to it being submitted to the United Nations.

Although the ROC is unable to make a formal submission or present preliminary information to the CLCS or to deliver a diplomatic note to that body or to the United Nations, its Ministry of Foreign Affairs issued a formal statement regarding Taiwan's position toward the submissions made by the countries surrounding the South China Sea. This statement is found in Appendix 1.

The CLCS has no authority to make recommendations on bilateral maritime boundaries. Thus, it has to defer any recommendations on the limits of the continental shelf where disputes exist. As a result, the entire South China Sea will be off limits to this body for years to come. Resolution to the numerous issues in this region will have to be found elsewhere.

Allocation Lines: Not Boundaries or Claim Limits

There are several "lines" that have appeared on maps and charts over the years that have caused confusion as to what exactly is being claimed in the South China Sea. The map that China attached to its 2009 note in which it protested the Joint Submission by Malaysia and Vietnam is one example.[54] (See the PRC map in Hu's article.[55]) This map has created confusion among scholars and Governments for decades. One analyst provided a succinct history of this line that first appeared on Chinese maps in 1947.[56] This dashed line has been labeled a "historic claim line" or "traditional sea boundaries line."[57] What is clear is that the Chinese Government has never published a law or decree giving these dashed lines any domestic legal significance.

These dashed lines that extend around the perimeter of the South China Sea can best be labeled as lines of allocation. The intent of these lines is to surround those islands and cays that China claims. It does not apply to the waters or seabed within these dashed lines. Any sovereign or jurisdictional rights must come from ownership of the islands, not from the dashed lines. The dashed lines do not imply any maritime boundary claim by China. Thus, these lines that have appeared on Chinese maps for more than 60 years merely reflect China's long-standing claim of sovereignty over all the geographical features within the dashed lines in the South China Sea. They have no significance in resolving any maritime boundary dispute.

Another set of lines that has caused confusion in the South China Sea has been the Philippine "treaty limits" and the "Kalayaan claim" line. (See Figure 3.) Treaties between Spain and the United States (1898 and 1900) and between the United Kingdom and the United States in 1930 defined what was to become the Republic of the Philippines in 1946.[58] The limits established by these treaties were lines of allocation; inside the lines defined in these treaties were the Philippine islands. The limits did not establish any sovereignty,

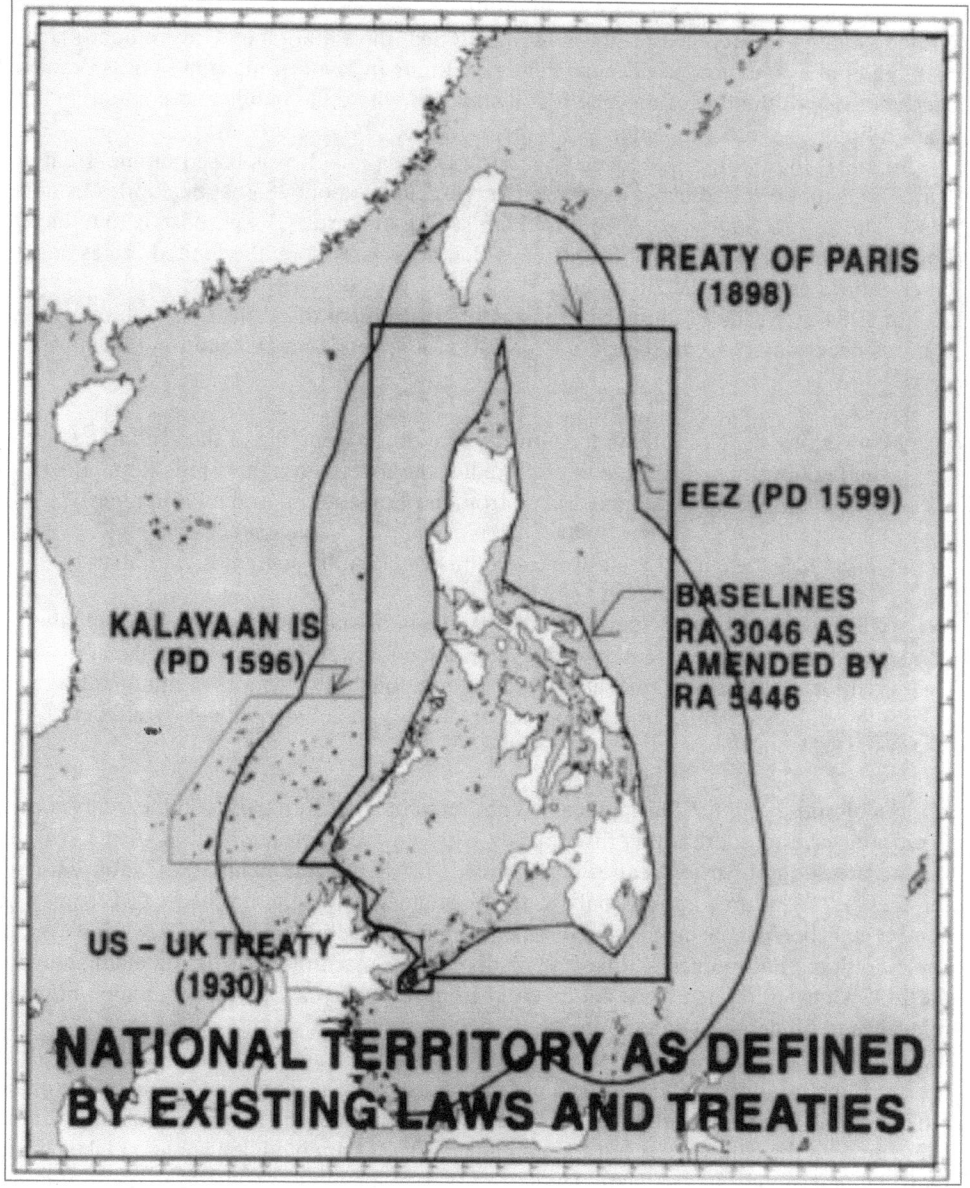

Figure 3. Philippine claims: Kalayaan Claim, Treaty of Paris and Archipelagic Straight Baselines.

sovereign rights, or exclusive jurisdiction over the waters, seabed, or air space. However, subsequent to its independence, the Philippines enacted laws that have treated the waters inside these limits as Philippine territory. It has been unclear as to whether they considered them internal waters or territorial seas.

Except for the area in the southwest, the "treaty limits" is essentially a rectangle that Spain and the United States found convenient in late nineteenth century to define the Philippine territory. There is no relationship, under modern international law of the sea principles, of this treaty box to maritime zones. During, and following, the Third United Nations Conference on the Law of the Sea, the Philippines Government knew it had a dilemma as to how to disavow the treaty limits in favor of maritime limits drawn in accordance with the law of the sea. It is a situation where the public had come to believe that Philippine sovereignty extended to these limits.

In 1961, the Philippines enacted its territorial sea law. It was based on the Treaty of Paris limits that resulted in the outer limit varying, up to about 285 nautical miles from the coast. The United States protested this claim saying, in part: "[I]ts purpose is to reduce to Philippine sovereignty large areas of sea which are regarded by the United States and all other nations as part of the High Seas."[59]

In 1984 when the Philippines deposited its instrument of ratification with the United Nations becoming party to the LOS Convention it appended a Declaration that stated, in part:

> By signing the Convention the Government of the Republic of the Philippines shall not in any manner impair or prejudice the sovereign rights of the Republic of the Philippines under and arising from the Constitution of the Philippines.[60]

In January 1986, the United States protested this Declaration stating, in part, that,

> with respect to other States and the nationals of such other states, the rights and duties of states are defined by international law, both customary and conventional. The rights of States under international law cannot be enlarged by their domestic legislation, absent acceptance of such enlargement by affected States.[61]

As of mid-2009, the Philippines had not retracted its claim based on the treaty limits. It did not have to address this discrepancy between the international law of the sea and its interpretation of earlier treaties when it made its partial continental shelf submission to the CLCS.[62] That area applied only to the Benham Rise, to the northeast of Luzon. The continental shelf can be considered distinct from its EEZ claim, made in 1978. However, at some point the Philippines will have to distinguish its maritime jurisdiction claimed under the LOS Convention and those limits emanating from the earlier treaties, which have no relevance to modern-day international law.

The other non-LOS–related limit found on Philippine maps is the Kalayaan line.[63] This is also a line of allocation based on a claim first asserted by Thomas Cloma, a Philippine citizen, in 1956 to islands in the South China Sea, adjacent to the Philippine islands. Cloma came up with the name Kalayaan (Freedomland). The claim included about 33 islands and reefs, but not Spratly Island itself, which is located to the west of Kalayaan. The Philippine Government has not used this limit for any official claim.

Malaysia's Continental Shelf Claim

Malaysia is the only claimant that has produced an official map depicting its continental shelf claim, at least as it was defined in 1979 when the map was produced. There is no Malaysian law or decree associated with the map that depicts Malaysia's continental shelf limit. This map was produced following a 1978 visit by Malaysian troops to some of the southern South China Sea islands. In 1983, Malaysian troops again went to the area and landed on Swallow Reef. Malaysia has maintained a base there since that time. It is unclear how Malaysia views that 1979 map in light of the LOS Convention and its Joint Submission with Vietnam in May 2009.

Thoughts on South China Sea Boundary Delimitations

It may be premature to title this section "Thoughts on Possible Solutions" because it seems that, in 2009, tensions have been raised as a result of the 13 May continental shelf submission deadline. Thus, it is instead titled "Thoughts on South China Sea Boundary Delimitations." Each country likely is reflecting on what next steps should and can be taken. There is much at stake: natural resources, national pride, foreign relations, and regional stability. If compared to land-based territorial disputes elsewhere in the world, the claims made by each of these countries to these dot-like features are very recent and somewhat weak. It is questionable exactly when some of these islands were first occupied, if there has been continuous occupation, and if some of these islands are even islands at all (e.g., above water at high tide). The charting and surveying of many of these islands are quite poor.

The real boom in asserting sovereignty claims to these features came only in the mid-1960s when reports were published suggesting a distinct possibility that hydrocarbons may exist in the seabed underlying the South China Sea. A few years later, the 200-nautical-mile EEZ became an internationally accepted regime giving coastal States the right to claim exclusive jurisdiction over economic activities (e.g., fishing and exploiting the seabed resources). Thus, control and sovereignty over any piece of territory meant large areas of ocean space and seabed.

Reviewing the status of the claims, statements, and actions of each party shows that only the two Chinas and Vietnam have claimed all the islands and reefs in the South China Sea. The Philippines claims most, but not all, of the islands. It does not claim the Paracel Islands or Spratly Island itself and several islands in that immediate vicinity. Malaysia asserts sovereignty over only a few southern islands and Brunei's claim (an extension of its 1958 boundaries seaward) includes perhaps one small reef and continental shelf in the southern area.

How should these countries proceed? In the past year or so, there have been attempts by certain countries to enter into joint survey projects. The Philippines and China expressed an interest in jointly conducting survey work. South Korea and Vietnam have announced a similar plan to jointly survey a part of the South China Sea. While cooperation is a good thing, what happens if any of these surveys discover a worthy-looking geological area? Tensions would likely arise, competing claims reiterated, and so forth. It might be a wiser step for the States to put in motion a reasonable plan to identify and agree on certain areas where particular countries will jointly work before the next Persian Gulf is discovered in their own backyard.

A starting proposal would be "to agree to disagree" on who owns all the small islands in the South China Sea and to ignore the features. It is highly unlikely any boundaries can be negotiated in the near future. It is possible that partial boundary treaties may be concluded, delimiting lines on the fringe of South China Sea such as short continuation of the China-Vietnam boundary from the Gulf of Tonkin. However, the States need to look for ways to carve up, or jointly develop, the region without using any of these small islands. As can be seen in Figure 1, if 200-nautical-mile limits were drawn from the "mainlands," ignoring the small islands in the South China Sea, then there would be a donut hole in the middle.

Many law of the sea experts would argue that most, if not all, the islands in the South China Sea should be considered Article 121, paragraph 3 rocks, and thus should not receive any EEZ or continental shelf. Even if the argument is persuasive that a given island is an island and not a rock, it is likely that the feature may be discounted, or given less than full consideration, in a maritime boundary delimitation. When reviewing the State practice of how States have negotiated maritime boundary treaties, it becomes apparent that a key element is one of geographic balance between the coastlines of two States. In situations where an island of one State is situated in front of the other State, it often is given less than full consideration. This would be the situation in the South China Sea.

One long-term solution scenario would be to identify areas of the South China Sea over which only two countries dispute the area. For example, in the north, the two Chinas and Vietnam are the only claimants to the Paracel Islands. To the north and east of the Paracel Islands, the area would involve only the two Chinas and the Philippines.

The interests of Brunei and Malaysia would be kept to some designated area in the southern part of the South China Sea. The possibility exists that, depending on how Malaysia and Brunei resolve their dispute, Brunei's maritime jurisdiction may not even reach the area where the other States claim. The tricky part comes in the center of the South China Sea, and here the players would be China, Taiwan, Vietnam, and the Philippines. Proximity as a criterion in any proposed solution puts China and Taiwan at a disadvantage because most of the disputed parcels of territory are closer to Vietnam and the Philippines. But, a tri- or quadruple-State commission (China-Taiwan-the Philippines-Vietnam) could be established to create a development strategy by which shares in certain areas could be based on nondistance criteria.

To begin this process, the States may wish to call in an outside entity (an organization, Government, group of experts) which could offer nonbinding advice and recommendations on how to allocate the area to the respective States, or to create joint development schemes. In addition to developing the nonliving resources, other aspects requiring cooperation among the parties would be: fishing, navigation, surveying, weather alerts (tsunamis), environment protection, and so forth. The opportunities are endless for these countries to work together and to enjoy the fruits of what the waters and seabed have to offer. The political will of all entities involved needs to be present for any scenario to have a chance of succeeding.

Postscript: The View of the United States

The United States has a vested interest in a stable East Asian region. All the countries are trading partners of the United States, and key commercial and military shipping plies the waters of the South China Sea. On 15 July 2009, Ambassador Scot Marciel, deputy assistant secretary of state for East Asian and Pacific affairs, appeared before the Senate Foreign Relations' East Asian and Pacific Affairs Subcommittee to give a statement on "Maritime Issues and Sovereignty Disputes in East Asia."[64] The fact that Ambassador Marciel appeared before this subcommittee to present the State Department's views on the South China Sea signals the importance that the United States gives to this region. The thrust of the statement is that the United States has vital interests in the region, that stability and peace here serves the entire international community including U.S. interests. Marciel referred to the 2002 Declaration on the Conduct of the Parties in the South China Sea[65] as a key document with useful principles such as that all claimants should "resolve disputes . . . by peaceful means" and "exercise self-restraint." Ambassador Marciel has put the U.S. Congress on notice as well as the countries surrounding the South China Sea that the U.S. Government places a high priority on this region and that it urges the claimant States to seek a peaceful resolution to the dispute claims.

Notes

1. Heda Bayron, "New Philippine Border Law Re-ignites Territorial Disputes in the South China Sea," 17 March 2009, Voice of America, available at www.voanews.com/english/archive/2009-03.
2. Central News Agency, 9 May 2009, www.etaiwannews.com/etn/print.php. (This URL no longer exists.)
3. Reuters, 12 May 2009, available at www.reuters.com/article/oilRpt/idINPEK14634720090512.
4. 2 June 2009, Stratfor Global Intelligence, available at www.us.mc01g.mail.
5. Gabe Joselow, 16 July 2009, available at www.voanews.com/english/2009-07-16.
6. 1833 *U.N.T.S.* 397.
7. Currently the "two Chinas," the Republic of China (ROC, or Taiwan) and the People's Republic of China (PRC, or mainland China), possess the same position on their common claims in the South China Sea. It is noted that there are special international issues pertaining to the role Taiwan can play in international organizations and conventions. Since both Chinas make the same claims, references in this article to "Chinese claims" apply to both the ROC and PRC.

The "China" claim to islands, rocks, and shoals was first claimed, and illustrated, in a 1946 map produced by the Government of the ROC's Department of the Territories and Boundaries of the Ministry of the Interior. It designated its claim to the territories by depicting a "U-shaped" discontinuous line around the perimeter of the South China Sea. After 1949, the PRC has succeeded the ROC's claims to the South China Sea islands with a similar U-shaped discontinuous line on maps. The ROC has maintained its claims. See the 1946 ROC Map and the recent PRC Map attached to its 2009 Note CML/17/2009 in Nien-Tsu A. Hu, "South China Sea: Troubled Waters or a Sea of Opportunity?" in this Special Issue.

8. *North Sea Continental Shelf Cases*, [1969] *I.C.J. Reports*, 22 (emphasis added).
9. Daniel J. Dzurek, "The Spratly Islands Dispute: Who's on First?" *Maritime Briefing*, Vol. 2, No. 1, International Boundaries Research Unit, 1996, 1.
10. Spratly Island is located at approximately 8°38.5′ N, 111°55′ E and is situated in the southwest portion of these features. Vietnam occupies the island.
11. The map can be found in Dzurek, supra note 9, at 38.
12. *Ibid.*, at 48.
13. John M. Glionna, "Squatters in Paradise Say It's Job from Hell," 26 July 2009, available at www.latimes.com/news/nationworld/world/la-fg-paradise-prison26-2009jul26,0,7243566.story.
14. Tripartite Agreement for Joint Marine Seismic Undertaking in the Agreement Area in the South China Sea, 2004. See Nguyen Hong Thao and Ramses Amer, "A New Legal Arrangement for the South China Sea," *Ocean Development and International Law* 40 (2009): 339.
15. For the treaty and analysis, see T. L. McDorman, "People's Republic of China-Vietnam," in *International Maritime Boundaries*, Vol. V, eds. David A. Colson and Robert W. Smith (Leiden, the Netherlands: Martinus Nijhoff, 2005), 3745–3758.
16. *Ibid.*, at 3746.
17. Brunei Darussalau, Preliminary Submission Concerning the Outer Limits of the Continental Shelf, May 2009, available at the Web site of the Commission on the Limits of the Continental Shelf at www.un.org/Depts/los/clcs_new/clcs_home.htm.

The North Borneo (Definition of Boundaries) Order in Council, 1958, Statutory Instruments 1958 No. 1517; and the Sarawak (Definition of Boundaries) Order in Council, 1958, Statutory Instruments 1958 No. 1518.

18. Malaysia-Vietnam, Joint Submission to the Commission on the Limits of the Continental Shelf in Respect of the Southern Part of the South China Sea, Executive Summary, May 2009, available at the Web site of the Commission, supra note 17.
19. R. Haller-Trost, "The Brunei-Malaysia Dispute over Territorial and Maritime Claims in International Law," *Maritime Briefing*, Vol. 1, No. 3, International Boundaries Research Unit, 1994, 4–5.

20. The Philippines, Republic Act No. 9522, An Act to Amend Certain Provisions of Republic Act No. 3046, as amended by Republic Act No. 5466, to Define the Archipelagic Baselines of the Philippines, and for Other Purposes, approved 10 March 2009, available at the Web site of the Philippine Law and Jurisprudence Database at www.lawphil.net/statutes/repacts/ra2009/ra_9522_2009.html (accessed 8 August 2009). See also the Philippines, "PGMA Signs Baselines Bill into Law," 11 March 2009, available at the official Government portal of the Philippines at (accessed 8 August 2009).

21. See J.Ashley Roach and Robert W. Smith, *United States Responses to Excessive Maritime Claims*, 2d ed. (The Hague: Martinus Nijhoff, 1996), 216–217.

22. Treaty of Peace Between the United States and Spain, 10 December 1898, 187 *Consolidated Treaty Series* 100.

23. It should be noted, however, that specific archipelagic sea-lanes have not been designated by the Philippines.

24. The Philippines, A Partial Submission of Data and Information on the Outer Limits of the Continental Shelf of the Republic of the Philippines Pursuant to Article 76(8) of the United Nations Convention on the Law of the Sea, Executive Summary, May 2009, available at the Web site of the Commission, supra note 17.

25. An Act to Amend Republic Act No. 3046, supra note 20, sec. 2.

26. See People's Republic of China, Letter to Secretary-General of the United Nations, Doc. CML/12/2009, New York, 13 April 2009, available at the Web site of the UN Division on the Law of the Sea at www.un.org/Depts/los/LEGISLATIONANDTREATIES/Statefiles/Phil.htm; Vietnam, Permanent Mission to the United Nations, "Vietnam's Response to Philippine President's Signing of Baseline Act," 13 March 2009, available at www.vietnam-un.org/en/news.php?id=77&act=print; and Bayron, supra note 1.

27. Robert W. Smith and Bradford L. Thomas, "Island Disputes and the Law of the Sea: An Examination of Sovereignty and Delimitation Disputes," *Maritime Briefing*, Vol. 2, No. 4, International Boundaries Research Unit, 1998.

28. Informal Single Negotiating Text, Doc. A/Conf.b2/WP. 8, 7 May 1975, in Third United Nations Conference on the Law of the Sea, *Official Records*, Vol. IV (New York), 170–171.

29. Robert D. Hodgson and Robert W. Smith, "The Informal Single Negotiating Text (Committee II): A Geographical Perspective," *Ocean Development and International Law Journal* 3 (1976): 230.

30. Robert D. Hodgson, "Islands: Normal and Special Circumstances," in *Law of the Sea; Emerging Regime of the Oceans, Proceedings of the Law of the Sea Institute*, eds. J. K. Gamble and G. Pontecorvo (Cambridge, MA: Ballinger, 1974), 150–151.

31. *Ibid.*, at 231.

32. It is noted in Hodgson and Smith, supra note 29, at 231, that there are many mainland coastal areas and larger islands that are uninhabited due to arid conditions, but they clearly can generate an EEZ or continental shelf.

33. *Ibid.*, at 232.

34. See D. H. Anderson, "British Accession to the UN Convention on the Law of the Sea," *International and Comparative Law Quarterly* 46 (1977): 778.

35. Hodgson and Smith, supra note 29, at 233.

36. See, generally, Yann-huei Song, "Okinotorishima: A 'Rock' of an 'Island'? Recent Maritime Boundary Controversy Between Japan and Taiwan/China," in *Maritime Boundary Disputes, Settlement Processes, and the Law of the Sea*, eds. Seoung-Yong Hong and Jon M. Van Dyke (Leiden, the Netherlands: Martinus Nijhoff, 2009), 151–161.

37. People's Republic of China, Letter to the Secretary-General of the United Nations, Doc. CML/2/2009, New York, 6 February 2009.

38. Korea, Letter to the Secretary-General of the United Nations, Doc. MUN/046/09, New York, 27 February 2009, available at the Web site of the Commission, supra note 17.

39. See Report of the Nineteenth Meeting of the States Parties, Doc. SPLOS/203, 24 July 2009, paras. 70–79 and 106–108.

40. Dzurek, supra note 9, at 1.

41. LOS Convention, supra note 6, art. 11.

42. It should be noted that the Commission has no competence to make judgments or recommendations on a coastal State's baseline.

43. Malaysia-Vietnam Joint Submission, supra note 18.

44. The Philippines Partial Submission, supra note 24.

45. Malaysia-Vietnam Joint Submission, supra note 18; and Vietnam Submission to the Commission on the Limits of the Continental Shelf pursuant to Article 76, paragraph 8 of the United Nations Convention on the Law of the Sea 1982, Partial Submission in Respect of Vietnam's Extended Continental Shelf: North Area (VNM-N), Executive Summary, April 2009, available at the Web site of the Commission, supra note 17.

46. Brunei Preliminary Submission, supra note 17.

47. People's Republic of China, Preliminary Information Indicative of the Outer Limits of the Continental Shelf Beyond 200 Nautical Miles, May 2009, available at the Web site of the Commission, supra note 17.

48. People's Republic of China, Letter to Secretary-General of the United Nations, Doc. CML/17/2009, New York, 7 May 2009; and Letter to Secretary-General of the United Nations, Doc. CML/18/2009, New York, 7 May 2009, available at the Web site of the Commission, supra note 17.

49. Malaysia, Letter to Secretary-General of the United Nations, Doc. HA 24/09, New York, 20 May 2009, available at the Web site of the Commission, supra note 17.

50. Vietnam, Letter to Secretary-General of the United Nations, Doc. No. 86/HC-2009, New York, 8 May 2009, available at the Web site of the Commission, supra note 17.

51. PRC Letters, supra note 48, para. 2.

52. Vietnam Letter, supra note 50, para. 3.

53. Malaysia Letter, supra note 49, para. 3.

54. PRC Letters, supra note 48.

55. See Figure 1 in Nien-Tsu Alfred Hu, "South China Sea: Troubled Waters or a Sea of Opportunity?" (in this Special Issue).

56. Dzurek, supra note 9, at 11–15.

57. *Ibid.*

58. For a review of the history of the Philippine claim, see Dzurek, supra note 9, at 21; and J. R. V. Prescott, *The Maritime Political Boundaries of the World* (New York: Methuen, 1985), 217–225.

59. U.S. Embassy in Manila, Diplomatic Note No. 836 of 18 May 1961, State Department File No. 796.022/5-2461. On this topic, see Roach and Smith, supra note 21, at 216–222.

60. See Roach and Smith, supra note 21, at 220–221.

61. *Ibid.*, at 221.

62. The Philippines Partial Submission, supra note 24.

63. See Dzurek, supra note 9; and Prescott, supra note 58, for further historic analysis of the Philippine claim.

64. See Appendix 2.

65. Declaration on the Conduct of Parties in the South China Sea, 4 November 2002, available at the Web site of ASEAN at www.aseansec.org/13163.htm.

Appendix 1

Declaration of the Republic of China on the Outer Limits of Its Continental Shelf

No. 003 12 May, 2009
(ROC Ministry of Foreign Affairs, at www.mofa.gov.tw/webapp/fp.asp?xItem=38077 &ctnode=1901.)

The Republic of China (ROC), as a Contracting Party to the 1958 Geneva Convention on the Continental Shelf, enjoys sovereign rights over its continental shelf under international law. The principles of the 1958 Convention have been incorporated into the relevant provisions of the 1982 United Nations Convention on the Law of the Sea (UNCLOS). Moreover, customary international law also confirms that coastal States possess sovereign rights over the exploration of continental shelf and the exploration of natural resources thereof. This Government has long supported such basic tenets. As a matter of fact, this Government promulgated the Law on the Exclusive Economic Zone and Continental Shelf of the Republic of China on 21 January 1998, in which Article 2 stipulates that the continental shelf of the Republic of China is the submerged area that extends throughout the natural prolongation of its land territory to the outer edge of the continental margin.

The Government of the Republic of China reiterates that the Diaoyutai Islands, Nansha Islands (Spratly Islands), Shisha Islands (Paracel Islands), Chungsha Islands (Macclesfield Islands), and Tungsha Islands (Pratas Islands) as well as their surrounding waters are the inherent territories and waters of the Republic of China based on the indisputable sovereignty titles justified by historic, geographic and international legal grounds. Under international law, the Republic of China enjoys all the rights and interests over the foregoing islands, as well as the surrounding waters and sea-bed and subsoil thereof. The claims made or occupation undertaken over them by any other State for whatever reason and by whatever means will be void and null in the eyes of international law.

As a coastal State, the Republic of China since 2006 has actively initiated an investigation and related preparatory work for collecting the scientific data needed to establish its claims over the outer limits of its continental shelf in accordance with Article 76 of the UNCLOS as well as the requirements of the Scientific and Technical Guidelines of the Commission on the Limits of the Continental Shelf.

As indicated by the materials collected through the said investigation undertaken by this Government, the continental margin to the east of Taiwan and the continental margin along the East China Sea to the northeast of Taiwan can be used by this country to claim its extended continental shelf. The related scientific evidence proves that the span of natural prolongation of the continental shelf of this country goes beyond 200 nautical miles from the territorial sea baselines in the "Eastern Taiwan Waters" and the "East China Sea Waters." Parts of such extended continental shelf overlap with the continental shelf claimed by the neighboring countries of the Republic of China.

This Government has recruited experts in the legal, policy, scientific and technical fields to make every endeavor in the preparatory work for the drawing up of the outer limits of the continental shelf of the ROC. As this Country was not invited to participate in the negotiation and signing of the UNCLOS, it was unable to become a party State to the UNCLOS. As a result, this Government is not legally bound by the SPLOS/72 and SPLOS/183 decisions made by the Meetings of the Contracting Parties to the UNCLOS. Accordingly, the making of claims over the extended continental shelf by this country is not constrained by the date of 12 May 2009. After this date, this country shall remain entitled to make claims on the outer limits of its extended continental shelf beyond 200 nautical miles with respect to the waters of the East China Sea, the Eastern Taiwan, and the South China Sea.

Article 76, paragraph 10 of the UNCLOS provides, "[t]he provisions of this article are without prejudice to the question of delimitation of the continental shelf between States with opposite or adjacent coasts." Since this country and its neighboring countries have not reached any agreements on the maritime delimitation of the surrounding waters, the resolution of the issues regarding the maritime delimitation between this country and its neighboring countries should be made in accordance with international law and the equitable principle through the conclusion of an agreement. Pending the conclusion of such an agreement, the Government of the Republic of China calls upon all concerned parties in the region to assist in preserving the regional maritime legal order. Together we should maintain regional peace and stable development and substantively promote positive relations under the principle of "joint exploitation and resources-sharing."

Appendix 2

Statement by U.S. Department of State
Deputy Assistant Secretary Scot Marciel
Bureau of East Asian and Pacific Affairs
Statement Before the Subcommittee on East Asian and Pacific Affairs
Senate Foreign Relations Committee, Washington, D.C.
July 15, 2009
Maritime Issues and Sovereignty Disputes in East Asia

(U.S. State Department, at www.state.gov/p/eap/rls/rm/2009/07/126076.htm)

Chairman Webb and Members of the Committee, I am pleased to testify before you today on maritime and sovereignty issues in East Asia. The sea lanes that run through East Asia are some of the world's busiest and most strategically important. They serve as the prime arteries of trade that have fueled the tremendous economic growth of the region and brought prosperity to the U.S. economy as well. Billions of dollars of commerce—much of Asia's trade with the world, including the United States—flows annually through those waters. Over half of the world's merchant fleet by tonnage sails through the South China Sea alone each year.

The United States has long had a vital interest in maintaining stability, freedom of navigation, and the right to lawful commercial activity in East Asia's waterways. For decades, active U.S. engagement in East Asia, including the forward-deployed presence of U.S. forces, has been a central factor in keeping the peace and preserving those interests. That continues to be true today. Through diplomacy, commerce, and our military presence, we have protected vital U.S. interests. Our relationships with our allies remain strong, the region is at peace, and—as you know well—the U.S. Navy continues to carry out the full range of missions necessary to protect our country and preserve our interests.

Our presence and our policy have also aimed to support respect for international maritime law, including the UN Convention on the Law of the Sea. Although the United States has yet to ratify the Convention, as you know Mr. Chairman, this Administration and its predecessors support doing so, and in practice, our vessels comply with its provisions governing traditional uses of the oceans.

Issues surrounding maritime and sovereignty disputes in East Asia are multifaceted and complex. With your indulgence, Mr. Chairman, I am going to focus on three topics:

—First, the multiple sovereignty disputes in the South China Sea;
—Second, recent incidents involving China and the activities of U.S. naval vessels in international waters within that country's Exclusive Economic Zone (EEZ);
—And finally, the strategic context of these distinct topics and how the United States should respond.

China, Vietnam, Taiwan, the Philippines, Malaysia, Indonesia, and Brunei each claim sovereignty over parts of the South China Sea, including its land features. The size of each party's claim varies widely, as does the intensity with which they assert it. The claims center on sovereignty over the 200 small islands, rocks and reefs that make up the Paracel and Spratly Islands chains.

Sovereignty disputes notwithstanding, the South China Sea is largely at peace. Tensions among rival claimants rise and fall. To date, the disputes have not led to sustained military conflict. In 2002, the ASEAN countries and China signed the "Declaration on the Conduct of Parties in the South China Sea." While non-binding, it set out useful principles, such as that all claimants should "resolve disputes ... by peaceful means" and "exercise self-restraint," and that they "reaffirm their respect for and commitment to the freedom of navigation in and overflight above the South China Sea, as provided for by the universally recognized principles of international law, including the 1982 UN Convention on the Law of the Sea."

More importantly, the 2002 document signaled a willingness among claimants to approach the dispute multilaterally. We welcomed this agreement, which lowered tensions among claimants and strengthened ASEAN as an institution. It has not eliminated tensions, nor has it eliminated unilateral actions by claimants in the South China Sea, but it's a start, and a good basis on which to address conflict in the region diplomatically.

U.S. policy continues to be that we do not take sides on the competing legal claims over territorial sovereignty in the South China Sea. In other words, we do not take sides on the claims to sovereignty over the islands and other land features in the South China Sea, or the maritime zones (such as territorial seas) that derive from those land features. We do, however, have concerns about claims to "territorial waters" or any maritime zone that does not derive from a land territory. Such maritime claims are not consistent with international law, as reflected in the Law of the Sea Convention.

We remain concerned about tension between China and Vietnam, as both countries seek to tap potential oil and gas deposits that lie beneath the South China Sea. Starting in the summer of 2007, China told a number of U.S. and foreign oil and gas firms to stop exploration work with Vietnamese partners in the South China Sea or face unspecified consequences in their business dealings with China.

We object to any effort to intimidate U.S. companies. During a visit to Vietnam in September 2008, then-Deputy Secretary of State John Negroponte asserted the rights of U.S. companies operating in the South China Sea, and stated that we believe that disputed claims should be dealt with peacefully and without resort to any type of coercion. We have raised our concerns with China directly. Sovereignty disputes between nations should not be addressed by attempting to pressure companies that are not party to the dispute.

We have also urged that all claimants exercise restraint and avoid aggressive actions to resolve competing claims. We have stated clearly that we oppose the threat or use of force to resolve the disputes, as well as any action that hinders freedom of navigation. We would like to see a resolution in accordance with international law, including the UN Convention on the Law of the Sea.

There are various other maritime-related disputes in East Asia. Japan and China have differences over EEZ limits in the East China Sea, and sovereignty over the Senkaku Islands. These disputes have drawn less attention than those in the South China Sea. We continue to monitor developments on all of these maritime disputes, as quarrels over sovereignty can escalate quickly in a region where nationalist sentiment runs strong.

I would now like to discuss recent incidents involving China and the activities of U.S. vessels in international waters within that country's Exclusive Economic Zone (EEZ). In March 2009, the survey ship *USNS Impeccable* was conducting routine operations, consistent with international law, in international waters in the South China Sea. Actions taken by Chinese fishing vessels to harass the *Impeccable* put ships of both sides at risk, interfered with freedom of navigation, and were inconsistent with the obligation for ships at sea to show due regard for the safety of other ships. We immediately protested those actions to the Chinese Government, and urged that our differences be resolved through established mechanisms for dialogue—not through ship-to-ship confrontations that put sailors and vessels at risk.

Our concern over that incident centered on China's conception of its legal authority over other countries' vessels operating in its Exclusive Economic Zone (EEZ) and the unsafe way China sought to assert what it considers its maritime rights.

China's view of its rights on this specific point is not supported by international law. We have made that point clearly in discussions with the Chinese and underscored that U.S. vessels will continue to operate lawfully in international waters as they have done in the past. I would note that there have been no further incidents of harassment by Chinese fishing vessels since mid-May.

In closing, I would like to look at both these concerns—the EEZ concerns with China and the overlapping South China Sea claims—in a broader strategic context. Specifically, what do these issues signify for international law and for the evolving power dynamics in East Asia, and how should the United States respond?

The *Impeccable* incident and the sovereignty disputes in the South China Sea are distinct issues that require distinct policy responses from the United States. On a strategic level, to an extent, both issues highlight a growing assertiveness by China in regard to what it sees as its maritime rights. In some cases, we do not share or even understand China's interpretation of international maritime law.

We believe that there are constructive ways, however, to tackle these difficult issues. With respect to freedom of navigation in the EEZ by U.S. naval vessels, we have urged China to address our differences through dialogue. Last month at the Defense Consultative Talks in Beijing, Under Secretary of Defense for Policy Michele Flournoy raised this issue, and the Chinese agreed to hold a special session of our Military Maritime Consultative Agreement (signed in 1998) to take up this issue and seek to resolve differences.

In the case of the conflicting sovereignty claims in the South China Sea, we have encouraged all parties to pursue solutions in accordance with the UN Convention on the Law of the Sea, and other agreements already made between ASEAN and China.

The assertions of a number of claimants to South China Sea territory raise important and sometimes troubling questions for the international community regarding access to sea-lanes and marine resources. There is considerable ambiguity in China's claim to the South China Sea, both in terms of the exact boundaries of its claim and whether it is an assertion of territorial waters over the entire body of water, or only over its land features. In the past, this ambiguity has had little impact on U.S. interests. It has become a concern, however, with regard to the pressure on our energy firms, as some of the offshore blocks that have been subject to Chinese complaint do not appear to lie within China's claim. It might be helpful to all parties if China provided greater clarity on the substance of its claims.

We need to be vigilant to ensure our interests are protected and advanced. When we have concerns, we will raise them candidly, as we have done over the pressuring of our companies.

We note that China has taken a more conciliatory approach to resolving some disputes over its land borders. Last year, for example, China and Vietnam concluded a land border demarcation agreement. China's general diplomatic approach to Southeast Asia has emphasized friendship and good-neighborliness. Likewise, China's anti-piracy deployment to the Gulf of Aden has been a positive contribution to a common international concern. We are encouraged by these steps, and hope that China will apply the same constructive approach to its maritime rights and boundaries.

We have a broad relationship with China, Mr. Chairman, which encompasses many issues of vital strategic importance to both countries. We agree closely on some issues; on others, we frankly have differences. Our bilateral relationship can accommodate and respect those differences, and address them responsibly through dialogue.

Thank you for your time, and I am pleased to answer your questions.

A Strategic Perspective on Security and Naval Issues in the South China Sea

CHRIS RAHMAN
MARTIN TSAMENYI

Australian National Centre for Ocean Resources and Security
University of Wollongong
Wollongong, New South Wales, Australia

Maritime security in the South China Sea faces a number of challenges, ranging from lower-level nontraditional threats to traditional politicostrategic considerations, including the potential for conflict between regional states over territory or marine resources and the possibility of conflict between major powers. This article focuses on the major South China Sea sea lines of communication, regional naval developments, and a case study of Chinese opposition to military operations in its South China Sea exclusive economic zone. It argues that Beijing is again exhibiting a more assertive posture to bolster its strategic position in the South China Sea while the other South China Sea states are also asserting their claims and developing naval capacity.

Introduction

Good order and security in the South China Sea face a number of challenges, ranging from nontraditional threats to the environment and the economic well-being of small coastal communities reliant on the sea; to more traditional concerns over piracy and other criminal activity at sea; to political considerations, including the potential for conflict between regional states over disputed territory, maritime jurisdiction, and related marine resources. At the highest level of the threat spectrum, the possibility of conflict between major powers is also rarely absent from such an important sea area, which involves some of the world's busiest and most important sea lines of communication (SLOC).

There are many reasons, on paper, why efforts to address and ameliorate challenges to order, security, and well-being in a semienclosed sea area, within which many of those challenges are transnational, ought to be shared cooperatively between littoral states. However, the political sensitivities involved in Southeast Asia, where national interests often clash, or at least diverge, as much as they are shared, make the achievement of a "stable maritime regime," as described by Michael Leifer in 1991, extremely unlikely.[1] The South China Sea is a difficult case due in large part to its complex geography and consequent jurisdictional quagmire. Moreover, the inconsistent perspectives and interpretations of the law of the sea held by both littoral and user states ensure that the UN Convention on the Law of the Sea (LOS Convention)[2] is an inadequate basis for the establishment of Leifer's stable maritime regime.[3]

Further, the region is becoming increasingly unsettled by strategic uncertainty and dynamism, with the rise of China and its growing assertiveness casting ever-longer shadows over long-standing territorial disputes and historical enmities. In addressing the strategic and naval aspects of South China Sea security, this article has selected three areas for more detailed analysis among the many possible candidate options: strategic geography, naval and strategic developments, and recent controversial episodes with respect to military operations in the exclusive economic zone (EEZ).

Strategic Geography

The South China Sea is a large space linking southern China and Taiwan to peninsular and archipelagic Southeast Asia and peninsular and continental Southeast Asia to archipelagic Southeast Asia. The South China Sea also constitutes a vital section of the seaborne trade route linking: both Europe and the Middle East to Northeast Asia; Southeast Asia to Northeast Asia; and much of Southeast Asia to the Pacific Ocean and North America.[4] The geography of the South China Sea area is an important factor in a strategic analysis. Its central location in East Asia ensures its importance for trade and strategic communications. Its complexity ensures both physical dangers for the safety of navigation and political dangers as a source of international dispute. Indeed, the varied political, cultural, ethnic, historical, and strategic identities of its littoral polities ensure a potential for dispute or conflict that is all but permanent.

The South China Sea is semienclosed by eight littoral polities: Brunei, China, Indonesia, Malaysia, the Philippines, Singapore, Taiwan, and Vietnam as well as Cambodia and Thailand within the Gulf of Thailand. The geographic limits of the South China Sea are poorly defined and to some extent contested. The International Hydrographic Organization (IHO), for example, has been trying to revise its published 1953 South China Sea limits for over 20 years.[5] The revised 2002 edition of its *Limits of Oceans and Seas* publication remains in draft form only.[6] The 2002 draft edition excludes significant areas incorporated within the 1953 edition: the Natuna Sea in the south (this revision seems to approximate Indonesia's archipelagic baselines); the Gulf of Tonkin in the west (in addition to the already excluded Gulf of Thailand); and the Taiwan Strait in the north.[7] This article takes no position on the limits of the South China Sea, simply noting the problematic nature of definition.[8] Nevertheless, no matter where exactly the limits are drawn, it is a large body of water encompassing a surface area of approximately 2.7 million to 3 million square kilometers.

Choke Points

The South China Sea's geographical complexity, largely due to the archipelagic nature of its eastern and southern bounds, means that most of its principal entry and exit points for maritime navigation are narrow and represent "choke points" in terms of maritime security. Some of these routes are very narrow and potentially hazardous, with others less so. The most significant of these potential choke points are:[9]

- the Straits of Singapore and Malacca—the shortest route connecting the South China Sea with the Indian Ocean, via the Andaman Sea;

- the Karimata Strait—connecting with the Java Sea and thence to the Sunda and Lombok Straits;
- the Balabac Strait—connecting with the southern part of the Sulu Sea (south of Palawan) and thence to the Pacific Ocean via the Surigao Strait and Philippine Sea;
- the Mindoro Strait—connecting via the Apo East Pass and Cuyo East Pass with the northern part of the Sulu Sea;
- the Verde Island Passage—an alternative route connecting to the Sulu Sea via the Cuyo East Pass and to the Philippine Sea and Pacific Ocean via the San Bernadino Strait;
- the Bashi Channel and Balintang Channel—connecting with the Philippine Sea and Pacific Ocean between Taiwan and Luzon; and
- the Taiwan Strait.

Sea Lines of Communication

As previously noted, the South China Sea represents one of the world's most important maritime thoroughfares. Quality data on shipping through the region are difficult to come by. However, some of the commonly cited figures include that trade across the South China Sea involves approximately half the annual global merchant fleet tonnage. In particular, it is a lifeline for seaborne energy supplies from the Middle East, Africa, Australia, and Southeast Asia to the large resource import-dependent economies of Northeast Asia. Oil, especially, is a strategically essential commodity, making the South China Sea important for both maritime and energy security. A significant proportion of the world's annual oil and gas shipments transit the South China Sea: in approximate terms, Japan, South Korea, and Taiwan each import over 80% of their crude oil via the South China Sea; and, for China, which now imports over 50% of its total oil consumption, around 80% to 90% of those imports cross the South China Sea.[10] The quantity of oil, gas, and other energy resources imported across these SLOC is expected to increase significantly over the next few decades.

As noted above, there is not a single sea-lane, but many, depending on the origins and destinations of voyages, direction of voyages, and the time of year and hence weather patterns. The most important sea-lane is the route that enters and exits the South China Sea via the Malacca and Singapore Straits, which will continue to see ever-greater quantities of shipping over time, despite the short-term dampening effects of the global economic crisis. Over the recent past, for example, the number of merchant ships on international voyages transiting the Malacca Strait increased from around 44,000 in 1999 to over 70,000 in 2007.[11]

The route followed once a ship has exited the Malacca and Singapore Straits (or taken on route to the straits), however, can differ depending on the factors noted above. Most typically ships leaving the Singapore Strait, and heading northeastward, pass to the west of the Anambas Islands of Indonesia, between Charlotte Bank and Prince Consort Bank (or Xiwei Tan 西衛灘 in Chinese) of the Spratly Islands, between Bombay Reef (or Langhua Jiao 浪華礁 in Chinese) of the Paracel Islands and Macclesfield Bank (or Zhongsha Qundao 中沙群島 in Chinese) and then to Hong Kong or through the Taiwan Strait; or to the east of Macclesfield Bank and then through either the Bashi or Balintang Channel to Japan or other Northeast Asian destinations. Other routes link Singapore to the Pacific Ocean, including the route passing Prince Consort Bank and then heading past North Danger Reef (or Shuangzi Qunjiao 雙子群礁 in Chinese) of the Spratly Islands to the Verde Island

Passage of the Philippines and then to the San Bernadino Strait of the Philippines; the route that passes close to the west coast of Borneo and then through the Palawan Passage (between Palawan and the Spratly archipelago) to the Verde Island Passage; or the route again passing close to the west coast of Borneo, via the Balabac Strait, the Sulu Sea, and Surigao Strait (or Basilan Strait and Celebes Sea).[12] While the main SLOC run north-south, there are also important east-west routes linking Southeast Asia with North America and the Panama Canal. Some routes connecting Hong Kong and the other ports of southern China with Californian ports and the Panama Canal also cross the northern section of the South China Sea, connecting to the Pacific via the Balintang Channel.[13]

The Straits of Lombok and Sunda are also feeders into the South China Sea. The Lombok Strait is an important route for large tankers with draughts too deep to undertake the Malacca Strait passage. Thus, shipping may transit through the Java Sea and Karimata Strait into the South China Sea using either of the two straits. Not all vessels transiting the Lombok Strait pass through the South China Sea, however, as many transit the Makassar Strait and the Celebes Sea to the Pacific Ocean. However, the Lombok-Makassar-Celebes route is used, for example, by Australian liquefied natural gas tankers bound for Guangdong Province in southern China, which then pass through the Sibutu Passage and Sulu Sea and via the Mindoro Strait to the South China Sea. The South China Sea-Mindoro Strait route also is used by southbound traffic from Shanghai heading to the Torres Strait.[14]

Although it is often noted that the disputed South China Sea island groups sit astride the major SLOC, Northeast Asia-bound shipping mostly sails west of the Spratlys—an area to be avoided by shipping as a navigation hazard—passing between the Paracels and Scarborough Shoal (or Huangyan Dao 黃岩島 in Chinese) and close to the Pratas Islands (or Tungsha Qundao 東沙群島 in Chinese) to the north, proceeding either through the Taiwan Strait or the Bashi or Balintang Channels. The Palawan Passage route skirts the Spratlys on the archipelago's eastern side.

South China Sea SLOC are not vital only to trade. They also constitute the essential and shortest routes linking the western Pacific with the Indian Ocean for the region's navies. The U.S. Pacific Command, in particular, with naval bases in Pearl Harbor, Guam, and Japan, has responsibilities throughout the Pacific and Indian Oceans. It was notable, for example, during the initial phases of Operation Enduring Freedom against al-Qaeda and the Taliban in Afghanistan in late 2001 and 2002, that U.S. naval assets and supplies transited from those bases into the Indian Ocean via the Malacca Strait. Other regional navies also make use of the South China Sea both as an operational area and transit route.

In theory, at least, SLOC security is a common concern of all littoral, maritime, and trading states. Cooperation in Asia to improve the safety and security of shipping from piracy and navigational hazards and even the potential threat of terrorism has been growing, albeit slowly. This has involved international, regional, subregional, and bilateral cooperative measures, none of which, however, have been able to mitigate the region's underlying strategic tensions.[15] China, for example, despite having a strong interest in the safety of its shipping through the South China Sea and associated straits, maintains a rather traditional view of SLOC security, with a possible U.S. blockade of China-bound shipping in the event of a conflict over Taiwan being a primary concern.

Naval and Strategic Developments

Although the defense budgets of most Southeast Asian states were badly hit by the Asian economic crisis of 1997–1998, in recent times defense spending has again been on the rise. It is not yet clear whether the current global financial crisis will have significant lasting effects on defense budgets, but thus far many players seem relatively immune. Of the major powers, the Chinese and Indian defense budgets, in particular, have consistently grown at a high rate over the past decade, with China having increased its defense budget annually at a double digit clip for two decades.[16]

Drivers of Naval Modernization

There have been a number of factors driving, or at least influencing, naval modernization, including simply the ability to afford new capabilities. A leading factor in the South China Sea has been the disputes over the territorial features and, as a consequence, the potential maritime jurisdiction to which such features may be entitled, including the related living and nonliving marine resources. Questions exist over the extent of possible hydrocarbon resources in the central South China Sea. Another factor often overlooked is the South China Sea's importance as a fishing ground, accounting for 10% of the global catch,[17] with the annual harvest of around 5 million tonnes representing the fourth largest of the world's 19 major fishing areas.[18] Seafood provides a high proportion of the regional population's protein intake as well as being an important source of livelihood. Across Southeast Asia it is estimated that there are 10 million fishermen, with up to 100 million people relying on regional fisheries for their economic well-being.[19] It therefore is not surprising that much of the low-level conflict in and around disputed island groups have involved fisheries.

One of the ways in which the Spratly Island disputes have been militarized by the claimant states has been occupation of territorial features by military personnel and the construction of military facilities. Vietnam is believed to occupy around 25 features (including Spratly Island, or Nanwei Dao 南威島 in Chinese), the Philippines 8 (including Thitu Island, or Pagasa in Tagalog, Zhongye Dao 中業島 in Chinese), Malaysia 3, and Taiwan the largest island (Itu Aba, or Taiping Island 太平島 in Chinese).[20] China is thought to occupy at least 8 features: Subi Reef (or Zhubi Jiao 渚碧礁 in Chinese), Gaven Reef (Nanxun Jiao 南熏礁 in Chinese), Johnson Reef (Chigua Jiao 赤瓜礁 in Chinese), Kennan Reef (Ximen Jiao 西門礁 in Chinese), Fiery Cross Reef (Yongshu Jiao 永暑礁), Cuarteron Reef (Huayang Jiao 華陽礁), North Danger (Shuangzi Qunjiao 雙子群礁), and Mischief Reef (Meiji Jiao 美濟礁).[21] Other sources have cited the total number of occupied features as ranging from 45 to 58, even though, as noted by one political geographer, only 36 of the features seem to lie above the water at high tide.[22]

The island disputes exacerbate an already complex tangle of maritime claims in the South China Sea, where many boundaries remain undelimited and jurisdiction over marine resources contested. A further irritant has been new maritime claims to extended continental shelf areas, particularly the joint submission to the UN Commission on the Limits of the Continental Shelf (CLCS) by Malaysia and Vietnam,[23] and the submission by Vietnam regarding the northern area of the South China Sea,[24] which elicited strongly worded protests from China.[25] Other claimants are likely to follow with their own claims, further escalating tensions,[26] and thus also influencing naval development.

The centrality of China's role as a claimant state, and the linkages between its interests in the South China Sea and the development of Chinese maritime power and its overall ambitions for regional hegemony, make the disputes important beyond the limited face value of a few small, scattered islands, rocks, and reefs—or even potential energy resources. China has long been wary of the strategic presence of opposing hegemonic powers in Southeast Asia, who might exploit Chinese weaknesses at sea to apply pressure on China from its southern maritime periphery. China's strategic ambitions in the South China Sea therefore involve the extension of its defensive perimeter, countering the presence of other major powers, countering threats to its territorial and maritime interests by other claimants, and, ultimately, seeking some measure of maritime command over the area to enforce its hegemonic pretensions.

Furthermore, China also has an interest in being able to exert control over East Asian sea-lanes, both to safeguard its own oil supplies and to threaten the economic lifelines of Taiwan and Japan if necessary. A permanent strategic presence in the South China Sea, particularly if it can successfully enforce its territorial claims, might conceivably provide China with such an ability in the future. The establishment of bases, staging, and surveillance posts along the vital sea-lanes has been described as China's "string of pearls" strategy by a U.S. report, *Energy Futures in Asia*, produced by consultants Booz Allen Hamilton for the Office of the Secretary of Defense.[27] A string of ports, bases, and listening posts stretching from the entrance to the Persian Gulf through to the South China Sea constitute the so-called "pearls." There has been some scepticism, however, over the status and utility of some of the alleged facilities.[28]

Although the Spratly Group itself is avoided by shipping, bases in the islands conceivably could be used to disrupt shipping, as was the case in World War II when Japan based submarines at Itu Aba for that purpose.[29] However, the small size of even the largest islands in the Spratly Group, their isolation and need for infrastructure and constant replenishment, mean that they would have minimal strategic value in any significant conflict. Instead, they are highly vulnerable, indeed probably incapable of being defended against concerted attack. Any strategic value they may hold pertains mostly during peacetime, as surveillance or staging outposts, and as political indicators of intent with respect to territorial and maritime claims.

Nevertheless, in a reflection of the string of pearls concept, two U.S. Naval War College researchers argued that Chinese strategists view China as a rising commercial power, supposedly dominant in the South China Sea yet living under the shadow of a globally preponderant maritime power, a geostrategic situation necessitating the establishment of "bases adjoining the sea lines of communication" in the South China Sea.[30] China has over a period of more than three decades slowly built up its military facilities throughout the South China Sea, including in the Spratlys. In recent years, it has significantly enhanced bases, in particular, on Hainan Island and in the Paracel archipelago. There have also been reports that the People's Liberation Army (PLA) Navy intends to bolster its forces in the area, with a senior PLA officer suggesting that the security situation was "very grim," requiring China to deploy more ships to the disputed region, and to enhance the militarization of occupied features in the Spratlys, including constructing a port for naval vessels and an airport on Mischief Reef, a Chinese occupied reef that lies inside the EEZ claimed by the Philippines.[31]

Chinese strategists also noted the geopolitical importance of controlling Taiwan and the Taiwanese-occupied islands in the Spratlys if China is to establish a dominating position into the "southernmost reaches of the South China Sea."[32] This view of Taiwan, as a "beachhead" through which to exert dominance over maritime Southeast Asia, seems to be part of Beijing's broader geostrategic perspective on Taiwan's importance, which in large part explains China's concerted efforts since the early 1990s to undermine Taiwan's de facto independence and eventually to gain control of the island itself.[33]

Another driver of naval modernization is the likelihood that these factors have led to a degree of hedging by the Southeast Asian littoral states against strategic uncertainty or the possibility of a significant conflict. Although rarely stated by the regional states, it is fair to suggest that the most likely contingencies that might directly affect the South China Sea area involve China. The possibilities include a conflict over Taiwan, with Japan or the United States, Chinese moves in the Spratlys or against Vietnam, or the external consequences of internal instability within China itself.

Although less likely to lead to armed conflict, the region is also rife with longstanding local rivalries. Some of these are historically based, such as between Singapore and Malaysia; related to territorial or maritime disputes, such as that between Indonesia and Malaysia over the Ambalat offshore development area on the east coast of Borneo; or both, such as the nascent Philippine claim to Sabah or the long-standing enmity and distrust between Vietnam and China. Religious and ethnic factors may also play a role in some rivalries. Even though many of the rival states would never admit to it, such relationships are factors in military modernization. Many of the specific irritants do not lie within the South China Sea itself but, as influences on naval development, do have implications for security in the area. Although the concept of an "arms race" is metaphorical and of dubious utility for policymakers, to some extent there does seem to be an element of competitive arms building throughout the region, even if some of it reflects "friendly rivalry" within the Association of Southeast Asian Nations (ASEAN) community rather than dangerous strategic competition.

The need to deal with piracy and armed robbery at sea, and the potential threat of maritime terrorism, has been a spur for naval and other maritime security force enhancements in some states, especially the three littoral states of the Malacca and Singapore Straits as well as the Philippines. However, these classes of threat have been most apparent in the straits themselves in the former case, and in the Sulu-Celebes Seas area of the southern Philippines in the latter, rather than in the South China Sea proper. There have been concerns more recently, however, that piratical attacks have been on the increase in the southern reaches of the South China Sea, around the Riau archipelago, where ships often are at anchor waiting to enter the Port of Singapore, and around Mangkai Island and the Anambas Islands.[34] This may result in greater efforts being made to secure this area through which the main route to Northeast Asia from Singapore and the straits passes.

Naval modernization in the South China Sea states thus cannot be attributed to any single factor. While each individual state may have its own priorities, all of the issues discussed above influence most of the littoral states of the South China Sea to a greater or lesser extent. However, the fluid state of great power relations and the rise of China should not be discounted as a leading driver of at least some of the higher end warfighting capabilities being procured, such as submarines.

Characteristics of Naval Modernization

One of the characteristics of naval modernization in the region has been the development of coast guards or coast guard-type civilian or paramilitary organizations with a focus on maritime enforcement, safety, marine environmental protection, and other nonmilitary tasks. South China Sea states with such organizations include Brunei, China, Indonesia (which has marine police, but is considering a full-fledged coast guard as well), Malaysia, the Philippines, Singapore, Taiwan, and Vietnam.[35] The coast guards of other states, particularly those of Japan and the United States, also frequently deploy into the South China Sea.

One of the consequences of this development, however, is that the navies have been able to focus more on warfighting roles and the types of disputes that conceivably might lead to armed conflict. A number of significant capabilities are being introduced into the forces of South China Sea states, including: submarines; new, larger surface combatants; maritime-capable combat aircraft and maritime patrol aircraft; and advanced antiship cruise missiles. The expansion of regional diesel-electric submarine fleets is particularly significant, with existing users modernizing their forces and other states becoming submarine operators for the first time.

For example, Singapore has introduced four old ex-Swedish Challenger class submarines over the past few years, its first ever submarines, while it is adding two newer (albeit still 20 years old) ex-Swedish Västergötland class (A-17) ships. Significantly, the A-17s will be the first submarines in the region equipped with air independent propulsion, which enables submerged operations to continue without the need to surface for more than 2 weeks. The first A-17 is likely to enter Singaporean service by late 2010, probably replacing one of the older types.[36] Malaysia's navy will also become submarine equipped for the first time when the first of two new Franco-Spanish Scorpene vessels becomes operational in 2010.[37] It is particularly significant that Vietnam has signed a deal for six new Kilo class boats from Russia,[38] which will be the first full-sized submarines operated by Hanoi. The decision was likely to have been influenced by Hanoi's concerns over China's more assertive position in the South China Sea. Meanwhile, Indonesia is seeking to recapitalize its largely moribund submarine force while Thailand also has shown an interest in joining the regional submarine club; although the aspirations of both navies have been continually frustrated by a lack of funds.[39] Taiwan continues to pursue options to replace its small and aging submarine fleet, despite the political obstacles that have stymied it in recent years.

It is also noteworthy that several South China Sea States have introduced modern frigate and corvette-sized surface combatants in recent years, including Brunei,[40] Indonesia, Malaysia, and Singapore, while China and Taiwan have added to their own surface combatant fleets. The introduction of more of these types of vessels, including by navies with little or no experience in operating major combatant units, indicates a growing offshore emphasis to their military priorities. Together with the other navies that regularly use the South China Sea, the inescapable reality is that naval traffic and activity is thus likely to increase in the future.

Some regional states have also been developing flat deck amphibious ships, which might see deployments in the South China Sea area, especially in response to natural disasters and humanitarian crises. Thailand has long had a small aircraft carrier, although it is rarely operational. The U.S. Navy has a large carrier and amphibious force. India has long operated carriers. Japan has small helicopter carriers of the Osumi class, soon to be joined by the larger 18,000-ton Hyuga class. South Korea has built two 19,000-ton Tok-do class helicopter carriers. Australia is procuring two large (c. 27,000-ton) landing helicopter dock (LHD) vessels of Spanish design.[41] China is expected soon to develop LHD-type vessels or an aircraft carrier capability.

One of the more notable capability developments, which also indicates greater offshore priorities, is the proliferation of modern antiship cruise missiles, whether land, air, or sea (from surface ships and submarines) launched. Land-attack cruise missiles (LACMs) have also started to appear in the inventories of regional states, most notably China and Taiwan. The land-attack capabilities of some external states are also relevant to the strategic situation, especially those of the United States with respect to its deterrent posture against potential Chinese aggression. Other states developing such capabilities with relevance to security in the South China Sea include India and most recently, Australia, which announced in its 2009 Defence White Paper that its three new Aegis destroyers (to enter service over the next 5 years) and next generation frigates and submarines will all be equipped to carry LACMs, almost certain to be the U.S. *Tomahawk*.[42]

In China, the process of naval modernization and expansion has been relatively slow, but inexorable, creating real improvements in China's maritime power.[43] China has introduced several new classes of surface ships and submarines over the past decade, including: three classes of indigenous destroyers and one Russian; two classes of indigenous diesel-electric submarines and one Russian; and new nuclear powered attack (SSN) and ballistic missile-carrying (SSBN) submarines. The PLA Navy Air Force and PLA Air Force have both introduced highly capable Russian Su-30 multirole combat aircraft, with maritime strike a primary role as well as indigenous JH-7 and B-6 maritime strike aircraft.[44]

There are thought to be approximately 25–30 major surface combatants based with China's South Sea Fleet (out of a total force of around 80 ships), including both ships of the new Type 052C Luyang II and the 052B Luyang I class indigenous guided missile destroyers, and vessels of the latest frigate class, the Type 054A Jiangkai II. Interestingly, the majority of the PLA navy's amphibious warfare and transport ships are based with the South Sea Fleet, including 11 of the 19 072 II and 072 III heavy landing ships. The sole Type 071 landing platform dock (LPD) large amphibious ship (of approximately 20,000 tonnes) commissioned into the South Sea Fleet in late 2007 is based at the Zhanjiang naval base in Guangdong Province.[45] This force posture should enable rapid deployments of marines or other ground forces into the South China Sea or against Taiwan.

China's strike and antiaccess capabilities have widespread coverage, even excluding naval platforms, which are, of course, inherently mobile.[46] It is clear that, even from the Chinese mainland, the entire South China Sea now falls within range of the PLA's conventional missile and airpower. With two major naval air bases on Hainan Island, as well as bases on Woody Island (or Yungxing Dao 永興島 in Chinese, which hosts deployments of combat and other aircraft) and other islands of the Paracel Group, in addition to significant intelligence-gathering and communications facilities both in the Paracels (and to a lesser extent in the Spratlys) and on Hainan Island, China is well equipped for surveillance of the entire region.[47]

An important strategic development in the South China Sea is the expansion of the Yulin (榆林) naval base located at Sanya (三亞) on the southern tip of Hainan Island. Traditionally, the main base for the conventional submarines of the South Sea Fleet, it has undergone major expansion since the late 1990s. It now also hosts a surface fleet base for the South Sea Fleet's 9th Destroyer Flotilla, with two piers of about 1 kilometer in length, meaning that it can host very large ships, including in the future the much-anticipated Chinese aircraft carrier. The second major development is the construction of a nuclear submarine base, or 2nd Submarine Base, including three piers, an underground submarine facility, and submarine demagnetization facilities. The entrance to the underground facility is 23 meters wide, capable of housing any of the PLA Navy's submarines. The Federation of American Scientists claim that one of the PLA Navy's new 094 Jin class nuclear ballistic missile submarines is based there.[48] The waters to the south of Hainan Island exceed 5,000 meters in depth, which would enable SSBN patrols in the South China Sea.[49] However, if China wishes to transform the South China Sea into an SSBN bastion to enable a secure operating environment for its sea-based nuclear second strike capability,[50] it will need to be able to effectively deny access to the area to rival major powers, an unlikely proposition. Nevertheless, China's sensitivity to offshore surveillance of the likely SSBN operating area and the tracking of its submarines were likely behind the March 2009 *Impeccable* incident, discussed below.

The Chinese position on aircraft carriers has notably changed in recent times. While the notion of a PLA navy aircraft carrier was previously rejected out of hand, the position now seems to be that not only is it possible, but likely, even inevitable. Statements by a number of senior PLA Navy officers seem to confirm that an aircraft carrier program will soon be publicly announced.[51] Rear Admiral Professor Zhang Zhaozhong (張召忠) stated in the *Global Times* newspaper in April 2009, for example, that "[d]eveloping aircraft carriers is our first imperative."[52] The South Sea Fleet—possibly Yulin—is the most likely basing location for aircraft carriers due to the proximity to disputes where power projection capabilities would be important, and also to the major SLOC, both for protection and interdiction.

Military Operations in the EEZ

Military operations by foreign states in maritime zones of jurisdiction claimed by coastal states is a controversial issue throughout Asia, where sensitivities over sovereignty and sovereign rights at sea are strongly felt.[53] The most contentious of the maritime zones with respect to foreign military operations is the EEZ. One interpretation of the LOS Convention, which seems at least implicitly to be favored by several South China Sea states,[54] is that the EEZ constitutes a special zone of coastal waters in which the coastal state has been granted jurisdiction to make and enforce laws and regulations concerning certain activities.[55]

Some South China Sea states claim security zones at sea that attempt to restrict the activities of foreign warships or other military activities, or otherwise assert rights affecting such activities. These include China, Indonesia, Malaysia, the Philippines, and Vietnam.[56] The sensitivities of some littoral states, most notably China, have led to legal, political, and naval efforts to assert such restrictive views of navigational freedoms. China's naval or "enforcement" efforts in this regard, resulting in diplomatically significant incidents at sea, are discussed below.

The proliferation of naval capabilities and activities throughout the region's often difficult or dangerous maritime geography leads to the inevitable conclusion that incidents and accidents at sea are likely to become more common and, thus, pose a potential trigger for conflict. In particular, accidents or unexpected encounters at sea are potential consequences of increased submarine activity due to the often difficult operating conditions in the South China Sea and sometimes constrained or complex underwater geography and unhelpful acoustic conditions. Such difficulties are indicators that there is likely to be much more military hydrographic surveying and acoustic data gathering throughout the area, which will itself create tensions, especially when such activities occur in the EEZs of certain coastal states. Undelimited and disputed maritime boundaries will further complicate matters. Without such surveys, however, accidents involving submarines are even more likely.[57]

Moreover, the fact that many of the region's submarine operators are inexperienced—and some arguably of limited competence—makes the situation more dangerous. And yet it is not only the inexperienced or poorly trained that can run into difficulties with submarine operations. While doubts have been raised, for example, over the competence and training of Chinese submarine crews as a result of past accidents, experienced operators such as the United States, Australia, Britain, France, and Russia have all had serious incidents in recent years. In the Russian and Chinese cases, the outcomes were catastrophic. Thus, the idea that there will be many more submarines operating within the South China Sea, especially in the littoral areas, raises real issues of operational safety. However, greater transparency in submarine operations is unlikely because transparency would undermine the primary tactical advantage and operating characteristic of submarines—stealth.

China's Response to U.S. Military Operations

China has been the most assertive state in the region with respect to attempting to restrict, or even curtail, foreign military activities in and above areas it claims as its EEZ. There have been a number of incidents between Chinese and U.S. naval forces, including in the South

China Sea. The most explosive incident to date was the 1 April 2001 collision between a U.S. Navy EP-3E electronic intelligence-gathering aircraft and a PLA F-8 fighter aircraft, 70 nautical miles southeast of Hainan Island. The incident was the unwitting culmination of a growing aggressiveness by Chinese interceptor pilots toward similar surveillance flights over the preceding 2 months. The damaged EP-3E managed to land on Hainan Island while the Chinese fighter pilot was never found. There is little doubt that reckless flying by the Chinese pilot caused the incident. As commander of the U.S. Pacific Fleet, Admiral Dennis Blair stated at the time:

> Big airplanes like [the EP-3E] fly straight and level on their path, little aeroplanes zip around them. Under international airspace rules, the faster and more manoeuvrable aircraft has an obligation to stay out of the way of the slower aircraft. It's pretty obvious who bumped into who.[58]

The Chinese nonetheless impounded the U.S. aircraft (and detained its crew), managing to remove valuable systems before allowing its removal.[59]

Despite the fact that the collision occurred in international airspace, China asserted a right to keep foreign surveillance aircraft and warships out of its 200-nautical-mile EEZ. In the EEZ, a coastal state has sovereign rights over marine resources and jurisdiction regarding marine scientific research and the protection and preservation of the marine environment.[60] Such provisions create ambiguity, often intentionally, and have led to disputes with respect to military operations. China's arguments focused on issues of security and coastal state rights under LOS Convention Article 58, which defines the rights and duties of "other States" in the EEZ. Article 58 confers on all states the freedoms of the high seas referred to in Article 87 of navigation, overflight, and the laying of submarine cables and pipelines, including those associated with the operations of ships and aircraft, compatible with other LOS Convention provisions. Such rights must be exercised with "due regard" for the rights and duties of the coastal state and comply with the laws and regulations of the coastal state with regard to its sovereign rights.[61] It should also be noted that the "due regard" provision is reciprocal in view of the text of Article 56(2).

The LOS Convention does not specifically allocate rights for naval activities in the EEZ. Some states make the argument that military uses of the EEZ by foreign states is prohibited by Article 58 because they are either incompatible with the reservation of the highs seas for (undefined) peaceful purposes (LOS Convention Article 88), or not "lawful uses" of the sea.[62] Freedom of the seas is reduced in the EEZ, however, for non-navigation uses in that coastal states are given exclusive jurisdiction over the construction of artificial islands, installations, and structures concerned solely with resource, marine scientific research, or environmental purposes. This does not necessarily prohibit the construction or placement of military installations or devices, however, that are unrelated to the environment, resources, or marine scientific research.[62]

Contrary to China's arguments, the waters of the EEZ are best understood as being high seas, with the coastal state having sovereign rights to adopt laws and regulations with respect to the use of resources and the management of certain other activities. Other states thus retain all high seas freedoms, including the conduct of military activities, albeit noting the undefined "due regards" requirements. With respect to overflight, such as in the EP-3E case, neither the LOS Convention nor the Convention on International Civil Aviation[64] grant coastal states powers to control the airspace over the EEZ. Airspace is not part of the EEZ, and all aircraft have freedom of overflight and, therefore, the right to conduct military operations. Thus, the adoption of laws or policies for the EEZ not related to using resources; establishing artificial islands, installations, or structures; conducting marine scientific research; or protecting the marine environment are not consistent with the LOS Convention. China's objections to U.S. military activities in the EP-3E incident were not related to any of those issues.

Another significant South China Sea incident occurred on 8 March 2009, 75 nautical miles south of the coast of Hainan Island, in China's EEZ. The unarmed and civilian-manned ocean surveillance ship, USNS *Impeccable*, part of the U.S. Military Sealift Command's Special Mission Ships Program and designed to map the seabed using active low-frequency towed sonar arrays and conduct underwater acoustic data gathering, was harassed by five Chinese vessels. One was a PLA Navy intelligence-gathering ship, another a Bureau of Fisheries patrol vessel, a third vessel from the State Oceanic Administration, plus two fishing trawlers. The *Impeccable* was variously described at the time as conducting a routine seabed mapping or using a surveillance towed-array sensor system (SURTASS) to listen for and track submarines. Chinese sailors used a long grappling hook to try to snare the cable towing the deployed array and two vessels closed in to within 15 meters of the *Impeccable* and ordered it to leave the area. The *Impeccable* responded by opening its fire hoses at the Chinese, who in turn stripped to their underwear! The two Chinese vessels then closed to within 8 meters, moving directly in front of the *Impeccable* dropping pieces of wood in its path, forcing it to an emergency halt in order to avoid a collision.[65]

A Chinese Foreign Ministry spokesman stated that the *Impeccable* had "conducted activities in China's special economic zone in the South China Sea without China's permission" and demanded that the United States "put an immediate stop to related activities and take effective measures to prevent similar acts from happening," adding that U.S. claims of harassment were "gravely in contravention of the facts and ... are totally unacceptable to China."[66] Further, a PLA Navy political commissar stated that: "Innocent passage by naval vessels from other countries in the territorial waters [or] in the special economic zone is acceptable, but not allowed otherwise."[67] Another spokesman from China's Defence Ministry asserted several days later that:

> The Chinese side's carrying out of routine enforcement and safeguarding measures within its exclusive economic zone was entirely appropriate and legal.... We demand that the United States respect our legal interests and security concerns, and take effective measures to prevent a recurrence of such incidents.[68]

These statements clearly confuse the EEZ regime with that of the territorial sea and seem to be asserting territorial sea rights in the EEZ. The statements reflect Chinese laws that require warships to seek authorization prior to entering Chinese territorial waters, and further security rights in the contiguous zone.[69] Under the LOS Convention, military activities are controlled only with respect to innocent passage, transit passage, and archipelagic sea-lanes passage, none of which apply to the EEZ.[70]

Another argument made by a Chinese analysis is that the activities of the *Impeccable* were not consistent with the LOS Convention's "peaceful uses of the seas" provision,[71] stating that its operations were

> obviously aimed at collecting military information and are not for peaceful purposes. They openly encroach on the national security and peaceful order of China and constitute a threat of force against its territorial integrity and political independence.[72]

LOS Convention Article 301 prohibits "any threat or use of force against the territorial integrity or political independence of any State" and, together with the Article 88 reservation of the high seas for "peaceful purposes," is generally accepted to be a reiteration of the customary prohibition on the use of force stated in Article 2(4) of the UN Charter.[73] No sound argument can be made in the context of the LOS Convention, or any other international legal instrument, that peacetime surveillance activities in the EEZ threaten either the territorial integrity or political independence of any coastal state. Like the official Chinese arguments, these arguments again imply coastal state sovereignty in the EEZ, which is inconsistent with the LOS Convention. Moreover, it also implies that military operations and information gathering are inherently nonpeaceful. This is a meaningless argument that logically could be applied to all military operations and forces.

If China's assertions of sovereignty in the EEZ are unjustified, the interpretations of the LOS Convention over whether military surveys in the EEZ equate to marine scientific research are more ambiguous. Coastal states possess the right to regulate marine scientific research in the EEZ.[74] However, the Convention does not define marine scientific research. It can be argued that the LOS Convention regime does not encompass military intelligence-gathering activities and naval hydrographic surveys. Furthermore, such activities neither impinge upon the use of EEZ resources nor damage the marine environment. Thus, it can be argued that these activities should be deemed not to be restricted by provisions of the LOS Convention.[75] As Sam Bateman has commented on the incident:

> There are good grounds for the U.S. feeling justified in claiming the right of the *Impeccable* to work in the South China Sea. It was not marine scientific research under the jurisdiction of the coastal state and requiring prior permission of that state. Rather it was part of the high seas freedoms of navigation that UNCLOS specifically extends to an EEZ ... the tasking of the *Impeccable* ... [is] clearly military in nature. Military uses of the seas are a recognised right under international law, and it would be difficult for China to sustain an argument that the activities of these ships posed a direct threat to its national security.[76]

The *Impeccable* incident represented the most dangerous of a pattern of incidents that had occurred between China and the United States at sea in a 2-week period. A Chinese Bureau of Fisheries patrol vessel on 4 March 2009, without warning, used a high-intensity spotlight to illuminate a sister ship of the *Impeccable*, the USNS *Victorious*, 125 nautical miles off the Chinese coast in the Yellow Sea. This was followed the next day by 12 low-level passes over the ship by a Y-12 maritime surveillance aircraft. Also on 5 March, the *Impeccable* was approached by a Chinese frigate at close range, which twice crossed the surveillance ship's bow, once at a range of only 100 yards, and a Y-12 aircraft conducted 11 low-level flyovers. On 7 March, a Chinese intelligence collection ship (presumably the same one involved in the 8 March incident) asserted via radio that the *Impeccable* was conducting illegal operations and that it should leave the area or "suffer the consequences."[77] This series of events seemingly represents a growing pattern of increasing Chinese assertiveness at sea. As the U.S. Director of National Intelligence testified at the Senate Armed Services Committee: "In the past several years, they have become more aggressive in asserting claims."[78] The hardening Chinese attitude may be reflected by a 19 February Communist Party newspaper article from Inner Mongolia, which reputedly stated that: "If an American spy ship enters China's sea area again, China will sink it."[79]

The U.S. response to the *Impeccable* incident was to divert a destroyer, the USS *Chung-Hoon*, to escort the *Impeccable*, which continued its survey work.[80] China, in turn, stated that it would increase patrols in the South China and build new patrol boats.[81] A U.S. Defense Department official made it clear in Senate testimony that the United States will not back away either from its strategic role as the guarantor of regional stability or its stance on asserting its freedom of navigation rights.

> U.S. Pacific Command will continue to assert freedom of navigation rights in the region. U.S. Pacific Command will continue to conduct operations in the South China Sea, in strict compliance with customary international law as reflected in the UN Convention on Law of the Sea. The United States' activity will be governed by our interests in the region, and our desire to preserve security and stability throughout the western Pacific.[82]

A further incident occurred in June 2009 when a Chinese submarine collided with the underwater sonar array being towed by the U.S. destroyer, USS *John S. McCain*, in the South China Sea off the coast of the Philippines, during the U.S. Navy's annual naval exercises with Philippine forces. Both sides downplayed the incident, with the Americans calling it an "inadvertent encounter"[83] and the Chinese concurred. Nevertheless, a senior PLA researcher at the Academy of Military Sciences added that: "The best way to avoid such collisions is for the Pentagon to stop its unfriendly moves towards China in the region,"[84] despite the fact that the incident seems to have occurred far from waters under any form of Chinese jurisdiction.

The 1998 Military Maritime Consultative Agreement[85] between Washington and Beijing has proven ineffective in preventing such at-sea incidents or even managing incidents or crises when they occur. The United States has called for a more formal incidents-at-sea style agreement, such as that made with the Soviet Union during the cold war,[86] but thus far seems to have been either rebuffed or ignored. Yet, the expansion of the Chinese navy and China's more assertive stance at sea—as well as a general growth in naval and maritime enforcement capacity throughout the region—suggest that such incidents are likely to become more, rather than less, common.

These incidents indicate that China's practice is not consistent with the LOS Convention. China seems to be claiming some kind of jurisdiction over most of the South China Sea (i.e., all of the waters within its U-shaped line claim), stating in May 2009 that:

> China has indisputable sovereignty over the islands in the South China Sea and the adjacent waters, and enjoys sovereign rights and jurisdiction over the relevant waters as well as the seabed and subsoil thereof.[87]

Any attempt to impose its expansive EEZ views could represent an attempt to exclude foreign military aircraft and warships from the entire region. Although such a position is unenforceable in practical terms, it would reflect a Chinese desire to turn the South China Sea into a Chinese lake.

Indeed, the contested interpretation of the EEZ regime is exacerbated in enclosed or semienclosed sea areas such as the South China Sea, as the entire sea space potentially is encompassed if all littoral states claim the maximum EEZ to which they may be entitled and if EEZs are claimed for the features of the Spratly Islands. In the South China Sea, only the waters surrounding parts of the disputed Spratly Islands are not currently claimed as EEZs, although such claims are possible in the future. If EEZs were claimed from the

Spratlys features, there would be no area of high seas; if not, then a high seas enclave would exist in the center of the South China Sea. However, as argued above, this should be immaterial with respect to the rights of foreign states to conduct military activities in those areas.

Conclusion: China, Geopolitical Competition, and the South China Sea

For some years, it appeared that China had reined it its assertiveness in the South China Sea, choosing instead a conciliatory approach (or "charm offensive") of diplomacy and economic integration with its Southeast Asian neighbors. However, Beijing has returned to type and exhibited a more assertive—even aggressive—posture. China is increasing its pressure on other claimant states in the South China Sea and "unwelcome" forces such as those of the United States in a concerted fashion. This pressure, which hitherto had been primarily political and economic, is becoming increasingly militarized. There seems to be a concerted effort to bolster its strategic position in the South China Sea, returning to a trend that had been evident since the early 1970s, but which is now enabled by far greater resources and military capabilities than before.

Other South China Sea states are also asserting their own claims and developing their own naval capacity, albeit to a lesser degree than China. Combined with other drivers of regional naval modernization discussed earlier, there exists a trend to naval growth in the region. Unless the global financial crisis worsens, that trend is likely to continue. Supposedly common regional interests in SLOC security, marine environmental protection and conservation of fish stocks, energy security, combating transnational crime, and even mitigating the potential negative effects of climate change all require cooperative approaches if they are to be satisfactorily addressed. However, the region still lacks effective mechanisms by which to achieve practical cooperation, and the reality of regional political life means that those challenges are as likely to divide states as to unite them.

Underpinning all of these challenges is the growing strategic competition focused on the rise of China, which has already set in motion balancing or hedging strategies by several states, including some from the South China Sea region. Great power competition in the region—particularly centered around constraining China—inevitably will have a South China Sea element. The U.S. Navy has been a constant factor in the area since before World War II. Japan, and especially the Japan Coast Guard, and even India, make deployments into the South China Sea. The presence of these and other "external" maritime forces will probably only grow and, in combination with the naval forces of the South China Sea states themselves, will create a more complex and potentially more dangerous operating environment into the future. Any thoughts that the South China Sea can become a zone of peace and cooperation may have to be placed on hold for some time.

Notes

1. Michael Leifer, "The Maritime Regime and Regional Security in East Asia," *Pacific Review* 4 (1991): 126–136. See also, more recently, Sam Bateman, "Building Good Order at Sea in Southeast Asia: The Promise of International Regimes" in *Maritime Security in Southeast Asia*, eds. Kwa Chong Guan and John K. Skogan (London: Routledge, 2007), 97–116.

2. U.N. Convention on the Law of the Sea, 1833 *U.N.T.S.* 397.

3. Sam Bateman, "UNCLOS and Its Limitations as the Foundation for a Regional Maritime Security Regime," IDSS Working Paper No. 111 (Singapore: Institute for Defence and Strategic Studies, April 2006), 2.

4. John H. Noer, with David Gregory, *Chokepoints: Maritime Economic Concerns in Southeast Asia* (Washington, DC: NDU Press, 1996), Figures 17–20, 63–66.

5. International Hydrographic Organization, *Limits of Oceans and Seas*, Special Publication No. 23, 3rd ed. (Monte Carlo: IHO, 1953), 30–31.

6. International Hydrographic Organization, *Limits of Oceans and Seas*, IHO Publication S-23, draft 4th ed. (IHO, 2002).

7. *Ibid.*, at 6-6-6-8.

8. For a discussion on the geographical scope of the South China Sea, please refer to Nien-Tsu Alfred Hu, "Semi-enclosed Troubled Water: A New Thinking on the Application of the 1982 UNCLOS Article 123 to the South China Sea," *Ocean Development & International Law* 41(3), 2010, pp. 281–314, at 299–301.

9. See (UK) Admiralty, *Ocean Passages for the World*, 5th ed., NP 136 (Taunton: United Kingdom Hydrographic Office, 2004), chap. 7.

10. Data averaged and compiled from various U.S. government sources, including the Department of Defense, Energy Information Administration, and Office of Naval Intelligence.

11. Data from the Port Klang Vessel Traffic Service.

12. *Ocean Passages for the World*, supra note 9, at 166–172.

13. *Ibid.*, at 240–243.

14. *Ibid.*, at 203–204.

15. See Chris Rahman, "The International Politics of Combating Piracy in Southeast Asia," in *Violence at Sea: Piracy in the Age of Global Terrorism*, ed. Peter Lehr (New York: Routledge, 2007), pp. 183–198.

16. United States, Office of the Secretary of Defense, *Military Power of the People's Republic of China 2009*, Annual Report to Congress (Washington, DC: Department of Defense, 2009), 31.

17. Clive Schofield, "Dangerous Ground: A Geopolitical Overview of the South China Sea" in *Security and International Politics in the South China Sea: Towards a Cooperative Management Regime*, eds. Sam Bateman and Ralf Emmers (London: Routledge, 2009), 14–18.

18. United Nations Environment Programme (UNEP), *Global International Waters Assessment. South China Sea: Regional Assessment 54* (Kalmar, Sweden: University of Kalmar, 2005), 40–41.

19. Meryl J. Williams, *Enmeshed: Australia and Southeast Asia's Fisheries*, Lowy Institute Paper 20 (Sydney, Australia: Lowy Institute for International Policy, 2007), 27.

20. See Clive Schofield, "A Code of Conduct for the South China Sea?" *Jane's Intelligence Review*, November 2000, 37. Itu Aba is now manned by the civilian Taiwan Coast Guard Administration.

21. Greg Austin, *China's Ocean Frontier: International Law, Military Force and National Development* (St Leonards, New South Wales, Australia: Allen & Unwin, 1998), 132 and 380–381.

22. Schofield, "Dangerous Ground," supra note 17, at 11 and 22, n. 24.

23. Malaysia-Vietnam Joint Submission to the Commission on the Limits of the Continental Shelf Pursuant to Article 76, paragraph 8 of the United Nations Convention on the Law of the Sea 1982 in Respect of the Southern Part of the South China Sea, Executive Summary, May 2009, available at the Web site of the Commission on the Limits of the Continental Shelf at www.un.org/Depts/los/clcs_new/clcs_home.htm.

24. Vietnam Submission to the Commission on the Limits of the Continental Shelf Pursuant to Article 76, paragraph 8 of the United Nations Convention on the Law of the Sea 1982, Partial Submission in Respect of Vietnam's Extended Continental Shelf: North Area (VNM-N), Executive Summary, April 2009, available at the Web site of the Commission, supra note 23.

25. People's Republic of China, Letter to Secretary-General of the United Nations, Doc. CML/17/2009, New York, 7 May 2009; and Letter to Secretary-General of the United Nations, Doc. CML/18/2009, New York, 7 May 2009, available at the Web site of the Commission, supra note 23.

26. See Sam Bateman and Clive Schofield, "Outer Shelf Claims in the South China Sea: New Dimension to Old Disputes," *RSIS Commentaries*, 1 July 2009 (Singapore: S. Rajaratnam School of International Studies, Nanyang Technological University).

27. The report was first publicized by Bill Gertz, "China Builds Up Strategic Sea Lanes," *Washington Times*, 18 January 2005.

28. See, for example, Andrew Selth, "Burma, China and the Myth of Military Bases," *Asian Security* 3 (September 2007): 279–307.

29. See Geoffrey Till, "The South China Sea Dispute: An International History," in Bateman and Emmers, supra note 17, at 36.

30. James R. Holmes and Toshi Yoshihara, *Chinese Naval Strategy in the 21st Century: The Turn to Mahan* (London: Routledge, 2008), 53.

31. L. C. Russell Hsiao, "In a Fortnight: PLA General Advises Building Bases in the South China Sea," Jamestown Foundation, *China Brief*, 24 June 2009, 1–2.

32. Holmes and Yoshihara, supra note 30, at 53.

33. See Alan M. Wachman, *Why Taiwan? Geostrategic Rationales for China's Territorial Integrity* (Stanford, CA: Stanford University Press, 2007).

34. Eric Frécon, "Piracy in the South China Sea: Maritime Ambushes off the Mangkai Passage," *RSIS Commentaries*, 20 February 2009.

35. Sam Bateman, "Coast Guards: New Forces for Regional Order and Security," *AsiaPacific Issues*, No. 65, January 2003, 5.

36. Tim Fish, "Submarine Programmes Top SE Asian Wish Lists," *Jane's Navy International*, April 2010, 27.

37. Ibid., at 26.

38. Ibid., at 27.

39. Ibid., at 27.

40. Brunei, however, is now trying to sell its relatively new ships, probably because they are too large and sophisticated for Brunei's needs and its capacity to operate them.

41. See Eric Grove, "Carrier Waves: Programmes Speak of an Enduring Appeal," *Jane's Navy International*, November 2007, 31–32.

42. Commonwealth of Australia, *Defending Australia in the Asia Pacific Century: Force 2030*, (Canberra: Department of Defence, May 2009), 81. For an analysis, see Jack McCaffrie and Chris Rahman, "Australia's 2009 Defense White Paper: A Maritime Focus for Uncertain Times," *Naval War College Review* 63 (Winter 2010): 69.

43. See, generally, Chris Rahman, "The Rise of China as a Regional Maritime Power: Strategic Implications for a New Century," PhD dissertation, University of Wollongong, 2003.

44. For details on PLA maritime forces, see the generally reliable SinoDefence.com Web site, available at www.sinodefence.com/navy/default.asp.

45. Ibid.

46. See the map *Military Power of the People's Republic of China* 2009, supra note 16, at 23.

47. See Bruce A. Elleman, "Maritime Territorial Disputes and Their Impact on Maritime Strategy: A Historical Perspective," in Bateman and Emmers, supra note 17, at 46–48.

48. See the SinoDefence Web site, supra note 44; and Richard D. Fisher, "Satellite Imagery Confirms Nuclear Sub Base in China," *Jane's Defence Weekly*, 16 April 2008, 4.

49. Ibid.

50. The concept of SSBN bastions, protected by concentric layers of defensive capabilities, was developed by the Soviet Union during the cold war. For analysis, see Bryan Ranft and Geoffrey Till, *The Sea in Soviet Strategy*, 2nd ed. (Annapolis, MD: Naval Institute Press, 1989), 193–197.

51. See "Naval Chief Details Chinese Wishlist," *Jane's Navy International*, May 2009, 5; and "Speculation Mounts over PRC's Aircraft Carrier Plan," *Taipei Times*, 7 March 2009.

52. Kang Jua, "China Doesn't Need Super Navy: Military Analysts," *Global Times*, 21 April 2009.

53. See the two special issues of the journal *Marine Policy* devoted to the topic: Vol. 28 (January 2004) and Vol. 29 (March 2005).

54. For a further discussion on the debate as it stands in East Asia, see, for example, EEZ Group 21, *Guidelines for Navigation and Overflight in the Exclusive Economic Zone: A Commentary* (Tokyo: Ocean Policy Research Foundation, 2006).

55. For a forceful but unconvincing Malaysian argument to this effect, see B. A. Hamzah, "EEZs: U.S. Must Unclench Its Fist First," *RSIS Commentaries*, 9 April 2009.

56. See Stuart Kaye, *Freedom of Navigation in the Indo-Pacific Region*, Papers in Australian Maritime Affairs No. 22 (Canberra: Sea Power Centre–Australia, 2008), 8–12 and 31–35.

57. See Sam Bateman, "Perils of the Deep: The Dangers of Submarine Operations in Asia," *RSIS Commentaries*, 21 February 2007 (Singapore: S. Rajaratnam School of International Studies, Nanyang Technological University).

58. As quoted in "Trapped Behind the Lines," *The Australian*, 3 April 2001, 1.

59. "'Spyplane' Loss a Big Blow for U.S. Intelligence," *Jane's Navy International*, May 2001, 8.

60. LOS Convention, supra note 2, art. 56(1).

61. For an analysis, see Martin Tsamenyi and Barry Snushall, "The Legal Dimension of Maritime Military Operations," in *Positioning Navies for the Future: Challenge and Response*, ed. Jack McCaffrie (Sydney: Sea Power Centre—Australia and Halstead Press, 2006), 111–132.

62. *Ibid.*, at 122.

63. *Ibid.*, at 116.

64. *Ibid.*, at 116. See also Convention on International Civil Aviation, Chicago, 7 December 1944, 9th ed., 2006, ICAO Doc. 7300/9, arts. 1–3.

65. See "U.S. Angered by Chinese Naval Manoeuvres," *The Australian*, 10 March 2009; "USN-PLA South China Sea Incident," Associated Press, 10 March 2009; "China Says U.S. Provoked Naval Incident," *International Herald Tribune*, 10 March 2009; and "Surveillance Ship 'Did Not Violate Law,' Says DoD," *Jane's Navy International*, April 2009, 6.

66. As quoted in "FM: U.S. Naval Ship Violates Int'l, Chinese Law," *China Daily*, 10 March 2009.

67. As quoted in "Violation of China's Sovereignty Never Allowed," *China Daily*, 10 March 2009.

68. As quoted in "Obama–Yang Discuss U.S.-China Sea Dispute on the Sidelines of Improved Cooperation," Associated Press, 15 March 2009.

69. See Kaye, supra note 56, at 31.

70. Tsamenyi and Snushall, supra note 61, at 113–121.

71. LOS Convention, supra note 2, art. 301.

72. Ji Guoxing, "The Legality of the '*Impeccable* Incident,'" *China Security* 5 (Spring 2009): 18–19.

73. Tsamenyi and Snushall, supra note 61, at 122.

74. LOS Convention, supra note 2, arts. 56, 87, 238–241.

75. Tsamenyi and Snushall, supra note 61, at 128.

76. Sam Bateman, "Clashes at Sea: When Chinese Vessels Harass U.S. Ships," *RSIS Commentaries*, 13 March 2009, 2 (Singapore: S. Rajaratnam School of International Studies, Nanyang Technological University). For an explanation of the U.S. position, see Patrick J. Neher, Raul A. Pedrozo, and J. Ashley Roach, "In Defence of High Seas Freedoms," *RSIS Commentaries*, 24 March 2009 (Singapore: S. Rajaratnam School of International Studies, Nanyang Technological University); and Captain Raul Pedrozo, JAGC, USN, "Close Encounters at Sea: The USNS *Impeccable* Incident," *Naval War College Review* 62 (Summer 2009): 106–107.

77. "USN-PLA South China Sea Incident," Associated Press, 10 March 2009.

78. Cited in "Blair: China Gets 'More Aggressive' Against U.S. Ships," *Washington Times*, 11 March 2009.

79. Cited in *ibid*.

80. "Destroyer to Protect Ship Near China," *Washington Post*, 13 March 2009.

81. "Beijing to Deploy More Ships to the South China Sea," *Times* (UK), 19 March 2009.

82. Testimony of Deputy Assistant Secretary of Defense Robert Scher, Asian and Pacific Security Affairs, Office of the Secretary of Defense, Before the Subcommittee on East Asian and Pacific Affairs, Senate Committee on Foreign Relations, United States Senate, on "Maritime Issues and Sovereignty Disputes in East Asia," 15 July 2009, 5.

83. "Chinese Sub Smashes U.S. Destroyer's Sonar," *The Australian*, 13 June 2009.

84. As quoted in "Sub, Sonar Collision 'Inadvertent,'" *Global Times*, 15 June 2009.

85. Agreement Between the Department of Defense of the United States of America and the Ministry of National Defense of the People's Republic of China on Establishing a Consultation Mechanism to Strengthen Military Maritime Safety, Beijing, 19 January 1998.

86. Agreement Between the Government of the United States of America and the Government of the Union of Soviet Socialist Republics on the Prevention of Incidents On and Over the Sea, Moscow, 25 May 1972, as amended by a 1973 Protocol and a 1998 Exchange of Diplomatic Notes. The latter was agreed by the Russian Federation, which succeeded the Soviet Union with respect to all rights and obligations relating to the agreement.

87. See PRC Letters, supra note 25.

The ROC's Maritime Claims and Practices with Special Reference to the South China Sea

KUAN-HSIUNG WANG

Institute of Political Science
National Taiwan Normal University
Taipei, Taiwan, Republic of China

The South China Sea is an area of disputes on sovereignty and resource jurisdiction claims. As one of the six claimants, the Republic of China (Taiwan) has played an important role not only because it is the originator of the U-shaped lines, but also it has continuously occupied the largest island, Tai-Ping-Dao, in the Spratlys. This article reviews the ROC's position on the issues through an exploration of its maritime claims to the territorial sea, continental shelf, and exclusive economic zone.

Introduction

The littoral States surrounding the South China Sea claim sovereignty over all or part of the islands, rocks, reefs, or sandbanks in the area. The two Chinese Governments, the Republic of China (ROC) and the People's Republic of China (PRC),[1] have similar, or even the same, positions toward the legal status of the geographical features in the South China Sea because they draw on the same historic evidence and practices. There are also the U-shaped lines declared by the ROC Government in 1947. Many scholars have studied the definition, explanation, and legal situation of the U-shaped lines.[2] This article will review from a legal and historic perspective the position or maritime claims of the original creator of the U-shaped lines (i.e., the ROC Government) and detail the offshore zones and claims of Taiwan.

The ROC's Maritime Claims

Territorial Sea Claim

In July 1912, the year immediately after the Ching Dynasty was overthrown by Sun Yat-Sen and the Republic of China, the first republic in Asia, was established, the Department of the

Navy, taking sea power into consideration, sent a memo to the Ministry of Foreign Affairs (MOFA) and suggested that:

> Normally, the limits of territorial sea is up to three nautical miles. This is correspondent to the range of cannon-shot in the past. Lately, the more advanced the technology is, the longer the cannon-shot can reach. . . . Consequently, in order to protect our rights, the width of our territorial sea should be extended to this range.[3]

But the ROC Government took no action.

In May 1924, about 100 Japanese fishing boats engaged in fishing along the coast of Shantung (山東) Province. They destroyed the nets and equipment of the nearby Chinese fishermen. The Chinese Government intended to enter into negotiations with the Japanese over the issue, but the Japanese claimed that their boats were fishing on the high seas and had not intruded into the Chinese territorial sea. The situation worsened during 1929–1931 and the coastal provinces frequently requested the central Government to establish the territorial sea scheme and settle on its breadth.[4]

At the Hague Conference on Codification of International Law of 1930, the ROC, with 19 other States, took the position that the breadth of the territorial sea should be 3 nautical miles, measured from the low-water mark along the coast and that, within such area, the coastal State enjoyed full sovereignty, subject to the right of innocent passage by foreign vessels.[5] The breadth of the territorial sea was probably the most controversial topic considered by the 1930 Hague Conference. General agreements on the law of the sea were reached at the conference such as the high seas being free for the use of all; a narrow belt, generally 3 nautical miles in width, of territorial sea subject to the sovereignty of the coastal State; and a contiguous zone recognized for the control of sanitary, defense, immigration, and smuggling problems.[6]

Taking into account national security, the livelihood of fishermen, and in accordance with its position in the Hague Conference, the ROC Government declared the breadth of its territorial sea to be 3 nautical miles.[7] In addition, it also declared there to be an additional zone of 12 nautical miles, measured from the territorial sea baselines, within which there existed jurisdiction with regard to the arrest of smuggling.

Along with the international expansion of maritime jurisdiction after the Truman Proclamations in 1945,[8] the ROC Government became aware of the development of the law of the sea and took under consideration a 12-nautical-mile territorial sea. The Chinese delegate to the UN International Law Commission,[9] Shu-Hsi Hsu (徐淑希), said that the 12-nautical-mile territorial sea would meet the demands of most States.[10]

Following the beginning of the Third United Nations Conference on the Law of the Sea (UNCLOS III) in 1973, the issues of the breadth of territorial sea, the establishment of the exclusive economic zone (EEZ), as well as the definition on continental shelf were core areas of discussion. The ROC Government was anxious about the development of the international law of the sea and the possible impact on its fishing industry, especially distant water fisheries. Accordingly, on 9 December 1974, the ROC Executive Yuan[11] held a meeting and established an ad hoc committee, the Committee on the Territorial Sea Issues, to study those issues under the lead of the Ministry of the Interior.

The problems presented to the ROC by the international developments in the law of the sea were peculiarly difficult because of the adverse diplomatic situation that the ROC Government was confronting. Not only was the ROC excluded from UNCLOS III, but it did not have diplomatic relations with many countries. In the face of these difficulties, negotiating any solution to disputes that arise from time to time made it desirable for the ROC to take a cautious position on claiming rights or privileges.[12]

Nevertheless, the ROC was concerned by other coastal States' extending territorial seas and establishing 200-nautical-mile EEZs, especially after Philippine President Marcos declared in Presidential Decree No. 1599 a 200-nautical-mile EEZ on 11 June 1979.[13] The Philippine Decree had a significant impact on Taiwan because the northern limits of the Philippine EEZ, measured from its northernmost base point on the Yami Island, could cross through the middle of Taiwan Island and make all the waters south of that limit the Philippine EEZ. The ROC Executive Yuan responded by declaring an extension of the territorial sea from 3 to 12 nautical miles and the establishment of the 200-nautical-mile EEZ on 6 September 1979.[14] The Declaration was as follows:

1. The territorial sea of the Republic of China shall be measured from the baselines and shall extend to the outer limits of the water area of twelve nautical miles from such baselines.
2. The exclusive economic zone of the Republic of China shall be measured from the baselines from which the territorial sea is measured and shall extend to the outer limits of the water area of two hundred nautical miles from such baselines.

   A. The Republic of China shall have in the exclusive economic zone sovereign rights for purposes of exploitation, conservation and utilisation of the natural resources, and such jurisdiction the exercise of which are recognised under international law.
   B. Where the exclusive economic zone of the Republic of China extends over any part of the exclusive economic zones as proclaimed by other states, the boundaries shall be determined by agreement between the states concerned or in accordance with generally accepted principles of international law on delimitation.
   C. Other states may enjoy in the exclusive economic zone of the Republic of China the freedom of navigation and overflight and of the laying of submarine cables and pipelines, and engage in such other activities with respect to navigation and communication as permitted by international law.

3. The sovereign rights enjoyed by the Republic of China over the continental shelf contiguous to its coast as recognised by the Convention on the Continental Shelf of 1958 and the general principles of international law shall not be prejudiced in any manner by the proclamation of the present exclusive economic zone or the establishment of such zones by any other state.

This Declaration was endorsed by the Presidential Decree issued on 8 October 1979.[15] The Presidential Decree stated:

1. The territorial sea of the Republic of China shall be measured from the baselines and shall extend to the outer limits of the water area of twelve nautical miles from such baselines.
2. The exclusive economic zone of the Republic of China shall be measured from the baselines from which the territorial sea is measured and shall extend

to the outer limits of the water area of two hundred nautical miles from such baselines.
3. The sovereign rights enjoyed by the Republic of China over the continental shelf contiguous to its coast shall not be prejudiced in any manner by the proclamation of the present exclusive economic zone or the establishment of such zones by any other State.

The 1979 Declaration creates an overlapping EEZ area with that of the Philippines in the Bashi Channel. Moreover, due to sovereignty claims by the ROC over the Pratas Islands, Paracel Islands, Macclesfield Bank, and the Spratly Islands, Taiwan also has overlapping maritime claims with Malaysia, the Philippines, the PRC, and Vietnam in the South China Sea. There is no specific delimitation method mentioned in the Declaration but, according to paragraph 2(B): "the boundaries shall be determined by agreement between the States concerned or in accordance with generally accepted principles of international law on delimitation." This illustrated the ROC Government's aspiration and position in negotiating with its neighboring countries on maritime delimitation issues.

Continental Shelf Claim

Although the continental shelf had been an important issue in the field of international law of the sea and an international practice since the 1949 Truman Proclamation, scholars within East Asia and the Government of the ROC did not pay much attention to this topic until release in 1969 of the Emory Report that raised, for the first time, the hydrocarbon resource potential of the Asian seas.[16] Nonetheless, it is worthwhile examining the Taiwanese fishery industry's attitude toward the continental shelf.

When the 1956 International Law Commission Draft Articles on the Law of the Sea[17] were sent to States for comments, the Taiwanese fishing industry expressed the view that the sea area above the continental shelf should be considered as a part of the territorial sea and the coastal State should have the preferential rights and duties with respect to the living resources therein.[18] However, the ROC Government did not adopt this view and made no comments on the articles concerning the regime of the continental shelf.[19]

The ROC signed the 1958 Geneva Convention on the Continental Shelf on 29 April 1958.[20] No further action was taken to ratify the Convention. This changed after the release of the Emory Report, which stated that: "A high probability exists that the continental shelf between Taiwan and Japan may be one of the prolific oil reservoirs in the world. It also is one of the few large continental shelves of the world that has remained untested by the drill."[21] Soon after, the ROC Government asserted its claim to its adjacent continental shelf. In July 1969, the Executive Yuan issued a Declaration as follows:

> The Republic of China is a State signatory to the Convention on the Continental Shelf which was adopted by the UN Conference on the Law of the Sea in 1958. For the purposes of exploring and exploiting natural resources and in accordance with the principles embodied in the said Convention, the Government of the Republic of China declares that it may exercise its sovereign rights over all the natural resources of the seabed and subsoil adjacent to its coast outside its territorial sea.[22]

In early 1970, the Legislative Yuan decided to ratify the Continental Shelf Convention with the following reservation to Article 6:

With regard to the determination of the boundary of the continental shelf as provided in Paragraphs 1 and 2 of Article 6 of the Convention, the Government of the Republic of China considers:

1. that the boundary of the continental shelf appertaining to two or more States whose coasts are adjacent to and/or opposite each other shall be determined in accordance with the principle of the natural prolongation of their land territories; and
2. that in determining the boundary of the continental shelf of the Republic of China, exposed rocks and islets shall not be taken into account.[23]

With respect to the ROC reservation, its main point was regarding the Tiao-Yu-Tai (or 釣魚台 in Chinese and Senkaku Islands 尖閣諸島 in Japanese) issue or dispute with Japan. Both the ROC and Japan claim sovereignty over the Tiao-Yu-Tai Islands, which are situated on the edge of the continental shelf extended from Chinese mainland and the island of Taiwan. From the view of both the PRC and the ROC, these islands are continental in nature, appertaining to Taiwan, and are distinct from the oceanic Ryukyus in the east; therefore, claiming a continental shelf on the basis of natural prolongation would be favorable.[24] The Japanese Government takes the position that the status of Tiao-Yu-Tai Islands was *terra nullius* when it took control of the islands in 1895 as a result of the Treaty of Shimonoseki with the Chinese Government.[25] By denying the exposed rocks and islets' use as a base for claiming continental shelf, the ROC apparently was preparing its second line of defense (i.e., even if the ROC lost in the territorial sovereignty dispute over the Tiao-Yu-Tai Islands, it would still deny Japan's right to claim a continental shelf emanating from the islets). On the other hand, it can be pointed out that such a reservation would have had the undesirable effect of weakening the ROC claim to a continental shelf in the South China Sea region, if such continental shelf claim is to be based on the "exposed islets and rocks."[26]

Exclusive Economic Zone Claim

The ROC was reluctant to accept the concept of the EEZ when it first arose in the 1970s. The Executive Yuan held two meetings to examine the issues of the EEZ. Both meetings concluded that it was not appropriate to establish an EEZ or an exclusive fishery zone for three reasons:

1. The deep-sea fishery plays an important role in the ROC fishing industry. The Government deeply wishes that other States would not establish EEZs. Therefore, the ROC Government would not establish its own EEZ.
2. When the ROC Government ratified the Convention on the Continental Shelf, it declared that the delimitation of continental shelf boundary should correspond with the principle of natural prolongation of the land territory of coastal States.
3. If the ROC Government establishes EEZ, the disputes of delimitation would be arisen between it and Korea, Japan, and the Philippines. At this moment, none of those States had established any similar zone. Thus, the ROC should not establish any similar zone either.[27]

Nonetheless, as already noted, as a result of the 1979 Philippine EEZ Decree, the ROC Government declared its 200-nautical-mile EEZ on 6 September 1979. The EEZ declaration was welcomed domestically, especially by the fishing industry. The general feeling was that it was overdue because the neighboring countries, such as Japan and the Philippines, had already claimed similar zones.[28] Thus, the declaration made by the ROC Government was seen as a countermeasure to protect its fishing fleets, which had often been fined or seized by neighboring countries in disputed waters. Although the announcement did not solve the issues of maritime delimitation and fishery disputes, it did serve the purpose of notifying the neighboring countries of Taiwan's concern over these issues.

Related Legislation

Clear and unambiguous maritime zone laws and related regulations can serve the interests of both fishermen who fish in the marine environment and Government officials and administrators who may have to deal with potential fisheries conflicts or disputes.

The ROC Government declared the extension of the territorial sea and the establishment of EEZ on 6 September 1979, but there was no domestic law or regulation applied to such maritime zones so as to detail rights and obligations on the exploration and exploitation, conservation, and management of the natural resources within the EEZ in general, and to regulate fishing and other activities in particular. Moreover, without clear legal authorization, the relevant authorities may not be able to visit, inspect, detain, try, and punish those foreign vessels that intruded into the ROC's EEZ. For example, it is recorded that Japanese fishing vessels frequently intruded in and operated in the ROC's EEZ. For instance, on 19 September 1984, 40 Japanese fishing vessels were found operating in the EEZ of Pen-Chia-Yu Island.[29]

Owing to the growing concern over the lack of jurisdiction or authority to take action in the EEZ, on 11 September 1989 the ROC Ministry of the Interior convened an Ad Hoc Committee on Base Points and Baselines and Law of EEZ and Territorial Sea to study the issues. This committee, chaired by the minister of the interior, was composed of staff from the Secretariat of the Executive Yuan, the Deputy Ministers of Foreign Affairs, National Defence, Justice, Economic Affairs, Communications, Council of Agriculture, Administration of Environmental Protection, and scholars.[30] After almost 2 years of discussion and research, the committee produced two draft laws and sent them to the Legislative Yuan. The two drafts were the Draft of the Territorial Sea and the Contiguous Zone and Draft of EEZ and Continental Shelf.

The content of the two drafts was declarative rather than practical. Owing to the committee's consideration that the ROC's sovereignty and jurisdiction reaches the Chinese mainland, the baselines were drawn from the mouth of Yalu River[31] in the northeast along the coastal islands to the mouth of Peilun River in the southeast.[32] It also covers the Taiwan area, Nansha Chun-Tao (Spratly Islands) in the South China Sea, and the Tiao-Yu-Tai Islands in the East China Sea. The declaration of the sovereignty and jurisdiction over the Chinese mainland and Taiwan was a reiteration of the ROC's "Mainland Policy." As to the island groups in the South China Sea and the East China Sea, the draft laws served as a declaration of jurisdiction over them. With regard to the Spratly Islands in the South China Sea, Brunei, China, Malaysia, the Philippines, Taiwan, and Vietnam claim ownership over all or some of the islands. As for the Tiao-Yu-Tai Islands, China, Japan, and Taiwan claim sovereignty. The ROC declaration of the baselines of the territorial sea and its sovereignty over those areas would help to strengthen its position in negotiating with its neighboring countries. Nevertheless, the shortcoming would be that it was not practical to declare the ROC's sovereignty and jurisdiction over the Chinese mainland.

Only in January 1998 did the ROC Government promulgate the Law on the Territorial Sea and the Contiguous Zone, which declared its sovereignty over the territorial sea and the rights in the contiguous zone,[33] and the Law on the Exclusive Economic Zone and the Continental Shelf.[34]

Apart from the above legislation, the Executive Yuan declared, on 10 February 1999, "The First Part of the Baselines of the Territorial Sea of the Republic of China."[35] The way in which the islands in the South China Sea are described is noteworthy:

> All islands and atolls of the Nansha Islands surrounded by the Chinese traditional U-shape lines are the territory of the Republic of China. The delimitation of the baselines in this region shall be determined by a combination of straight baselines and normal baselines. The related information concerning names of the base points, their co-ordinates, and charts shall be promulgated in the future.[36] (emphasis added)

The ROC's Claim in the South China Sea: State Practice

The ROC Government was the first in the twentieth century to claim sovereignty over the Pratas Islands, Macclesfield Bank, the Paracel Islands, and the Spratly Islands, basing its claim on discovery and continuous patronage of these islands dating back to the first century.[37] When the Spratly Islands were "retroceded" to the ROC in 1946, the Kwangtung provincial Government was given jurisdiction over them.[38] In 1947, the ROC Ministry of the Interior's subsequent proposal to the central Government to "temporarily transfer jurisdiction of the islands to the ROC Navy" was approved.[39] In addition, an official map titled as "Map of the Location of the South China Sea Islands" was released that showed the Pratas Islands, Macclesfield Bank, Paracel Islands, and Spratly Islands within the 11 dotted U-shaped lines (Figure 1).

In 1948, the ROC dispatched warships to the archipelago to conduct surveys and erect landmarks.[40] In 1949, the ROC President promulgated the "Organisational Statutes Governing the Office of the Special Administrator of Hainan" and transferred the jurisdiction of the Spratly Islands from the Kwangtung provincial Government to the Hainan Special Administrative District.[41] Owing to its defeat in the civil war in May 1950, the ROC Government withdrew its forces from Hainan Island and the Paracels as well as the Spratly Islands.

According to the Treaty of Peace between the ROC and Japan signed on 28 April 1952, Japan "renounces all right, title, and claim to Taiwan (Formosa) and Penghu (the Pescadores) as well as the Spratly Islands and the Paracel Islands."[42] Although no sovereign successor was named in the Peace Treaty, the ROC claims that this treaty is proof that the ROC exercised complete sovereignty over these island groups.[43]

When, on 15 May 1956, a Philippine named Tomas Cloma claimed ownership, by discovery and occupation, of "Freedomland," the ROC Government immediately protested to the Philippine Government.[44] A naval contingent was sent to patrol the Spratly Islands, but found the Philippine had already left. Later, a Taiwanese garrison force of about 600 troops was sent to Tai-Ping-Dao (Itu Aba Island or 太平島), the largest island in the Spratly Islands, and has remained there ever since.[45] The Taiwanese Navy has patrolled Itu Aba Island and supplied the garrison there every 3 or 4 months ever since. In February 1990, the Executive Yuan placed Tung-Sha-Dao (Pratas Island) and Tai-Ping-Dao (Itu Aba Island) under the jurisdiction of the Kaohsiung city Government and set up a postal system on the

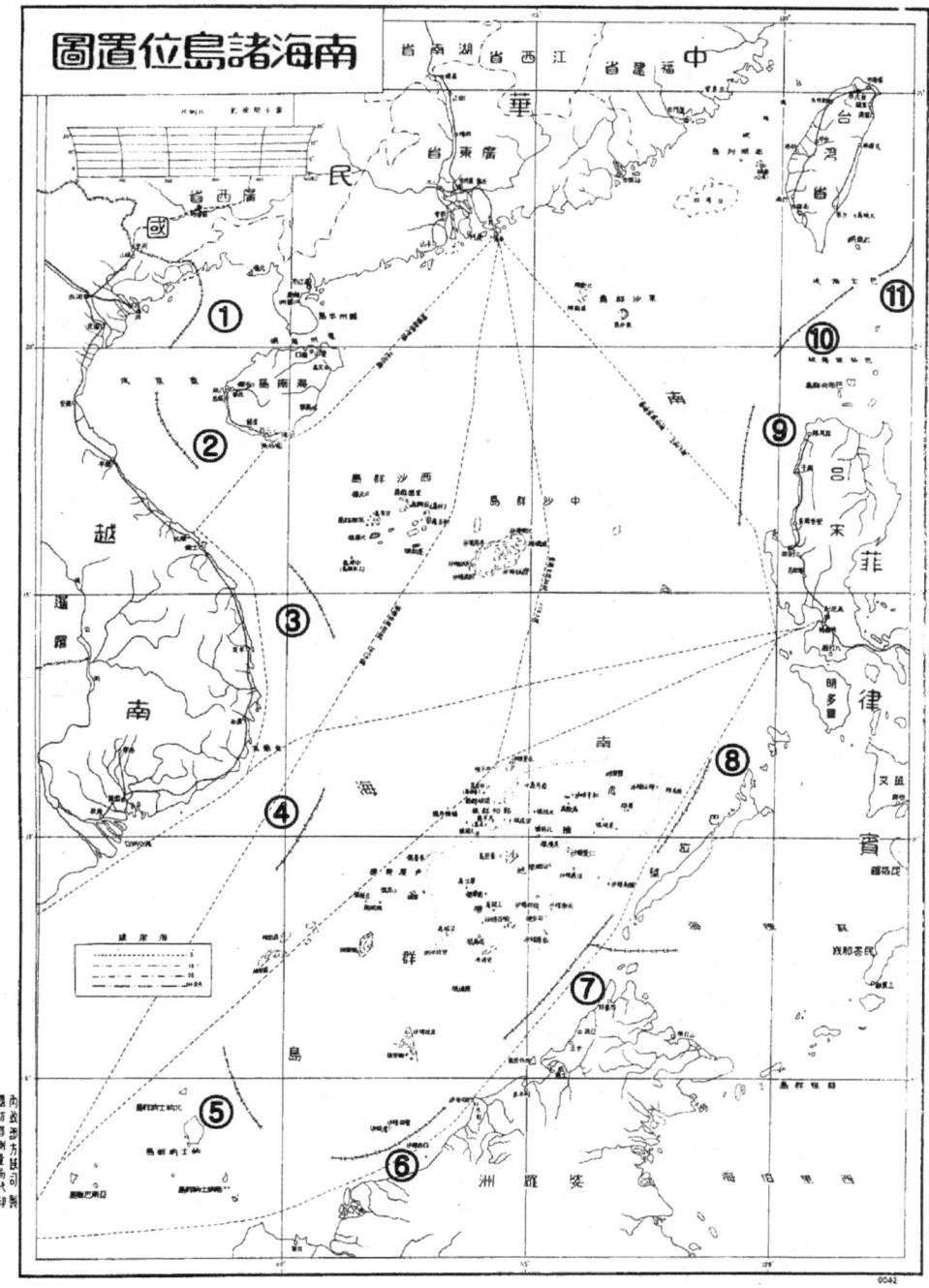

Figure 1. "Map of the Location of the South China Sea Islands" released by the ROC Government. (*Source:* See a reproduction of the original U-shaped lines map issued by the ROC Government on December 1946 in Nien-Tsu Alfred Hu, "South China Sea: Troubled Waters or a Sea of Opportunity", Figure 2, p. 6, in this Special Issue.)

islands as well as brought them under a unified administrative system.[46] In February 2000, the garrison shifted from the Marine to the Coast Guard Administration.[47]

On 13 April 1993, the ROC Executive Yuan approved the Policy Guidelines for the South China Sea, in which it stated that:

> In terms of history, geography, international law and facts, the Nansha Islands [Spratly Islands], Shisha Islands [Paracel Islands], Chungsha Islands [Macclesfield Islands], Tungsha Islands [Pratas Islands] are part of inherent territory of the Republic of China; the sovereignty over those islands belongs to the Republic of China. The South China Sea area within the historic water limit is the maritime area under the jurisdiction of the Republic of China, where the Republic of China possesses all rights and interests.[48]

In order not to create any unfavorable situation that would damage the ROC's legal claim, the MOFA has made numerous statements in response to the actions of other littoral States occurring in the South China Sea. The following are examples.

On 10 June 1997, in response to the election held by the Government of the Philippines for the village chief in the so-called Kalayaan Islands, the Government of the ROC stated that:

> The Nansha (Spratly) Islands, like the Chungsha (Macclesfield Bank) Islands, the Shisha (Paracel) Islands, and the Tungsha (Pratas) Islands, are an *integral part of the territory* of the Republic of China. The Government of the Republic of China has on numerous occasions reaffirmed its *sovereignty over these islands*.[49] (emphasis added)

Three days later, on 13 June 1997, the MOFA made almost the same statement of claiming sovereignty over the islands.[50] However, they did not touch on the status of the water area.

On 1 July 1999, the ROC lodged a protest against the occupation of Investigator Shoal and Erica Reef in the Spratly Islands by the Malaysian Government and the inclusion of the disputed Scarborough Shoal on a territorial map of the Philippine Government. In its statement, the ROC MOFA reiterated its position in the South China Sea with strong wording on both the islands and the water area.

> The Nansha (Spratly) Islands, like the Shisha (Paracel) Islands, the Chungsha Islands (Macclesfield bank) and the Tungsha (Pratas) Islands, is part of the territories of the Republic of China, whether legally, historically, geographically or in reality. *Its sovereignty undoubtedly belongs to the Republic of China*. No country or civilian group can claim or occupy these islands for any reason whatsoever.
>
> *The South China Sea is a body of water of the Republic of China. The Republic of China has all rights and privileges in the South China Sea.* Any activities (including the discussion on joint cooperation or on Code of Conduct, etc.) in the South China Sea region must acquire the approval of the Government of the Republic of China.
>
> *The Government of the Republic of China reiterates its aforementioned position and emphasises that its sovereignty, including rights and privileges,*

over the said islands, cannot be altered by any regional bilateral agreements or unilateral resolutions made by the ASEAN Regional Forum or any other forms of organisations.[51] (emphasis added)

On 5 November 2002, the ROC MOFA made a statement concerning the Declaration on the Conduct of Parties in the South China Sea signed by the Association of Southeast Asian Nations (ASEAN) and the PRC in Cambodia.[52] The MOFA stated:

> 1) The Government of the Republic of China reiterates its *territorial sovereignty* over Dongsha (the Pratas Islands), Xisha (the Parcel Islands), Zhongsha (the Macclesfield Bank) and Nansha (the Spratly Islands) in the South China Sea, over which it has all lawful rights according to international law.[53] (emphasis added)

The ROC Government has undertaken construction of an airstrip on Tai-Ping-Dao since 2006. The Vietnamese Government took the view that was a violation of Vietnamese sovereignty and heightened tensions in the area. The ROC MOFA responded on 20 November 2007:

> The Spratly Islands, the Paracel Islands, Macclesfield Bank and the Pratas Islands have always been an intrinsic part of Taiwan's territories, whether looked at from the perspective of history, geography, international law or plain fact. According to the principles of international law, the Government of Taiwan's sovereignty over these islands is unquestionable and it enjoys all rights accordingly.
>
> Taiwan has long stationed troops on Taiping Island (known to Vietnam as Itu Aba), the largest among the Spratly Islands. Basic airport facilities were established on the island years ago to transport essential supplies, to safeguard marine resources and for emergency humanitarian rescue.[54]

In August 2008, the Malaysian deputy prime minister led media members to Swallow Reef (Layang-Layang Atoll in Malaysian) and proclaimed Malaysia's sovereignty over the island. The MOFA stated that:

> 1. *The Spratly Islands, including the Swallow Reef, are located in Taiwan's territorial waters*. From either a historical, geographical or international legal perspective, the Spratly Islands, Paracel Islands, Macclesfield Islands, Pratas *Islands and nearby waters are part of Taiwan's territory and territorial waters.*[55] (emphasis added)

In 2009 the Philippines adopted legislation incorporating Huangyan Dao (or the Scarborough Shoal for the Philippines), in Macclesfield Islands, and part of the Spratly Islands into Philippine territory.[56] The ROC MOFA declared that:

> 1. In terms of either history, geography, reality or international law, the Spratly Islands, Paracel Islands, Macclesfield Islands, Pratas Islands, as well as the surrounding waters, are the existent territories of the Republic of China. The fact that sovereignty of these areas belongs to our Government is undeniable, Taiwan enjoys and deserves all rights accordingly. Any sovereignty claims

over, or occupation of, these islands and their surrounding waters will not be recognized by the Government of the Republic of China.[57] (emphasis added)

On 6 May 2009, Malaysia and Vietnam filed a Joint Submission to the Commission on the Limits of the Continental Shelf of the United Nations, with respect to their proposed outer limits of the continental shelf beyond 200 nautical miles.[58] On 7 May 2009, Vietnam filed a Submission to the Commission, with respect to the proposed outer limits of its continental shelf beyond 200 nautical miles in the northern area of the South China Sea.[59] The ROC responded:

> 1. In terms of either historical, geographical or international legal perspective, the Nansha Islands (Spratly Islands), Shisha Islands (Paracel Islands), Chungsha Islands (Macclesfield Islands), Tungsha Islands (Pratas Islands), *as well as their surrounding waters, their respective sea bed and subsoil belong to the existent territories of the Republic of China.* The *sovereignty of these archipelagoes* belongs to our Government is an undeniable fact, Taiwan therefore enjoys and deserves all rights accordingly. Any sovereignty claims over, or occupation of, these islands and their surrounding waters will not be recognized by the Government of the Republic of China.[60] (emphasis added)

On 12 May 2009, in a statement on the outer limit of the continental shelf, the ROC MOFA declared that:

> In terms of either historical, geographical or international legal perspective, Tiao-Yu-Tai Islands and the Nansha Islands (Spratly Islands), Shisha Islands (Paracel Islands), Chungsha Islands (Macclesfield Islands), Tungsha Islands (Pratas Islands), *as well as their surrounding waters, their respective sea bed and subsoil are the existent territories of the Republic of China.* The *sovereignty of these archipelagoes* belongs to our Government is an undeniable fact. The ROC enjoys and deserves all rights given by international law over the said islands and the surrounding waters, sea-bed and subsoil. Any sovereignty claims over or occupation of these islands under any reason or any means by any other country shall be null and void.[61] (emphasis added)

From the above statements made by the ROC Government, it is plain that there has been a moderation of position regarding the claims in the South China Sea. Recent ROC statements have focused more on the islands and the surrounding waters rather than the whole water body enclosed by the U-shaped lines. This shift will be discussed in the following section.

The U-Shaped Lines: Policy Implications

This section will examine the U-shaped lines on the 1947 map released by the ROC Government in the context of the aforementioned practices of the ROC Government. The map showing the U-shaped lines has taken on even greater importance since it was attached to communications from the PRC to the United Nations in 2009.[62]

First, what is the method utilized in the making of the U-shaped lines? An examination of the map titled "Map of the Location of the South China Sea Islands (*Nan-hi Chu-dao*

Wei-zhi Tu)" shows that there are 11 intermittent dotted lines encompassing most of the islands and islets in the South China Sea (See Figure 1). The series of lines starts from the estuary of Bei-Lun River, which is the boundary river between China and Vietnam. The first two segments go through the middle part of Tonkin Bay. The third and the fourth segments are located between Vietnam and the Paracel Islands as well as the Spratly Islands, respectively. Then, the fifth and the sixth lines take a circumgyration back toward the north. At the southernmost, the lines include James Shoal, which is claimed as the southernmost territory of China. The position of the seventh and the eighth lines are in the middle between the Spratlys and the north coast of Borneo as well as Palawan Island. The last three segments could be treated as a subseries of the U-shaped lines because they represent the continuation of the previous lines and they also imply a maritime division between Taiwan and the Philippines.

It is reasonable to derive that the median line principle was applied in making the U-shaped lines.[63] This presumption can be clarified by the seventh segment, which not only demonstrates the division between Spratlys and Sabah (the northern part of Borneo), but also shows a delimitation between the Philippine Balabac Island and Malaysian State of Sabah with a short side segment connected with the seventh one.[64]

Furthermore, the manner of depicting the dotted lines is the same as the one applied on the map to the national boundaries between China and Vietnam as well as Vietnam and Cambodia. However, the ROC Government took a conservative position by using dotted lines in an inconsecutive fashion. The implication for this is possibly to leave room for future negotiations with the respective countries.

Second, what is the status of the 11 U-shaped dotted lines? According to the 1982 UN Convention on the Law of the Sea, two baseline systems might be employed for measuring the breath of the territorial sea (i.e., the normal baseline or straight baselines).[65] In other words, the "low-water line along the coast as marked on large-scale charts officially recognized by the coastal States" or "straight baselines joining appropriate points." Examining the 1947 map, it is easy to recognize that its function was as a general description of the location of the different island groups within the U-shaped lines. Moreover, according to later practices, the ROC Government took the U-shaped lines to justify its position that they are a series of lines that embrace all the islands and represent sovereignty over those islands. This can be seen from the declaration made by the ROC Executive Yuan on 10 February 1999: "All islands and atolls of the Nansha Islands surrounded by the Chinese traditional U-shape lines are the territory of the Republic of China"[66] and other similar statements made by MOFA.[67] Under these circumstances, the ROC Government's intention when it produced the 1947 map was to demonstrate that sovereignty over the island groups belongs to the ROC.

Third, what is the status of the water body enclosed by the U-shaped lines? Some have argued that the water enclosed by the U-shaped lines are the internal waters. This is disputable. Article 8 of the LOS Convention provides that "[w]aters on the landward side of the baseline of the territorial sea form part of the internal waters of the State." Since the U-shaped lines are not a baseline system, either from the perspective of the normal baseline or straight baselines, then the fundamental basis for internal waters as well as territorial sea does not exist. Moreover, according to the theory and practices of international law of the sea, the coastal State enjoys full territorial sovereignty within its internal waters. Consequently, there is no right of innocent passage for any foreign ships through such water areas.[68]

Therefore, State practices in the South China Sea region do not support the claim of internal or territorial waters. The South China Sea constitutes one of the busiest sea transport routes in the world. As far as the living resources are concerned, the South China Sea is one of the most important maritime areas for commercial fisheries in the world. Stocks, such as scad and mackerel, and highly migratory species, such as tuna, are the most common and important commercial fish stocks. All these practices from the littoral States or other countries—heavy transportation, hydrocarbon resources exploration and exploitation, and fisheries resources management and conservation—create a detriment to claiming the water body enclosed by the U-shaped lines as a territorial sea, not to mention as internal waters.

Maritime claims to sovereignty over those islands and waters enclosed by the U-shaped lines could be a basis or leverage to advocate a claim to a territorial sea, contiguous zone, EEZ, and continental shelf surrounding the islands. Therefore, it is legitimate for the ROC Government to claim that all islands and atolls surrounded by the traditional U-shape lines are part of its territory.

Conclusion

The development of the law of the sea has been heavily influenced by national security concerns and economic interests. With regard to security interests, a broad band of territorial sea offers a form of security; in modern times, this is more of a psychological or political security than a practical defense against foreign attacks. In terms of economic interests, coastal States are primarily interested in the resources of their adjacent marine areas.

The ROC was the first country in the South China Sea region to claim sovereignty over the islands and islets enclosed by the unique U-shaped lines system. Moreover, there was no objection or protest against such claim when the ROC declared it, which could constitute estoppel for them.[69] Nonetheless, the ROC Government obscurely set out its claim to the status of the waters enclosed by the U-shaped lines, which has subsequently drawn more discussion and even challenges from other claimants.

It would be difficult to claim the water body within the U-shaped lines as internal waters or territorial sea since the South China Sea area is one of the busiest transport routes in the world. Because there is no restriction on the transport traffic administered by the ROC or the PRC, proclaiming sovereignty to the water area would be difficult. Therefore, from the examination of the 1947 map, the purpose of the U-shaped lines was to claim sovereignty over those islands and islets through applying the median line principle. Accordingly, claiming a territorial sea or contiguous zone surrounding those islands and islets might be justifiable for the ROC or the PRC. As to the possibility of extending EEZs or continental shelf from the islands, that would be the discussion as well as debate on the definition of islands or rocks in Article 121 of the LOS Convention.

Notes

1. For convenience, Taiwan will be used in reference to the Republic of China (ROC) and China will be used for the People's Republic of China (PRC).

2. See Yann-Huei Song, "Cross-Strait Interactions on the South China Sea Issues: A Need for CBMs," *Marine Policy* 29 (2005): 265–280; Zou Keyuan, "Maritime Boundary Delimitation in the Gulf of Tonkin," *Ocean Development and International Law* 30 (1999): 235–254; Yann-Huei Song and Zou Keyuan, "Maritime Legislation of Mainland China and Taiwan: Developments, Comparison, Implications, and Potential Challenges for the United States," *Ocean Development and International Law* 31 (2000): 303–345; Zou Keyuan, "Historic Rights in International Law and in China's Practice," *Ocean Development and International Law* 32 (2001): 149–168; Peter Kien-Hong Yu, "The Chinese (Broken) U-shaped Line in the South China Sea: Points, Lines, and Zones," *Contemporary Southeast Asia* 25 (2003): 405–430; Li Jinming and Li Dexia, "The Dotted Line on the

Chinese Map of the South China Sea: A Note," *Ocean Development and International Law* 34 (2003): 287–295; Peter Kien-Hong Yu, "Setting Up International (Adversary) Regimes in the South China Sea: Analyzing the Obstacles from a Chinese Perspective," *Ocean Development and International Law* 38 (2007): 147–156; Nguyen Hong Thao and Ramses Amer, "Managing Vietnam's Maritime Boundary Disputes," *Ocean Development and International Law* 38 (2007): 305–324.

3. Cited in Hwang Kang (黃剛), *The Republic of China's Territorial Sea and Its Related System* (*Jong-hwa-ming-gwo De Ling-hai Ji-jyh Shiang-guan Jyh-duh 中華民國的領海及其相關制度*) (Taipei, Taiwan: Commercial Press, 1973), 50.

4. Shih-Hao Lee and Juo-Tsian Chu (李士豪與屈若搴), *History of Chinese Fishery* (*Jong-gwo Yu-yeh-shyy 中國漁業史*) (Taipei, Taiwan: Taiwan Shan-Wu, 1970), 188–209.

5. See Conference for the Codification of International Law, Hague 1930, *Final Act*, Report of the Second Committee (Territorial Sea), reprinted in *American Journal of International Law* 24, Suppl. (1930): 234–235, 254; and Green Haywood Hackworth, *Digest of International Law*, Vol. 1 (Washington, DC: Department of State Publications, 1940), 628. See also C. J. Colombos, *International Law of the Sea*, 6th rev. ed. (London: Longmans, 1967), 99; and Y. L. Wu, ed., *China—A Handbook: Theory and Practice of International Law with Respect to Selected Issues* (New York: Praeger, 1973), 400.

6. See, generally, *Final Act*, supra note 5, at 234–247.

7. Ministry of Transportation and Communication, Decree No. 1612 of 20 April 1931. *Gazette of the Ministry of Transportation and Communications* (*Jiau-tong-bu Gong-bao 交通部公報*), No. 244 (9 May 1931), 1–2.

8. United States, Executive Order 9633 of 28 September 1945, 10 *Fed. Reg.* 12303, 59 *U.S. Stat.* 884.

9. Although the PRC was established in 1949, the ROC retained its membership status in the United Nations and other related organizations until 1971.

10. See *Yearbook of the International Law Commission*, Vol. 1 (1952), 153, para. 80; 158, para. 54; and Vol. 1 (1955), 154, para. 61; 172–173, para. 15; 186, para. 43.

11. The Executive Yuan is the highest administrative organ of the ROC Government and is led by the premier.

12. Joseph W. Dellapenna and A. Y. Wang, "The Republic of China's Claims Relating to the Territorial Sea, Continental Shelf, and Exclusive Economic Zones: Legal and Economic Aspects," *Boston College International and Comparative Law Review* 3 (1980): 357.

13. Philippine Presidential Decree No. 1599 of 11 June 1978 establishing an Exclusive Economic Zone and for other purposes available at www.un.org/Depts/los/LEGISLATIONANDTREATIES/PDFFILES/PHL_1978_Decree.pdf (accessed 18 March 2010).

14. Documents released at the Government Information Office Press Conference, 6 September 1979.

15. The Presidential Decree can be found in the *Gazette of the Presidential Office* (*Tzoong-toong-fuu Gong-bao* or *總統府公報*), No. 3575, 10 October 1979, 2. The Decree was issued with a document code (68)Tai-Tung(1)I-Tze No. 5046 ((六八)台統(一)義字第5046號令).

16. K. O. Emory, et al., "Geological Structure and Some Water Characteristics of the East China Sea and the Yellow Sea," *Technical Bulletin, Technical Advisory Group Report*, Vol. 2 (1969); and see infra note 21.

17. See "Report of the International Law Commission to the General Assembly," in *Yearbook of the International Law Commission*, Vol. 11 (1956), 254–301.

18. "Our Fishing Industry's Recommendation on the Law of the Sea (我漁業界對海洋法之建議)," *Yu-Yo* (*漁友*), No. 74 (August 1957), 13.

19. See UN Doc. A/CONF.13/5/Add 2, 29 January 1958, available at untreaty.un.org/cod/diplomaticconferences/lawofthesea-1958/docs/english/vol_I/8_A-CONF-13-5_PrepDocs_vol_I_e.pdf (accessed 19 March 2010).

20. Continental Shelf Convention, 499 *U.N.T.S.* 311.

21. Emory, supra note 16, at 39–41.

22. Reproduced in Hungdah Chiu, "Chinese Contemporary Practice and Judicial Decisions Relating to International Law, 1968–1970," *Annuals of the Chinese Society of International Law* 7 (1970): 84.

23. *Gazette of the Legislative Yuan* (立法院公報) 59, No. 64, 22 August 1970, 3.

24. For a more recent declaration made by the ROC Government concerning its position on the status of Tiao-Yu-Tai as well as the natural prolongation of continental shelf in the East China Sea area, see "Declaration of the Republic of China on the Outer Limits of Its Continental Shelf", 12 May 2009, available at www.mofa.gov.tw/webapp/ct.asp?xItem=38077&ctNode=1901&mp=6 (accessed 12 March 2010).

25. Japan Ministry of Foreign Affairs, "The Basic View on the Sovereignty over the Senkaku Islands," available at www.mofa.go.jp/region/asia-paci/senkaku/senkaku.html (accessed 16 March 2010).
Convention of Armistice Between Japan and China, 30 March 1895, reproduced in Clive Parry, ed., *Consolidated Treaty Series*, 1648–1918 (Dobbs Ferry, NY: Oceana, 1969), 198–199.

26. Hungdah Chiu, *Chinese Attitude Toward Continental Shelf and Its Implication on Delimiting Seabed in Southeast Asia* (Baltimore: School of Law, University of Maryland, 1977), 9–10.

27. *China Daily News* (*Jong-Gwo-Shyr-Bao* or 中國時報), 7 September 1979, 3.

28. Japan declared its EEZ in 1996. See *Law of the Sea Bulletin*, No. 35 (1997), 78. Prior to this, Japan had claimed a 200-nautical-mile fishing zone.

29. Pen-Chia-Yu is an island located in the northeast sea area of Taiwan. The sea area around that island provides an excellent fishing ground. The Taiwanese Navy had expelled those Japanese fishing vessels. See *United Daily News*, 20 September 1984, 5.

30. *Taiwan Daily News*, 10 September 1989, 2.

31. The Yalu River is the border river between China and North Korea.

32. The Peilun River is the border river between China and Vietnam.

33. Presidential Decree, 21 January 1998, with document code (87) Hwa-Tzoong(1)I-Tze No. 8700010340 ((87)華總(一)義字第8700010340號令).

34. Presidential Decree, 21 January 1998, with document code (87) Hwa-Tzoong(1)I-Tze No. 8700010350 ((87)華總(一)義字第8700010350號令).

35. See *Executive Yuan Gazette*, Vol. 5, No. 6, 10 February 1999, 36–37. For an English translation, see United States, Department of State, *Limits in the Seas*, No. 127, "Taiwan's Maritime Claims," 15 November 2005, Annex 2.

36. *Limits in the Seas*, ibid.

37. Pao-Min Chang, "A New Scramble for the South China Sea Islands," *Contemporary Southeast Asia* 12, no. 4 (1990): 22.

38. Government Information Office, ROC, "The Republic of China's Sovereignty over the Spratly Islands," Reference: ROC on Taiwan, No. RR-93–02, 30 April 1993, 2.

39. *Ibid.*

40. Chang, supra note 37, at 22.

41. *Ibid.*

42. Treaty of Peace Between the Republic of China and Japan, 1858 *U.N.T.S.* 38–44, art. II. See Gerardo M. C. Valero, "Spratly Archipelago Dispute: Is the Question of Sovereignty Still Relevant?" *Marine Policy* 18 (1994): 319.

43. Hungdah Chiu and Choon-ho Park, "Legal Status of the Paracel and Spratly Islands," *Ocean Development and International Law* 3 (1975): 14.

44. *United Daily News*, 24 May 1956, 1; and 25 May 1956, 1.

45. *Central Daily News*, 2 December 1992, 4. Itu Aba Island is 1,358 meters long and 350 meters wide, the total area is about 0.5 square kilometers.

46. *United Daily News*, 6 February 1990, 4.

47. *United Daily News*, 28 January 2000, 8.

48. "Policy Guidelines for the South China Sea (Nan-Hai Jeng-Tseh Gang-Liing or 南海政策綱領)," 13 April 1993. An unofficial English translation can be found in Kuan-Ming

Sun, "Policy of the Republic of China Towards the South China Sea: Recent Developments," *Marine Policy* 19 (1995): 408.

49. Statement made by the ROC MOFA on 10 June 1997, available at www.mofa.gov.tw.

50. Statement made by the ROC MOFA on 13 June 1997, available at www.mofa.gov.tw.

51. Statement made by the ROC MOFA on 1 July 1999, available at www.mofa.gov.tw.

52. Declaration on the Conduct of Parties in the South China Sea, 4 November 2002, available at the Web site of ASEAN at www.aseansec.org/13163.htm (accessed 19 July 2009); and as an appendix to Nguyen Hong Thao, "The 2002 Declaration on the Conduct of Parties in the South China Sea: A Note" *Ocean Development and International Law* 34 (2003): 282–285.

53. Statement made by the ROC MOFA on 5 November 2002, available at www.mofa.gov.tw.

54. Press Release, the ROC MOFA, 20 November 2007, available at www.mofa.gov.tw.

55. Press Release, the ROC MOFA, 15 August 2008, available at www.mofa.gov.tw.

56. The Philippines, Republic Act No. 9522, An Act to Amend Certain Provisions of Republic Act No. 3046, as amended by Republic Act No. 5466, to Define the Archipelagic Baselines of the Philippines, and for Other Purposes, approved 10 March 2009, available at the Web site of the Philippine Law and Jurisprudence Database at www.lawphil.net/statutes/repacts/ra2009/ra_9522_2009.html (accessed 8 August 2009). See also the Philippines, "PGMA Signs Baselines Bill into Law," 11 March 2009, available at the official Government portal of the Philippines at www.gov.ph/index.php?option=com_content&task=view&id=21961&itemid=2 (accessed 8 August 2009).

57. Statement made by the ROC MOFA, 6 February 2009, available at www.mofa.gov.tw.

58. Malaysia-Vietnam Joint Submission to the Commission on the Limits of the Continental Shelf pursuant to Article 76, paragraph 8, of the United Nations Convention on the Law of the Sea 1982 (1833 *U.N.T.S.* 397) in Respect of the Southern Part of the South China Sea, Executive Summary, May 2009, available at the Web site of the Commission on the Limits of the Continental Shelf at www.un.org/Depts/los/clcs_new/clcs_home.htm.

59. Vietnam Submission to the Commission on the Limits of the Continental Shelf pursuant to Article 76, paragraph 8, of the United Nations Convention on the Law of the Sea 1982, Partial Submission in Respect of Vietnam's Extended Continental Shelf: North Area (VNM-N), Executive Summary, April 2009, available at the Web site of the Commission, supra note 58.

60. Statement made by the ROC MOFA, 11 May 2009, available at www.mofa.gov.tw.

61. Chinese text version, available at www.mofa.gov.tw, translated by the author.

62. People's Republic of China, Letter to Secretary-General of the United Nations, Doc. CML/17/2009, New York, 7 May 2009; and Letter to Secretary-General of the United Nations, Doc. CML/18/2009, New York, 7 May 2009, available at the Web site of the Commission, supra note 58 (accessed 19 July 2009).

63. A *median line* is defined as every point of the line is equidistant from the nearest points on the baselines from which the breadth of the territorial seas of each of the two States is measured.

64. The maritime boundary delimitation is still a disputed issue between the Philippines and Malaysia. See Jonathan I. Charney, "Central East Asian Maritime Boundaries and the Law of the Sea," *American Journal of International Law* 89 (1995): 724–726.

65. LOS Convention, supra note 58, arts. 5 and 7.

66. "The First Part of the Baselines of the Territorial Sea," supra note 36.

67. See, for example, supra notes 48, 51, 53, 55, 57, 60, and 61.

68. Robin Churchill and A. V. Lowe, *The Law of the Sea*, 3rd ed. (Manchester, England: Manchester University Press, 1999), 61.

69. Kuen-Chen Fu, *A Study on the Legal Status of the ROC's Historic Waters in the South China Sea* (我國南海歷史性水域法律地位之研究) (Taipei, Taiwan: Research, Development and Evaluation Commission, Executive Yuan, 1992), 16–17.

The South China Sea Workshop Process and Taiwan's Participation

YANN-HUEI SONG

Graduate Institute of International Politics
National Chung Hsing University
Taichung, Taiwan, Republic of China
and
Institute of European and American Studies
Academia Sinica
Taipei, Taiwan, Republic of China

> *Since 1990, 19 Workshops on Managing Potential Conflicts in the South China Sea have been held. The Workshop, attended by Government and military officials in their private capacities as well as by academics mainly from the littoral States of the South China Sea (SCS) and from the non-SCS countries, is a continuing dialogue process that aims to manage potential conflicts by exploring areas of cooperation among the littoral States in the SCS area. It is also the only regional dialogue mechanism dealing specifically with the SCS issues, where scholars and Government officials from Taiwan and China can meet regularly and exchange views. This article reviews and evaluates the SCS Workshop process and discusses Taiwan's participation in the process. In the concluding section, the adoption of the China-Taiwan South-East Asia Network for Education and Training (SEA-NET) joint project at the nineteenth SCS Workshop, a big step regarding Taiwan's participation in the Workshop process, is discussed. And it is suggested that there likely will be more cooperative measures taken by Taipei and Beijing regarding the SCS area in the future.*

Introduction

Since 1990, nineteen Workshops on Managing Potential Conflicts in the South China Sea (hereinafter, SCS Workshops)[1] have been held under the auspices of the Policy Planning and Development Agency within the Indonesian Department of Foreign Affairs. The SCS Workshop, attended by Government and military officials in their private capacities as well as by academics mainly from mainly the littoral States of the South China Sea (SCS)[2] and from the non-SCS countries,[3] is a continuing dialogue process that aims to manage potential conflicts by exploring areas of cooperation among the littoral States in the SCS area. In addition to the Workshops, since 1993 a series of Technical Working Group (TWG) meetings,[4] Group of Experts (GE) meetings,[5] and other cooperative meetings have been held.

Given that Taiwan has been excluded from the track-one security dialogue processes in the Asia-Pacific that also address SCS issues, such as the ASEAN (Association of Southeast Asian Nations) Regional Forum (ARF),[6] the SCS Workshop is the only regional dialogue mechanism where scholars and Government officials from Taiwan, China, and the member States of ASEAN meet regularly and exchange views on a variety of SCS issues even though it is in their personal capacity.

In November 2008, at the eighteenth SCS Workshop held in Manado, Indonesia, the Taiwanese and Chinese participants for the first time expressed a willingness to work together and come up with a joint SCS project proposal. The China-Taiwan South-East Asia Network for Education and Training (SEA-NET) joint project was adopted at the nineteenth SCS Workshop held at Makassar, Indonesia, in November 2009.[7] The China-Taiwan joint project was considered "a milestone in the Workshop process"[8] and will first be implemented in Taiwan in 2010 and then in China in 2011.

The purpose of this article is to review the SCS Workshop process and Taiwan's participation. After the introductory section, a summary report on the recent rising tensions in the SCS will be provided. The development of the SCS Workshop and an evaluation of its performance will be given next. This will be followed by a discussion of Taiwan's new SCS policy,[9] its recent participation in the SCS Workshops, and the interactions between the Chinese and Taiwanese participants at the Workshops held between 2004 and 2009. The article will conclude with remarks on possible cooperation between Taiwan and China in dealing with the SCS issues.

Rising Tensions in the SCS: June 2008–February 2010

While relations between Taiwan and China appear to be rapidly improving, tensions in the SCS have escalated over the past few years. In June 2008, China asked the U.S. corporation ExxonMobil to withdraw from an exploration deal it had with Vietnam in the SCS, claiming that the blocks under contract are in Chinese waters and therefore constitute a breach of Chinese sovereignty.[10] In August 2008, Taiwan issued a statement reiterating its sovereignty over the Spratly Islands after Datuk Seri Najib Tun Razak, deputy prime minister of Malaysia, led members of the media to Swallow Reef (Pulau Layang-Layang) and proclaimed Malaysia's sovereignty over the disputed island.[11] During the second half of 2008, under Chinese pressure, the Philippine Government suspended its legislative process for its archipelagic baselines bill. However, in January 2009, the legislative process resumed and ended with the approval of the Archipelagic Baselines Act by the Senate in February 2009, in which the Philippines claims sovereignty over part of the disputed Spratly Islands and Scarborough Shoal located in the SCS. On 10 March 2009, President Gloria Arroyo signed the Archipelagic Baselines Act, claiming that the Kalayaan Island Group in the Spratly Islands and Scarborough Shoal, classified as a "regime of islands," is part of the country's territory.[12] China, Taiwan, and Vietnam lodged protests against the legislation.[13] In March, China sent its largest fishery patrol ship *Yuzheng 311* to the SCS. Wu Zhuang, director-general of the Administration for Fishing Affairs and Fishing Ports on South China Sea, was quoted by *China Daily* as saying that "[t]he patrol ship will safeguard China's sovereignty in the South China Sea and protect the nation's marine rights and interests."[14]

In early March 2009, China, Taiwan, and Vietnam reiterated, respectively, their sovereignty claims over the Spratly Islands after Malaysian prime minister Badawi's visit to Swallow Reef.[15] On 8 March 2009, the U.S. surveillance ship USNS *Impeccable* was involved in a skirmish with five Chinese vessels 75 miles off the Hainan Islands in the SCS. The United States protested the Chinese actions and said that the U.S. Navy ships will continue to operate in international waters in the SCS.[16]

In mid-March 2009, Vietnam protested against China's decision to allow a company to operate tours to Phu Lam Island in the Paracel Islands. Vietnam stressed that this seriously infringed on its territorial sovereignty and was unhelpful to bilateral negotiations.[17] The incident was followed in April 2009 by Vietnam appointing a Government official to the disputed Paracel Islands and sending a high-ranking delegation of the Communist Party of Vietnam's Central Committee for Education and Propagation to visit the islands. China protested and called the acts "illegal and invalid."[18]

On 7 May 2009, China sent two notifications to the Secretary-General of the United Nations[19] in response to the joint submission made by Vietnam and Malaysia on 6 May 2009[20] and the separate submission made by Vietnam on 7 May 2009[21] delivered to the Commission on the Limits of the Continental Shelf (CLCS) in relation to two areas of outer continental shelf located beyond the two countries' respective 200-nautical-mile exclusive economic zones (EEZs) in the SCS.[22] In the two notifications, China stated that it "has indisputable sovereignty over the islands in the South China Sea and the adjacent waters" and "enjoys sovereign rights and jurisdiction over the relevant waters as well as the seabed and subsoil therefore."[23] This sovereign and jurisdictional claim is manifested in a map attached to the notifications. In mid-June 2009, China seized three Vietnamese fishing boats and arrested 37 fishermen in the waters near the Paracel Islands for violating China's fishing law. Vietnam protested and stated that China's actions had infringed its sovereignty and jurisdiction in the SCS.[24] In early August 2009, Chinese naval patrols again seized a Vietnamese fishing boat in the disputed Paracel Islands in the SCS.[25]

In June 2009, General Zhang Li, former deputy chief of the general staff of the People's Liberation Army (PLA), presented a proposal at the sixth meeting of the eleventh National Committee of the Chinese People's Political Consultative Conference's Standing Committee, calling for China to build an airport and naval dock on Mischief Reef located in the Spratly Islands in the SCS. The former PLA general stated that such facilities would permit China to carry out air patrols of the area, support Chinese fishing vessels, and underline the country's claims to sovereignty of the disputed Spratly Islands in the SCS.[26]

In response to the friction in the SCS area, the *Impeccable* incident, and possible challenges to the U.S. maritime strategy and interests, a hearing was held before the Committee on Foreign Relations of the U.S. Senate on 15 July 2009. During the hearing, Peter Dutton asserted:

> Since all of the islands in the South China Sea are claimed as Chinese territory and included in the baselines section of the 1992 Territorial Sea Law, the effect of the 1988 law [the People's Republic of China Law on Exclusive Economic Zone and Continental Shelf] is to claim an exclusive economic zone around each of them. In combination, therefore, the two Chinese laws effectively claim a Chinese EEZ covering nearly the entire South China.[27]

In November 2009, Vietnam protested the Chinese sending two fishery patrol ships to the Paracel Islands and one medical ship to the Spratly Islands. Vietnam considered the move a violation of its sovereignty over the two archipelagos.[28] In the same month,

Vietnam for the first time held an international conference on SCS issues in Hanoi, in which 150 scholars and officials participated. It was speculated that, because Vietnam is taking over the chair of ASEAN in 2010, it would try to persuade the ASEAN countries to come together in a territorial negotiation with China.[29] On 16 December 2009, it was reported that Vietnam had purchased six diesel-electric Kilo class submarines and was considering ordering 12 Sukhoi Su-30MK2 fighter jets from Russia, all aimed at bolstering its claims against China over the disputed Paracel and Spratly Islands.[30] In January 2010, Vietnam again protested against China's plan to develop tourism in the Paracel Islands,[31] and China warned the Philippine Government against conducting seismic tests in the Reed Bank Basin off the Kalayaan Island Group in the Spratly archipelago.[32]

That tensions in the SCS area continue to rise highlights not only the ineffectiveness of the 2002 ASEAN-China Declaration on the Conduct of Parties in the South China Sea (hereinafter, SCS Declaration),[33] but also the necessity of concluding a Regional Code of Conduct in the South China Sea. In addition, the rising tensions demonstrate the importance of the role played by the existing regional dialogue processes to help manage the territorial and maritime jurisdictional disputes in the area. If the potential conflicts in the SCS cannot be properly managed, "it may not be long before it [the SCS] is seen once again as a major potential regional flashpoint."[34]

The SCS Workshop Process and Its Achievements

The initiative to convene the SCS Workshop was the brainchild of Indonesia's ambassador Hasjim Djalal, a leading authority on ocean law and policy and one of the most influential participants at the Third United Nations Conference on the Law of the Sea. In the late 1980s, tensions had risen in the SCS area as a result of a combination of developments: (1) the end of the cold war and the decline in superpower deployments in Southeast Asia; (2) the new law of the sea, most particular the 200-nautical-mile EEZs; (3) the hydrocarbon exploration and exploitation activities by the SCS littoral countries in the disputed waters in the SCS; and (4) the expansion of naval and air capabilities of the SCS littoral States.[35] In March 1988, a naval battle took place between Chinese and Vietnamese forces over Johnson South Reef (Chigua Jiao) in the Spratly Islands.[36] Concerned with the potential developments and conflicts in the SCS and the threat to Southeast Asian peace and stability, Djalal in cooperation with Ian Townsend-Gault of the University of British Columbia in Vancouver, Canada, sought financial support from the Canadian Government to fund a process that might help to manage potential conflicts in the SCS.[37] The Canadian International Development Agency (CIDA) agreed to provide the support in January 1990. The first SCS Workshop was convened in Bali, Indonesia, but only participants from the (then six) ASEAN countries were invited.[38] In 1991 participants from China, Taiwan, Vietnam, and Laos, and in 1994 participants from Cambodia were invited to attend the SCS Workshops.

The basic objectives of the SCS Workshops are:

- to manage the potential conflicts by seeking an area in which everyone could cooperate;
- to develop confidence building measures or processes so that the various claimants would be comfortable with one another, thus providing an atmosphere conducive for the solution of their territorial or jurisdictional disputes; and
- to exchange views through dialogue on the issues involved in order to increase mutual understanding.[39]

The main goal of the SCS Workshops has never been to solve the territorial and maritime jurisdictional disputes in the SCS, but rather "to create a sense of community among the people and communities around the South China Sea area that in the end may encourage countries to solve one of the problems they have by themselves."[40]

The nature of the SCS Workshops, as a second-track activity, was informal, with all participants participating in their personal capacities. As Townsend-Gault pointed out, the SCS Workshop process "could not have been initiated, much less developed, had there been any attempt to establish it as an official activity, taking place on an inter-Governmental basis."[41] In line with this informal nature, the word "authorities" is used instead of "countries" and "no-one is a delegate or representative."[42] While Taiwan's participation was one of the reasons for convening the SCS Workshops on an informal basis, the attitude of officials and the concern of China with the regionalization or internationalization of the SCS issues were also factors in maintaining the SCS Workshops on an informal basis.[43]

To date, there have been 19 SCS Workshops. Prior to 2001, Canadian funds covered the expenses of inviting three participants from each country to the SCS Workshops. However, participants from Taiwan, Brunei, and later Singapore were always self-funded because they were not among those who received foreign aids from CIDA. Since 1993 and before 2001, 17 TWG, 11 GE, and 2 Study Group meetings on marine scientific research, marine environmental protection, safety of navigation, resource assessments and means of development, legal matters, and zones of cooperation had been held under the aegis of the SCS Workshop process. (See Table 1.) The scope of activities taking place under the aegis of the SCS Workshop has shrunk since 2001 when the Canadian Government decided not to continue its financial support of the Workshop process.

In response to the Canadian decision, participating authorities at a meeting in Jakarta in August 2001 agreed to continue the informal Workshop activities by focusing on confidence building and cooperation while avoiding controversial, political, and divisive issues. Since 2001, a series of SCS Workshops and Working Group meetings have been convened.

In March 2002, the Anambas Expedition was carried out around the undisputed Indonesian Islands of Anambas in the SCS, with 29 participating experts and researchers from Malaysia, the Philippines, China, Taiwan, Thailand, Vietnam, Singapore, and Indonesia. The Anambas Expedition was the first of its kind, organized voluntarily by the participating authorities in the SCS Workshop process and aimed to identify the biodiversity of resources in the SCS. It was also hoped that the joint expedition would promote cooperation in the area, regardless of disputes that may exist in or regarding the specific area of the SCS.[44] In addition to the cooperative project on biodiversity, two other projects have been agreed to by the participating authorities in the SCS Workshop process: a project on the study of sea-level rise and one on the exchange of marine data.[45] Implementation of these two agreed projects has been the topic of continuing discussions.

The SCS Workshop process is the only forum in which all six claimants to the Spratly Islands have regularly participated. It is also among the longest running of the Asia-Pacific dialogue mechanisms that aim to manage the potential conflicts in the SCS area or address the maritime security challenges in the region. However, after nearly two decades of efforts, can it be said that the SCS Workshop process has been successful? Some commentators, such as Mark J. Valencia argued at a very early stage that the SCS Workshops "have failed to deliver substantive progress and are ... in danger of being marginalized by unilateral actions and bilateral negotiations in the South China Sea."[46] In 1993, Ted L. McDorman posited that the most difficult question about the informal SCS Workshop process was whether the process "will become a 'talking club' accomplishing little beyond holding out a false promise or co-operation while unilateral claim consolidation and strengthening of

Table 1
Meetings held or activities carried out under the SCS Workshop process (tabulated by the author)

Year	Meetings	Venue
1990	1st SCS Workshop	Bali, Indonesia
1991	2nd SCS Workshop	Bandung, Indonesia
1992	3rd SCS Workshop	Yogyakarta, Indonesia
1993	TWG-MSR1	Manila, Philippines
	TWG-MSR2	Surabaya, Indonesia
	TWG-RA1	Jakarta, Indonesia
	4th SCS Workshop	Surabaya, Indonesia
1994	TWG-MSR3	Singapore
	TWG-MEP1	Hangzhou, China
	5th SCS Workshop	Bukittinggi, Indonesia
1995	TWG-MSR4	Hanoi, Vietnam
	TWG-SNSC1	Jakarta, Indonesia
	TWG-LM1	Phuket, Thailand
	6th SCS Workshop	Balikpapan, Indonesia
1996	TWG-SNSC2	Bandar Seri Begawan, Brunei
	TWG-MSR5	Mactan, Cebu, the Philippines
	GEM-BD	Mactan, Cebu, the Philippines
	7th SCS Workshop	Batam, Indonesia
1997	TWG-MEP2	Hainan, China
	TWG-LM2	Chiang Mai, Thailand
	GEM-MEP1	Phnom Penh, Cambodia
	GEM-ETM1	Singapore
	GEM-HDI1	Kuching, Malaysia
	SCSBTC	Singapore
	8th SCS Workshop	Puncak, Indonesia
1998	TWG-SNSC3	Singapore
	TWG-LM3	Pattaya, Thailand
	TWG-MSR6	Manila, the Philippines
	GEM-HDI2	Singapore
	GEM-MEP 2	Manila, Philippines
	GEM-NL/NHR	Jakarta, Indonesia
	SGZC1	Vientiane, Laos
	9th SCS Workshop	Jakarta, Indonesia
1999	GEM-SAR/IAS	Kota Kinabalu, Malaysia*
	SGZC2	Bali, Indonesia
	GEM-EL1	Shanghai, China
	TWG-LM4	Koh Samui, Thailand
	10th SCS Workshop	Bogor, Indonesia
2000	GEM-HDI3	Bali, Indoneisa
	TWG-LM5	Cha Am, Thailand
2001	11th SCS Workshop	Banten, Indonesia
	SCS Special Meeting	Jakarta, Indonesia
2002	12th SCS Workshop	Jakarta, Indonesia
	Anambas Expedition	SCS Anambas Islands Group

Table 1
Meetings held or activities carried out under the SCS Workshop process (tabulated by the author) *(Continued)*

Year	Meetings	Venue
2003	13th SCS Workshop	Medan, Indonesia
2004	14th SCS Workshop	Batam, Indonesia
	Exercise Palawan	Palawan, Philippines
2005	15th SCS Workshop	Anyer, Banten, Indonesia
2006	16th SCS Workshop	Bali, Indonesia
	Working Group Meeting on the Study of Tides and Sea Level Change and Their Impact on Coastal Environment in the SCS	Bali, Indonesia
2007	17th SCS Workshop	Yogyakarta, Indonesia
	Working Group Meeting on the Study of Tides and Sea Level Change and Their Impact on Coastal Environment in the SCS	Yogyakarta, Indonesia
2008	18th SCS Workshop	Manado, Indonesia
	Working Group Meeting on the Study of Tides and Sea Level Change and Their Impact on Coastal Environment in the SCS	Manado, Indonesia
2009	19th SCS Workshop	Makasar, Indonesia
	Working Group Meeting on the Study of Tides and Sea Level Change and Their Impact on Coastal Environment in the SCS	Makasar, Indonesia

*GEM on Law Enforcement and Unlawful Acts at Sea and GEM on Search and Rescue were combined.

Abbreviations: TWG = Technical Working Group meeting; GEM = Group of Experts meeting; SCS Workshop = Workshop on Managing Potential Conflicts in the South China Sea; MSR = marine scientific research; MEP = marine environmental protection; SNSC = safety of navigation, shipping, and communications; RA = resources assessment; LM = legal matters; ETM = education and training of mariners; HDI = hydrographic data and information exchange; NL/NHR = nonliving and nonhydrocarbon resources; SGZC = Study Group on Zones of Cooperation.

bargaining or military position takes place."[47] In 1995, Valencia and the two other U.S. scholars presented a paper in which they stated that the SCS Workshop "has reached a plateau."[48] While it has been recognized that the 2002 SCS Declaration[49] drew on materials discussed at the first three SCS Workshops, the territorial disputes and conflicting maritime claims still exist in the SCS area and, as mentioned above, tensions have risen in the area over the past two years.

In evaluating the success or failure of the SCS Workshops, it should be borne in mind, as already noted, that the process was not established for the purpose of solving the territorial disputes and conflicting maritime claims in the SCS area, but rather to transform "the threat of mutually destructive confrontation in the South China Sea into the reality of mutually beneficial cooperation among the countries of the region."[50] In October 1995, Ali Alatas, then minister for foreign affairs of Indonesia, stated at the opening of the sixth SCS Workshop:

Solving territorial and jurisdictional issues and conflicting claims is never easy anywhere in the world. And yet the Workshop process, although not intended to resolve the conflicting territorial and jurisdictional claims in the South China Sea, has managed to help prevent the disputes from erupting into a major conflagration. It has also been able to increase regional and global awareness of the danger posed by the conflicting claims in the South China Sea if they are not managed properly.[51]

Townsend-Gault, one of the key persons in developing the SCS Workshop process, stated in 1998 that "bringing together participants from the entire region was something of an accomplishment."[52] In May 2007 at a conference on the SCS held in Singapore, Townsend-Gault commented on the contributions of the SCS Workshop process, stating that the SCS Workshop process was vital on two grounds: (1) it facilitated frank and nonconfrontational dialogues between the individual claimant States, and (2) it created and explored alternative avenues for cooperation.[53] He also opined that the SCS Workshop process "was a step towards a peaceful response, if not resolution, to the conflicts in the South China Sea region."[54] Townsend-Gault indicated that "instead of constantly focusing on the sovereignty-dispute deadlock, the workshops have shown that much more could be achieved if resources and attention are diverted to functional areas of cooperation instead."[55]

In a comprehensive paper presented at a meeting held in Seoul in October 2008 that was made available to all participants at the eighteenth SCS Workshop held in Manado, Indonesia, in November 2008, Djalal, "founding father" of the SCS Workshop process, explained its origin, goal, nature, process, structure, funding, progress, meetings and activities, accomplishments, problems, and current situation.[56] Djalal stressed that the key factor for judging the success or failure of the SCS Workshop process should be the result of managing the potential conflicts in the SCS area. If the potential conflicts in the SCS area do not come to reality, the process will be successful. He further explained that "the moment the potential conflict become[s] a reality may be our failure. But the moment the potential conflict has not develop[ed] into conflict but we manage it and then convert it to cooperation, that is a success."[57]

While the SCS Workshop process has successfully set the pace for cooperation in the area, it must also be pointed out that several challenges remain. One is the lack of willingness or support to continue discussing nontraditional security issues, which include sea-lanes of communication management, living and nonliving resource management and conservation, and institutional mechanisms for cooperation. The second problem is the lack of discussion of current ocean law and politics issues at the SCS Workshops, such as the ineffectiveness of the 2002 SCS Declaration, the need for a regional code of conduct, the implications of outer continental shelf submissions, the need to cooperate to combat piracy or prevent the spread of weapons of mass destruction (WMD). A further challenge is the relationship between China and Taiwan in the SCS.

Taiwan's SCS Policy and Participation in the SCS Workshop Process

On 13 April 1993, the Executive Yuan (the cabinet) of Taiwan approved the "Policy Guidelines for the South China Sea."[58] The Guidelines stipulated that "[o]n the basis of history, geography, international law and the facts, the Spratly Islands, the Paracel Islands, Macclesfield Bank, and the Pratas Islands, have always been a part of the inherent territory of the Republic of China." The Guidelines also proclaimed that

The South China Sea area within the historic water limit is the maritime area under the jurisdiction of the Republic of China, in which the Republic of China possesses all rights and interests. The government of the Republic of China is willing, on the bases of peace and reason, and in accordance with the principle of safeguarding the sovereignty of the Republic of China, develop this maritime area. The government of the Republic of China is also willing to resolve disputes over the area in accordance with international law and the UN Charter.[59]

Based on these principles, the SCS policy goals were set as: (1) resolutely uphold Taiwan's sovereignty over the SCS, (2) enhance development and management in the area, (3) actively promote cooperation in the area, (4) peacefully handle the disputes over the SCS, and (5) maintain the ecological integrity of the area.[60] For the purpose of implementation, nine major areas were identified: domestic matters, international cooperation matters, safeguard of security; communications, sanitary matters, environmental protection, cross-strait relations, academic research, and development of the resources.[61]

In June 2005, the Taiwanese Government transferred policymaking responsibility from the South China Sea Task Force of the Ministry of the Interior to the National Security Council under the Presidential Office. In mid-August 2005, President Chen Shui-bian approved the proposal to set up a Joint Meeting for the Situation in Maritime Areas under the National Security Council. Taiwan also decided to build a runway on Taipeing Island (Itu Aba, the largest island in the Spratly archipelago). This was followed in December 2005 by a decision to end the application of the 1993 SCS Policy Guidelines.[62]

In February 2008, President Chen traveled to Taiping Island to inaugurate the runway and to assert Taiwan's territorial claims to the Spratly Islands. During the visit, he announced a "Spratly Initiative," which can be seen as Taiwan's new SCS policy.[63] Chen proposed the initiative in order to achieve three goals: (1) to find a way for Taiwan to participate in the SCS security dialogue process and cooperative activities; (2) to prevent others from competing for the marine resources that Taiwan claims, including energy resources such as oil, gas, and gas hydrates, and other resources such as fisheries; and (3) to prevent the maritime environment in the SCS from being further damaged.[64] In particular, President Chen urged that "sovereignty disputes should be replaced with environmental protection and depletion of resources should be substituted with a sustainable ecosystem."[65]

There are four paragraphs in Chen's Spratly Initiative, which contain several proposals and statements that relate to handling of future SCS issues. In paragraph 1, Chen said that Taiwan is willing to accept the principles and spirit of the 2002 SCS Declaration[66] on an equal footing of sovereignty. He called for resolution of sovereignty disputes through peaceful means and the formulation of a regional code of conduct for the SCS. After pointing out his concern over the current situation of competitive exploitation of natural resources in the SCS by other countries, Chen stressed in paragraph 2 that priority should be given to maritime ecological conservation and sustainable development. In paragraph 3, Chen promised that Taiwan would invite international ecologists and representatives of major environmental groups to make regular visits to SCS islands held by Taiwan, including the Tungsha (Pratas) Islands, Taiping Island, and Zhong Zhou Sand. Finally, in the first half of paragraph 4 of the Spratly Initiative, Chen urged that sovereignty disputes in the SCS should not block the development of cooperation among the countries in the area. In the second half of paragraph 4, he suggested that a nongovernmental SCS research center be established.

Chen's SCS policy has been more or less followed by the Ma Ying-jeou administration that came into office in May 2008. Ma has adopted a SCS policy that advocates the opening up of the SCS by seeking joint development of resources in the area and helping maintain peace and stability in the Asia-Pacific region.[67] The policy, based on the principle of "sovereignty belonging to us, putting aside the disputes, peace and reciprocity, and joint development," calls for doing more research and survey on the resources in the Pratas Islands and the SCS. In addition, the policy calls for working with international conservation organizations to establish an SCS peace park at Taiping Island and Zhong Zhou Sand in the Spratly archipelago for the purpose of enhancing international cooperation and protecting the ecological and human cultural resources of the SCS region.

In August 2008, Taiwan's Ministry of Foreign Affairs issued a statement in response to the visit by Datuk Seri Najib tun Razak, deputy prime minister of Malaysia, to the disputed Swallow Reef in the Spratly archipelago, citing the Spratly Initiative that had been announced by the previous Government.[68] In October 2008, it was reported that China and Taiwan were to cooperate to explore oil resources in the SCS and the East China Sea.[69] Due to the efforts made by the Ma administration, the cross-strait relations have improved rapidly, which not only has helped reduce the confrontation between the Taiwanese and Chinese participants in the SCS Workshop process, but made it possible for the first time for the two sides to talk about submitting a joint project in the Workshop.

Taiwan's participation in the SCS Workshops dates to July 1991, when both China and Taiwan, together with Vietnam and Laos, were invited to attend the second SCS Workshop held in Bandung, Indonesia. It is believed that the main reasons for China's willingness to sit down with Taiwan at the SCS Workshop were the One-China principle adhered to by the then Government of Taiwan and Taiwan's proposal to jointly defend the SCS islands with China. In addition, both China and Taiwan agreed to attend the SCS Workshop on the same condition that the question of sovereignty over the disputed SCS islands would not be raised.[70] As a result of these understandings, since 1991 both Taiwan and China have participated in all of the SCS Workshops, the TWG and GE meetings, and the activities carried out under the Workshop process.

As already noted, the SCS Workshop is the only regional dialogue mechanism dealing specifically with SCS issues, where scholars and Government officials from Taiwan, China, and the member States of ASEAN meet regularly to exchange views on SCS issues even though in their personal capacity. Nevertheless, the use of Taiwan's official or preferred names (in particular, the Republic of China or Taiwan) and Taiwan's offer to host TWG or GE meetings under the SCS Workshop framework have been the source of confrontation between the Taiwanese and Chinese participants.

At the fourteenth SCS Workshop held in Batam, Indonesia, in November 2004, Taiwan presented a proposal on South East Asia Ocean Network for Education (SEAONE), which would serve as a training platform for open ocean science research in the SCS. China had difficulties with the proposal, and due to the lack of consensus, the SEAONE proposal was not considered as a Workshop project.[71] Since 2004, the Chinese and Taiwanese participants at the Workshops have disagreed over the SEAONE proposal. At the seventeenth SCS Workshop, no consensus was reached on Taiwan's SEAONE proposal, mainly due to China's opposition. At the same time, China presented a preliminary concept paper on Education, Training Course and Exchange on Marine Science and Technology in the SCS as a counter to Taiwan's SEAONE project. No consensus was reach on the Chinese proposal. Djalal, as the resource person of the SCS Workshop, indicated it would be a "win-win situation for China to pursue its own proposal hand in hand with Taiwan's SEAONE project."[72]

At the eighteenth SCS Workshop held at Manado, Indonesia, in November 2008, the Taiwanese and Chinese participants for the first time expressed a willingness to work together during the Workshop's intersessional period and come up with a joint proposal before the nineteenth SCS Workshop.[73] The main reason for the change to possible cooperation was the return of the Nationalist Party (KMT) to the Government in Taiwan in the March 2008 presidential election. The Ma administration supports the consensus reached between Taipei and Beijing in 1992, where both sides agree on the One-China principle, subject, however, to different interpretations.

The willingness to cooperate between Beijing and Taipei in the Workshop process increased, along with the further improvement of political relations between the two sides. The SEA-NET project proposal was adopted at the nineteenth SCS Workshop in November 2009. The project, consisting of training and visiting scientific programs on marine sciences, ocean and coastal management, will last for 2 years and be implemented by Taiwan in 2010 and by China in 2011. All of the participants at the nineteenth SCS Workshop "agreed to endorse and support the project and considered it a milestone in the Workshop process."[74]

The implications of this development in cross-strait cooperation on the management of the territorial and jurisdictional disputes in the Paracel and Spratly Islands are to be watched closely. For Taiwan, will its foreign relations with ASEAN member countries be affected if Taipei moves too closely to China's position on the SCS issues? Will the increasing cooperation between Taiwan and China in the SCS area affect Taipei's maritime strategy and its military defense relations with the United States? Will the improvement of the cross-strait relations make it possible for Taiwan to join cooperative oil exploration projects such as the Tripartite Agreement signed between the national oil companies of the Philippines, Vietnam, and China in March 2005? Will the development make it possible for Taiwan to be invited to sign the 2002 SCS Declaration,[75] or to participate in the dialogue process that aims to adopt a regional code of conduct in the SCS? For ASEAN member countries, will the China-Taiwan cooperation affect their claims to the sovereignty and maritime jurisdiction in the disputed areas in the SCS? Will the cross-strait cooperation in the SCS enhance China's deployment and assertiveness in the area and, thus, increase the security threat to the ASEAN claimants? For China, the cooperation between Taipei and Beijing in the SCS will certainly be welcomed because it is consistent with the One-China principle and, thus, could be considered useful in the accomplishment of the policy goal of reunification between Taiwan and mainland China.

Concluding Remarks

Over the past 18 years, Taiwan's participation in the SCS Workshop process has been limited mainly by China's continuing adherence to the One-China principle. The Chinese participants consistently expressed their opposition whenever they found a written statement or a remark made by other participants that implied the recognition of Taiwan as a country. China insisted that Taiwan could not host any meetings relevant to the SCS Workshop process. China asked the Policy Planning and Development Agency of the Indonesian Ministry of Foreign Affairs, the organizing committee of the SCS Workshop, to handle the Taiwan issue in accordance with the One-China principle. Thus, China opposed any acts that either aimed to upgrade the position of the Taiwanese participants or that ran counter to the One-China principle.

While the role played by Taiwan in the SCS Workshop process has been constrained by China's position, Taiwan has been able to participate in it. An informal communication channel for dealing with the SCS issues and developing possible cooperation between Taiwan and China has been established. Moreover, the academic circles on both sides of the Taiwan Strait have played an important role in making policy recommendations for their respective Governments to consider.

There has been a rapid improvement in cross-strait relations over the past 20 months. Moreover, Taiwan has begun to participate in activities of specialized agencies of the United Nations. This is very likely to have a positive development on Taiwan's participation in the SCS Workshop process. Regarding the SCS more generally, Taipei and Beijing have begun to cooperate in exploring oil and gas resources and to conduct joint search and rescue exercises in the northern part of the SCS.[76] The adoption of the China-Taiwan SEA-NET joint project at the nineteenth SCS Workshop can be considered a big step regarding Taiwan's participation in the Workshop process.

However, the direction of possible cooperation between Taiwan and China in handling the SCS issues and jointly participating in the SCS Workshop process in the years to come will be affected by recent developments in the region that include:

1. The speculation about the formation of a so-called Spratly Group among some Southeast Asian countries with territorial claims in the SCS and non-SCS countries such as Australia and the United States, which aims to counter the growing Chinese power in the SCS area;[77]
2. The hearing on Maritime Disputes and Sovereignty Issues in East Asia that was held by the U.S. Senate Committee on Foreign Relations on July 15, 2009, in which the invited experts cited the recent incidents in the SCS area as evidence of a more assertive sea power by Beijing;[78]
3. The annual Cooperation Afloat Readiness and Training (CARAT) exercises held between the United States and some ASEAN countries, including Singapore, Thailand, Malaysia, Indonesia, the Philippines, and Indonesia in June and July 2009, that aimed to enhance the ability of the participating countries' defensive forces to work together in dealing with the maritime security challenges; and
4. The declaration that "the United States is back" made by U.S. Secretary of State Hillary Clinton in Bangkok on July 21, 2009, and the United States' signing of the Treaty of Amity and Cooperation in Southeast Asia in Phuket, Thailand, the next day.[79]

Obviously, both Taiwan and China will assess the impact of the cross-strait cooperation in dealing with the SCS issues on their respective diplomatic relationships with the ASEAN and non-SCS countries and the implications of the development for their maritime interests and strategy.

Notes

1. For the background of the SCS Workshop, visit the Web site of the South China Sea Informal Working Group, University of British Columbia, available at faculty.law.ubc.ca/scs/ (accessed 14 July 2009).
2. The countries bordering on the South China Sea include: China, Taiwan, the Philippines, Vietnam, Brunei Darussalam, Malaysia, Indonesia, Thailand, Singapore, and Cambodia.
3. Scholars from Canada, the United States, Australia, member States of the European Union, and other non-SCS countries have attended the SCS Workshop.
4. The Technical Working Groups include those on: marine scientific research, resource assessment, legal matters, shipping, navigation and communications, and marine environmental protection.

5. The Groups of Experts include those on: marine scientific research, resource assessment, legal matters, shipping, navigation and communications, and marine environmental protection.

6. The twenty-sixth ASEAN Ministerial Meeting and Post Ministerial Conference, which were held in Singapore on 23–25 July 1993, agreed to establish the ASEAN Regional Forum (ARF). The inaugural meeting of the ARF was held in Bangkok on 25 July 1994. On 23 July 2009 the sixteenth ARF was held in Phuket, Thailand. Further information about the forum and the chairman's statements at the sixteenth ASEAN Regional Forum are available at the Web site of ASEAN at www.14thaseansummit.org/pdf-AMM/39chairman_statement_final.pdf.

7. See the Statement of the 18th Workshop on Managing Potential Conflicts in the South China Sea, Manado, Indonesia, 28–29 November 2008, para. 21; and the Statement of the nineteenth Workshop on Managing Potential Conflicts in the South China Sea, Makassar, Indonesia, 13–14 November 2009, para. 21.

8. Statement of the nineteenth Workshop, supra note 7, para. 21.

9. Taiwan's SCS Policy and Participation in the SCS Workshop is discussed on pages 8–11 of this article.

10. "China Warns Exxon to Quit Vietnam Deal," *Asia Pacific Oil and Gas Insights*, 1 July 2008, LexisNexis (accessed 11 July 2009).

11. Media Center, Ministry of Foreign Affairs, Republic of China, 15 August 2008, available at www.mofa.gov.tw/webapp/fp.asp?xItem=32920&ctNode=1014 (accessed 11 July 2009); and see "Taiwan Lodges Protest Against Philippines Act to Annex Disputed Islands," *BBC Monitoring Asia Pacific—Political*, 13 March 2009, LexisNexis (accessed 11 July 2009).

12. The Philippines, Republic Act No. 9522, An Act to Amend Certain Provisions of Republic Act No. 3046, as amended by Republic Act No. 5466, To Define the Archipelagic Baselines of the Philippines, and for Other Purposes, approved 10 March 2009, available at the Web site of the Philippine Law and Jurisprudence Database at www.lawphil.net/statutes/repacts/ra2009/ra_9522_2009.html. See also the Philippines, "PGMA Signs Baselines Bill into Law," 11 March 2009, available at the official Government portal of the Philippines at www.gov.ph/index.php?option=com_content&task=view&id=21961&itemid=2; and "Arroyo Signs into Law Bill Claiming Islands' Sovereignty," *Gulf News* (United Arab Emirates), 12 March 2009, LexisNexis (accessed 11 July 2009).

13. See People's Republic of China, Letter to Secretary-General of the United Nations, Doc. CML/12/2009, New York, 13 April 2009, available at the Web site of the UN Division on the Law of the Sea at www.un.org/Depts/los/LEGISLATIONANDTREATIES/Statefiles/Phil.htm; Vietnam, Permanent Mission to the United Nations, "Vietnam's Response to Philippine President's signing of Baseline Act," 13 March 2009, available at www.vietnam-un.org/en/news.php?id=77&act=print; and, more generally, Heda Bayron, "New Philippine Border Law Re-ignites Territorial Disputes in South China Sea," 17 March 2009, Voice of America, available at www.voanews.com/english/archive/2009-03/2009-03-17-voa15.cfm?renderforprint=1 (accessed 8 August 2009). See also Kristina Kazmi, "China Protests Philippine Bill Laying Claim to Disputed Spratly Islands," *Global Insight*, 19 February 2009; and Joyce Pangco Panares, "Vietnam Joins Protest Against Baseline Bill," *Manila Standard*, 21 February 2009, LexisNexis (accessed 11 July 2009). The statement made by the Ministry of Foreign Affairs, Republic of China (Taiwan) on 4 February 2009 is available at www.mofa.gov.tw/webapp/fp.asp?xItem=36869&ctnode=1548 (accessed 8 July 2009) (in Chinese). See also "Taiwan Lodges Protest Against Philippines Act," supra note 11.

14. "China Sends Fishery Patrol to South China Sea After Skirmish," Bernama, the Malaysian National News Agency, 12 March 2009, LexisNexis (accessed 11 July 2009).

15. See "Vietnam Reiterates Sovereignty Claim After Malaysian PM's Island Visit," *BBC Monitoring Asia Pacific—Political*, 10 March 2009; "The Government of the Republic of China (Taiwan) Reiterates Its Sovereignty over the Nansha Islands and Surrounding Waters," Government Information Office, Republic of China (Taiwan), 11 March 2009, available at www.gio.gov.tw/ct.asp?xItem=46362&ctNode=2462 (accessed 11 July 2009); and "China—Beijing Reiterates Sovereignty over Disputed Islands," Periscope *Daily Defense News* Capsules, 10 March 2009, LexisNexis (accessed 11 July 2009).

16. Pauline Jelinek, "Pentagon: Chinese Vessels Harassed Unarmed Ship," *Associated Press Online*, 9 March 2009, LexisNexis (accessed 11 July 2009). For further on this issue, see Chris Rahman and Martin Tsamenyi, "A Strategic Perspective on Security and Naval Issues in the South China Sea" (in this Special Issue).

17. "Vietnam Reaffirms Sovereignty over Paracel and Spratly Islands," *Thai Press Reports*, 16 March 2009, LexisNexis (accessed 11 July 2009).

18. "World—China Slams Vietnam's Paracel Post," *Morning Star*, 29 April 2009; "Vietnam Appointment of Hoang Sa District's Mayor Is Normal and Legal, Says FM Spokesman," *Thai Press Reports*, 1 May 2009; and "Vietnam CPV's High-ranking Delegation Visits Truong Sa Archipelago," *Thai Press Reports*, 1 May 2009, LexisNexis (accessed 11 July 2009).

19. People's Republic of China, Letter to Secretary-General of the United Nations, Doc. CML/17/2009, New York, 7 May 2009; and Letter to Secretary-General of the United Nations, Doc. CML/18/2009, New York, 7 May 2009, available at the Web site of the Commission on the Limits of the Continental Shelf at www.un.org/Depts/los/clcs_new/clcs_home.htm (accessed 19 July 2009).

20. Malaysia-Vietnam Joint Submission to the Commission on the Limits of the Continental Shelf Pursuant to Article 76, paragraph 8 of the United Nations Convention on the Law of the Sea 1982 in Respect of the Southern Part of the South China Sea, Executive Summary, May 2009, available at the Web site of the Commission, supra note 19.

21. Vietnam Submission to the Commission on the Limits of the Continental Shelf Pursuant to Article 76, paragraph 8 of the United Nations Convention on the Law of the Sea 1982, Partial Submission in Respect of Vietnam's Extended Continental Shelf: North Area (VNM-N), Executive Summary, April 2009, available at the Web site of the Commission, supra note 19.

22. The Commission of the Limits of the Continental Shelf was established by Annex II of the 1982 UN Convention on the Law of the Sea, done at Montego Bay, Jamaica, 10 December 1982, entered into force 16 November 1994, 1833 *U.N.T.S.* 397. Regarding the work of the Commission, see its Web site at supra note 19.

23. PRC Letter, CML/17/2009 and Letter, CML/18/2009, supra note 19, para. 2.

24. "Politics & Law: China Asked to Release Vietnamese Fishermen," *Vietnam News Brief*, 29 June 2009; and Kristina Kazmi, "Tensions Rise Between China and Vietnam over Disputed Islands," *Global Insight*, 29 June 2009, LexisNexis (accessed 11 July 2009).

25. "China Detain Vietnamese Fishermen Fleeing Storms," *Earth Times*, 4 August 2009, available at www.earthtimes.org/articles/printstory.php?news=280123 (accessed 7 August 2009).

26. See Russell Hsiao, "PLA General Advises Building Bases in the South China Sea," *China Brief* 9, no. 13 (24 June 2009), available at www.jamestown.org/programs/chinabrief/single/?tx_ttnews%5Btt_news%5D=35169&tx_ttnews%5BbackPid%5D=414&no_cache=1 (accessed 11 July 2009).

27. Peter Dutton, Written Testimony Before the U.S. Senate Committee on Foreign Relations Hearing on Maritime Disputes and Sovereignty Issues in East Asia, 15 July 2009, at 1–2, available at the Web site of the U.S. Senate Foreign Relations Committee at foreign.senate.gov/testimony/2009/DuttonTestimony090715p.pdf.

28. "Vietnam Decries Chinese Ship Incursion," Vietnamese News Agency, 27 November 2009, LexisNexis (accessed 11 July 2009).

29. Edward Wong, "Vietnam, Taking on China, Seeks Allies in Island Clash," *International Herald Tribune*, 5 February 2010, 3.

30. Nga Pham, "Vietnam to Buy Russian submarines," BBC News, 16 December 2009, available at news/bbc.co.uk/go/pr/fr/-/2/hi/asia-pacific/8415380.stm (accessed 1 March 2010).

31. "Vietnam Demands China End Tourism on Hoang Sa Islands," *Thai Press Reports*, 6 January 2010, LexisNexis (accessed 11 July 2009).

32. "China Warns Philippines Against Conducting Seismic Tests in Kalayaan Islands," *BBC Monitoring Asia Pacific—Political*, 25 January 2010, LexisNexis (accessed 11 July 2009).

33. The text of the Declaration is available at the Web site of ASEAN at www.aseansec.org/13163.htm (accessed 15 July 2009).

34. Ian Storey, "Impeccable Affair and Renewed Rivalry in the South China Sea," *China* 9, no. 9, available at www.jamestown.org/programs/chinabrief/single/?tx_ttnews%5Btt_news%5D=34922&tx_ttnews%5BbackPid%5D=414&no_cache=1 (accessed 11 July 2009).

35. See Allan Shephard, "Maritime Tensions in the South China Sea and the Neighborhood: Some Solutions," *Studies in Conflict and Terrorism* 17 (1993): 181–187; and Allan Shephard, "Oil on Troubled Waters: Indonesian Sponsorship of the South China Sea Workshop," *Studies in Conflict and Terrorism* 18 (1995): 1.

36. For information about the battle, see "John South Reef Skirmish," Wikipedia, available at < en.wikipedia.org/wiki/Hohnson-South_Reef_Skirmish (accessed 13 July 2009).

37. Hasjim Djalal, "Managing Potential Conflicts in the South China Sea," paper circulated at the sixteenth SCS Workshop held in Bali, Indonesia, on 23 November 2006.

38. For details about the first SCS Workshop, see *Report of the Workshop on Managing Potential Conflicts in the South China Sea*, Bali, 22–24 January 1990.

39. Djalal, supra note 37.

40. Hasjim Djalal, "Transcript of Opening Remarks by Director of Center for Southeast Asia Studies," at the sixteenth Workshop on Managing Potential Conflicts in the South China Sea, Bali, Indonesia, 23 November 2006. See Annex 2 in *The 16th Workshop on Managing Potential Conflicts in the South China Sea*, Bali, 23 November 2006 (Policy Analysis and Development Agency, Ministry of Foreign Affairs, Republic of Indonesia, Jakarta, 2007), 13.

41. Ian Townsend-Gault, "Preventive Diplomacy and Pro-Activity in the South China Sea," *Contemporary Southeast Asia* 20 (1998): 183.

42. *Ibid.*, at 184.

43. *Ibid.*, at 183–184; and see also Hasjim Djalal, "Managing Potential Conflicts in the South China Sea," paper circulated at the eighteenth SCS Workshop held in Manado, Indonesia, 28–29 November 2008, 7. This paper can be found as a chapter with a different title, "The South China Sea: The Long Road Towards Peace and Cooperation," in *Security and International Politics in the South China Sea: Towards a Cooperative Management Regime*, eds. Sam Bateman and Ralf Emmers (London: Routledge, 2009), 175–188.

44. For the Scientific Results of the Anambas Expedition 2002, see *The Raffles Bulletin of Zoology*, 2004, Supplement No. 11, edited by Peter K. L. Ng, Daisy Wowor, and Darren C. J. Yeo. Information about the publication is available at rmbr.nus.edu.sg/exanambas/ (accessed 15 July 2009).

45. Djalal, "The South China Sea," supra note 43, at 183.

46. Mark J. Valencia, "Spratly Solution Still at Sea," *Pacific Review* 6, no. 2 (1993): 160.

47. Ted L. McDorman, "The South China Sea Islands Disputes in the 1990s—A New Multilateral Process and Continuing Friction," *International Journal of Marine and Coastal Law* 8 (1993): 281.

48. Mark J. Valencia, Jon M. Van Dyke, and Noel Ludwig, "The South China Sea: Approaches and Interim Solutions," paper presented at the First Technical Working Group Meeting on Legal Matters in the South China Sea, Phuket, Thailand, 2–5 July 1995.

49. ASEAN-China SCS Declaration, supra note 33.

50. Address by H.E. Mr. Ali Alatas, Minister for Foreign Affairs of Indonesia at the Third SCS Workshop, Yogyakarta, Indonesia, 29 June–1 July 1992.

51. Address by H.E. Mr. Ali Alatas, Minister for Foreign Affairs, Republic of Indonesia at the sixth SCS Workshop, Balikpapan, Indonesia, 10 October 1995.

52. Townsend-Gault, supra note 41, at 184.

53. See *The South China Sea Towards a Cooperative Management Regime*, 16–17 May 2007, Singapore, Conference Report by the Maritime Security Programme, S. Rajaratnam School of International Studies, Nanyang Technological University, 4, available at www.rsis.edu.sg/publications/conference_reports/South_China_Sea_Report.pdf (accessed 28 April 2010).

54. *Ibid.*

55. *Ibid.*

56. See Djalal, supra note 43.

57. Transcript of Opening Remarks by Director of Center for Southeast Asia Studies, Prof. Dr. Hasjim Djalal, at the sixteenth Workshop on Managing Potential Conflicts in the South China Sea, Bali, Indonesia, 23 November 2006. The transcript can be found in the *Proceedings of the 16th Workshop on Managing Potential Conflicts in the South China Sea*, Bali, 23–24 November 2006 (Policy Analysis and Development Agency, Department of Foreign Affairs, Republic of Indonesia, Jakarta, 2007), Annex 2, 13–19.

58. See Prologue of the Policy Guidelines for the South China Sea, 13 April 1993. The unofficial English version of the Guidelines can be found in Kuan-Ming Sun, "Policy of the Republic of China Towards the South China Sea: Recent Developments," *Marine Policy* 19 (1995): 408.

59. *Ibid.*

60. *Ibid.*

61. *Ibid.*

62. See the information provided by Taiwan's Ministry of Interior, available at www.land.moi.gov.tw/law/chthml/lawcontext.asp?lcid=224 (accessed 24 July 2009) (in Chinese).

63. See Edwin Hsiao, "Chen Urges Cooperation with 'Spratly Initiative,'" *Taiwan Journal* 25, no. 6 (February 2008): 1. See also Chen-yi Lin, "Buffer Benefits in Spratly Initiative," *Asia Times*, available at www.atimes.com/atimes/China?JB22Ad02.html (accessed 28 April 2010).

64. Hsiao, supra note 63.

65. *Ibid*. See also Yann-huei Song, "The Policy Implications of President Chen's Historic Visit to Taiping Island and His Spratly Initiative," *Taiwan Perspective*, No. 119, 27 February 2008, available at www.tp.org.tw/eletter/story.htm?id=20012527 (accessed 24 July 2009).

66. ASEAN-China SCS Declaration, supra note 33.

67. Ma Ying-jeou's blue strategy and ocean policy, available at www.rdec.gov.tw/public/Attachment/942417365271.pdf (accessed 24 July 2009).

68. "The Government of the Republic of China (Taiwan) Reiterated Its Sovereignty over the Spratly Islands and Has Proposed a Spratly Initiative that Focuses on Environmental Protection Instead of Sovereignty Disputes," Press Release, 15 August 2008, available at the Web site of the ROC Ministry of Foreign Affairs at www.mofa.gov.tw/webapp/fp.asp?xItem=32920&ctNode=497&mp=1 (accessed 24 July 2009).

69. "Cross-Strait Hand to Hand: Forwarding South China Sea and East China Sea Oil Exploration". The news report in Chinese is available at http://www.cooloud.org.tw/node/29076 (accessed July 7, 2010).

70. See Yann-huei Song, "Cross-Strait Interactions on the South China Sea Issues: A Need for CBMs," *Marine Policy* 29 (2005): 269–270.

71. Statement of the Fourteenth Workshop on Managing Potential Conflicts in the South China Sea, Batam, Indonesia, 24–26 November 2004, paras. 25–27.

72. See Statement of the 17th Workshop on Managing Potential Conflicts in the South China Sea, Yogyakarta, Indonesia, 23–24 November 2007, para. 19.

73. See Statement of the 18th Workshop on Managing Potential Conflicts in the South China Sea, Manado, Indonesia, 28–29 November 2008, para. 21.

74. Statement of the 19th Workshop on Managing Potential Conflicts in the South China Sea, Makassar, Indonesia, 13–14 November 2009, para. 21.

75. ASEAN-China SCS Declaration, supra note 33.

76. See "Across-the-Straits Search and Rescue Exercise Held," 24 October 2008, Bridging the Straits, available at english.cri.cn/4426/2008/10/24/2101s417651.htm (accessed 28 April 2010); and Yuanming Alvin Yao, "Energy Cooperation Beyond the Taiwan Strait," 12 May 2009, available at www.mac.gov.tw/public/Attachment/04115571725.pdf (accessed 28 April 2010).

77. See Li Mingjiang and Wendy Wang, "Anti-China 'Spratly Group' Not Likely," *Straits Times*, 14 July 2009. http://www.rsis.edu.sg/ForPress/op_eds.html (accessed July 7, 2010).

78. See supra note 27.

79. See "Clinton Declares the US 'Is Back' in Asia," *Yahoo News*, 21 July 2009, available at www.google.com/hostednews/ap/article/ALeqM5hGIXTMV1yK2R4TjMuMfMXIXJShdgD99JBF

200 (accessed 25 July 2009); and "Remarks from the Signing Ceremony of the Treaty of Amity and Cooperation Accession," Hillary Rodham Clinton, Secretary of State, Sheraton Grande Laguna, Laguna Phuket, Thailand, 22 July 2009, available at www.state.gov/secretary/rm/2009a/july/126334.htm (accessed 25 July 2009).

Treaty of Amity and Cooperation in Southeast Asia, done at Bali, Indonesia, 24 February 1976, entered into force 21 June 1976, 1025 *U.N.T.S.* 316. The ASEAN States were required to agree to the People's Republic of China becoming a party to the Treaty of Amity. This was formally signified through the Instrument of Extension of the Treaty of Amity and Cooperation in Southeast Asia, done at Bali, Indonesia, 8 October 2003, text available at the ASEAN Web site at www.aseansec.org/15269.htm (accessed 19 July 2009). The People's Republic of China formally became a party to the Treaty of Amity through its Instrument of Accession to the Treaty of Amity and Cooperation in Southeast Asia, done at Bali, Indonesia, 8 October 2003, text available at the ASEAN Web site at www.aseansec.org/15272.htm (accessed 19 July 2009).

Regional Cooperation in Marine Environmental Protection in the South China Sea: A Reflection on New Directions for Marine Conservation

ALDO CHIRCOP

Marine & Environment Law Institute
Schulich School of Law
Halifax, Nova Scotia, Canada

Despite ongoing conflict management and confidence-building efforts in the South China Sea (SCS), there is still no clear path to the resolution of the complex multilateral sovereignty and the maritime boundary disputes. Intergovernmental Panel on Climate Change assessments for the region forecast significant climate and ecological change to the detriment of the region's coastal inhabitants, ecosystems, and economies. SCS states need to place marine conservation cooperation at the center of all development activity in order to enhance the prospects of adaptation to climate change. This article explores and argues for more effective SCS Large Marine Ecosystem cooperation through transboundary networks of marine protected areas.

Introduction

The South China Sea (SCS) has experienced protracted territorial and maritime boundary disputes for several decades. Some bilateral disputes have been resolved through negotiation or third party assistance but others, in particular those involving the Paracel and Spratly archipelagos and surrounding waters, remain intractable. Despite ongoing dialogue, which has created a constructive political mood, there is still no clear path to resolution in sight. This dialogue has been facilitated by the South China Sea Workshop process that has engaged stakeholders in unofficial and informal dialogue to explore potential paths of functional cooperation.[1] From time to time, the SCS states have embarked on specific cooperative initiatives that build confidence without prejudicing claims.[2]

Over the past two decades, there has been a growing sense of urgency in the need to take action in marine environmental cooperation at the global and regional levels. The First Assessment of the Intergovernmental Panel on Climate Change (IPCC)[3] anticipated that the SCS would experience significant climate and ecological change to the detriment of the region's coastal inhabitants, ecosystems, and economies, among others.[4] The IPCC's forthcoming Fifth Assessment can be expected to forecast an equally pessimistic scenario for the SCS. No one regional state can effectively respond to this change alone, even within its own undisputed jurisdiction. It is clear from the IPCC's Fourth Assessment[5] that the threat of further losses to coastal and marine ecosystems should be particularly worrisome for SCS states. They have large numbers of people living in low-lying coastal regions that are normally protected by coastal systems against natural hazards as well as deriving health and economic values.[6] Degraded coastal ecosystems will exacerbate the effects of climate change and produce substantial economic losses for the region.[7]

The need for accelerated action to protect marine ecosystems is also justified on another front. While recognizing the threats faced by marine ecosystems globally and regionally, SCS states together with other parties to the Convention on Biological Diversity (CBD)[8] committed at the Seventh Conference of the Parties (COP) to achieve effective protection of 10% of marine ecoregions by 2012 (CBD COP VII target).[9] This effectively means that 10% of the 3.2 million km^2 that make up the SCS will need to be placed under "effective" protection. The actual area of the SCS under protection pales in comparison at 0.31%, well below the global figure of 0.7% of marine areas under protection.[10] In addition to domestic marine protected area (MPA)[11] initiatives, regional initiatives to establish MPA networks are needed in response to the call of the World Summit on Sustainable Development for a global system of MPA networks,[12] which SCS states supported, and also to further assist meeting the CBD COP VII target. The Millennium Development Goals similarly called for an increase in protected areas (including MPAs) by the year 2010.[13] In 2003 the Fifth World Parks Congress lent support to these calls and the 2012 deadline, and further elaborated that "these networks should be extensive and include strictly protected areas that amount to at least 20–30% of each habitat, and contribute to a global target for healthy and productive oceans."[14] More recently, Indonesia, Malaysia, and the Philippines joined Papua New Guinea, the Solomon Islands, and Timor-Leste to launch the Coral Triangle Initiative to strengthen MPA networks, protect threatened marine species, and build greater resilience to climate change impacts, with support from the Global Environment Facility and Asian Development Bank.[15]

Protecting the region's deteriorating marine ecosystems and undertaking adaptive actions in response to climate change requires more cooperative regional efforts in the SCS than are currently being pursued. Although SCS regional cooperation in marine environment protection and marine scientific research has been enhanced, there is insufficient conservation action to protect the region's marine ecosystems against the impact of climate change and to meet the CBD COP VII target.

This article addresses the marine conservation dimensions of marine environmental protection in the SCS region. The entities concerned are: Brunei Darussalam; the People's Republic of China (China); Indonesia; Malaysia; the Philippines; Singapore; the Republic of China (Taiwan); and Vietnam, all of which have coastal frontage on the SCS Large Marine Ecosystem (LME). This article sets out the ecosystemic and human security stakes as a result of developmental pressures and climate change impacts. It argues that the SCS states need to place marine conservation cooperation at the center of all development activity in order to enhance the prospects of adaptation to climate change, and to do this on a cooperative basis. More specifically, the article argues that the progress achieved to date on marine ecosystem protection through MPAs, although helpful to protect coastal ecosystems, needs to be accelerated and expanded beyond coastal and inshore areas to meet the CBD COP VII target. In particular, there is an argument for more effective LME cooperation through transboundary networks of MPAs, whether existing or to be established. Because there are major international maritime trade routes in the region and the threats these pose to the region's rich marine biodiversity, this article further suggests that regional states should consider cooperating through the International Maritime Organization (IMO) to adopt further measures to protect sensitive ecosystems from international shipping. Finally, this article underscores the need for broad regional cooperation for marine conservation of the SCS as an LME whole. Marine areas in dispute need to be conserved as much as undisputed areas and whether they are located in coastal or offshore waters.

The Need for Marine Conservation in the SCS

State of the Region's Marine Ecosystems and Related Knowledge

The SCS LME forms part of a family of LMEs in the East Asian seas that include the Gulf of Thailand, the Indonesian Sea, North Australian Shelf, Northwest Australian Shelf, the Sulu-Celebes Sea, and the West Central Australian Shelf.[16] For the purposes of this article, the focus is on the SCS LME as defined in a recent report of the United Nations Environment Programme (UNEP).[17] Bathymetry varies between 200 m or less for shallow areas to over 1,000 m in the South SCS Basin and Palawan Trough. The SCS has a moderate production ecosystem, although it still accounts for 7.04% of the world's coral reefs, 12% of all mangroves, and 0.93% of seamounts.[18] By some estimates, the SCS accounts for a large percentage of coral reef species. The coral reef presence mainly occurs in Indonesian and Filipino waters (77% of the regions' coral reefs). In addition to coral reefs and mangroves, the SCS has extensive sea grass beds and other critical habitats for many species. Mangroves provide US$16 billion and coral reefs US$2.4 billion a year of ecological goods and services.[19] Sea grass and coastal swamps are valued at US$190 billion per year.[20]

The region's great natural wealth is now being affected by a number of marine uses, expanding populations, and economic activity. Coastlines are experiencing growth in human settlements, urbanization, and industrialization at high rates, threatening sensitive coastal ecosystems. Food production pressures to address regional needs and market demand from outside the region are affecting mangroves. Many have been destroyed or damaged to make way for shrimp and fish pond farms. Mangroves have decreased by 70% in 70 years and 20% to 50% of sea grass has been damaged.[21] Unfortunately, the bad news does not end there: Risk analysis for coral reefs as reported in the IPCC's Fourth Assessment forecasts reef losses in Asia to be as high as 88% in the next 30 years due to multiple stresses and climate change.[22] With a 1-m sea-level rise extensive mangroves will be lost, including in the Mekong Delta and Red River Delta in the Gulf of Tonkin.[23]

The SCS LME is an important fishing region that nets an annual 6 million tons valued at US$6 billion (mostly reef fish and pelagic species). The fisheries concerned have major economic, food security, and cultural importance for the region's coastal communities. China accounts for the largest share of fishing in the SCS LME.[24] The region's fishing activity is not being undertaken in a sustainable manner and includes "fishing down" and excessive bycatch. Human activity further threatens the region's reefs, for example, from overfishing and use of destructive methods. Seventy percent of reefs are severely depleted.[25] As elsewhere around the world, overfishing is a major cause of environmental degradation.[26] The region has many charismatic and migratory species, including tuna, sharks, turtles (six of which are endangered or vulnerable), dugongs and other mammals whose status is affected by resource exploitation, bycatch, pollution, and loss of habitat.

In addition to unsustainable coastal ecosystem and marine resource use practices, there is also sedimentation and extensive pollution from land-based activities, much of which has resulted from rapid industrialization and urbanization of coastlines, agriculture, and aquaculture.[27] The region's population is expected to double within three decades, so all of the above pressures can be expected to increase. There are also major trade routes through the region and, consequently, shipping is also a source of pollution, although spills have been described as moderate.[28]

There have been and continue to be regional efforts at marine conservation, but such efforts are insufficient in basic research, volume of activity, and effectiveness of results. Writing in 2000, Ng and Tan noted that there has been "little or no coordinated regional effort to identify knowledge gaps and provide useful solutions" in marine biodiversity research.[29] The region is still "relatively unexplored biologically" and much is to be "gained from a more systematic and cooperative approach."[30] Surprisingly, limited knowledge is true not only of demersal and abyssal fauna, but also of "smaller organisms living in shallow-water ecosystems, such as in the mangroves, coral reefs, seagrass meadows and sandy shores (meiofauna)."[31] Although almost a decade has passed since then, the research insufficiency continues and, frequently, conservation measures are undertaken in the absence of adequate knowledge. The World Conservation Union (IUCN) has reported that "some of the protected areas in the region were declared not on the basis of biodiversity but for some other reasons such as for historical importance."[32]

Contemporary Framework and Actions for Marine Environmental Conservation

Global Framework

By and large, most SCS states are parties to the most important global international environmental law instruments relevant for marine conservation. (See Table 1.) Taiwan has a unique status in international relations, resulting in its practical inability to become a party to international marine and environmental agreements. In practice, Taiwan's position is to abide by relevant international agreements.[33] The average number of years for ratification or accession for most instruments by the other SCS states has tended to be high. SCS states have mainly been "late" supporters of the instruments considered, meaning that they became parties after an instrument entered into force. It has not always been clear why some states are parties to a particular agreement, but not to another, given the frequently similar conservation objectives of many agreements. The CBD received widespread SCS state support early, but the widely ratified 1971 Convention on Wetlands of International Importance Especially as Waterfowl Habitation (Ramsar Convention),[34] the 1972 Convention Concerning the Protection of the World Cultural and Natural Heritage (World Heritage Convention),[35] and the Convention on International Trade in Endangered Species of Wild Fauna and Flora (CITES)[36] averaged 15 years. Although these figures may be of concern to international environmental lawyers, it is important to note that in the contemporary context most SCS states have committed to conserving marine ecosystems by employing particular spatial and functional tools provided in those instruments and also to achieving international status for certain protected areas. The issue, rather, is whether those responses are sufficient, given the extent and nature of the threats faced by the CSC LME.

All SCS states, but Taiwan, are parties to the 1982 United Nations Convention on the Law of the Sea (LOS Convention), which provides a framework for individual and cooperative action for the protection and preservation of the marine environment.[37] In comparison, neighboring Cambodia and Thailand are not yet parties. The LOS Convention has equipped coastal states with comprehensive maritime zones with the authority necessary

Table 1
SCS coastal state ratification or accession of global instruments relevant to marine conservation in the region

State	LOS Convention	CBD	Ramsar	WHC	CMS	CITES
Year adopted	1982	1992	1971	1972	1979	1973
Year in force	1994	1993	1975	1975	1983	1975
Brunei Darussalam	1996	2008	—	—	—	1990
PR China	1996	1993	1992	1985	—	1981
Indonesia	1986	1994	1992	1989	—	1978
Malaysia	1996	1994	1994	1988	—	1977
Philippines	1984	1993	1994	1985	1994	1981
Singapore	1994	1995	—	—	—	1986
Taiwan	—	—	—	—	—	—
Vietnam	1994	1994	1988	1987	—	1994
Total	7/8	7/8	5/8	5/8	1/8	7/8
Average since adoption	10.28	3.85	21	14.80	15	11.28
Average since entry into force	0.86	2.86	17	11.80	11	8.86

Notes: Years represent the date of the deposition of the instrument of ratification or accession. "Average since adoption" represents the average number of years it has taken SCS states to become parties since an instrument was adopted. "Average since entry into force" represents the average number of years it has taken SCS states to become parties since an instrument came into force. Abbreviations: SCS, South China Sea; LOS Convention, United Nations Convention on the Law of the Sea; CBD, Convention on Biological Diversity; Ramsar, Convention on Wetlands of International Importance Especially as Waterfowl Habitation; WHC, Convention Concerning the Protection of the World Cultural and Natural Heritage; CMS, Convention on the Conservation of Migratory Species of Wild Animals; CITES, Convention on International Trade in Endangered Species of Wild Fauna and Flora.

to exercise jurisdiction over the marine environment.[38] Clearly, in disputed marine areas, SCS states are constrained from fully exercising the environmental jurisdiction. However, the LOS Convention still places a responsibility on them to cooperate for this purpose at various levels. In particular, Article 123 of the LOS Convention provides:

> States bordering an enclosed or semi-enclosed sea should co-operate with each other in the exercise of their rights and in the performance of their duties under this Convention. To this end they shall endeavour, directly or through an appropriate regional organization:
>
> (a) to co-ordinate the management, conservation, exploration and exploitation of the living resources of the sea In particular, states bordering the semi-enclosed SCS have a responsibility to cooperate;
> (b) to co-ordinate the implementation of their rights and duties with respect to the protection and preservation of the marine environment;
> (c) to co-ordinate their scientific research policies and undertake where appropriate joint programmes of scientific research in the area;

(d) to invite, as appropriate, other interested states or international organizations to co-operate with them in furtherance of the provisions of this article.

These undertakings cover the full range of actions that SCS states would need to take in cooperating on MPAs. The UNEP, the United Nations Development Programme (UNDP), IUCN, and the World Wildlife Fund (WWF) have provided assistance to facilitate cooperative marine conservation.

In an understanding culminating in the Declaration on the Conduct of Parties in the South China Sea, China and the Association of Southeast Nations (ASEAN) states agreed that, pending settlement of the SCS dispute, they may explore or undertake cooperative activities, including for marine environmental protection.[39] This constructive policy is subject to procedural constraints: "The modalities, scope and locations, in respect of bilateral and multilateral cooperation should be agreed upon by the Parties concerned prior to their actual implementation."[40] It is unclear to what extent, if at all, a party to the Declaration could proceed with marine conservation activities without prior consultation and also without raising objections from other states.

As seen in Table 1, the CBD enjoys widespread support in the SCS. In contrast to the other conservation conventions that took more than a decade to be embraced by most regional states, the CBD received the support of most SCS states within 3 years of adoption. Commitment to the CBD is important because, in providing for conservation at the ecosystemic, species, and genetic levels, the Convention provides for both ex situ and in situ protection.[41] In situ protection is a basis for the designation of MPAs and MPA networks.

Similarly important and applicable to the SCS are the Ramsar Convention[42] and the World Heritage Convention.[43] The Ramsar Convention provides a framework for the designation of national wetland sites (Ramsar sites) as part of an international List of Wetlands of International Importance. The worst record with the SCS is that concerning the Ramsar Convention, a worrying observation considering the important functions of wetlands for "water storage, groundwater recharge, storm protection, flood mitigation, shoreline stabilization, erosion control, and retention of carbon, nutrients, sediments and pollutants" as well as protecting coastal ecosystems against climate change impacts and to facilitate adaptation and mitigation.[44] States parties commit to protecting and conserving the fundamental ecological functions of wetlands, regulating water regimes, and protecting the habitats of flora and fauna therein, especially waterfowl. States parties commit to compensating for wetland sites on the international list lost to development by creating additional nature reserves or by protection of a suitable portion of the original habitat. The list of all Ramsar sites in SCS states is reproduced in Table 2, although it is unclear how many and what acreage are actually located in the SCS coastal region. None are transboundary or appear on the Montreux Record as experiencing or likely to experience change as a result of human activities.[45] As to be expected because of its size, China has the largest number and acreage of Ramsar sites, although the majority are clearly outside the SCS region or are located inland. Several sites in other SCS states are coastal sites, such as the Tubbataha Reefs in the Philippines and Xuan Thuy in Vietnam. Most of Taiwan's wetlands have been overutilized or polluted, although Taiwan has recently established a wetlands conservation program.[46]

The World Heritage Convention underscores the duty of states for the identification, protection, conservation, presentation, and transmission of natural and cultural heritage sites within their territories.[47] The Convention Secretariat maintains a World Heritage List of sites communicated to it by states parties in fulfillment of their responsibilities under the

Table 2
Ramsar sites of SCS states (as of 29 May 2008)

State	Name	Year	Location	Size
China (36 Ramsar sites, 3,168,210 ha)	Bitahai Wetland	07/12/04	Yunnan	1,985 ha
	Chongming Dongtan Nature Reserve, Shanghai	11/01/02	Shanghai	32,600 ha
	Dafeng (*Elaphurus davidianus*) National Nature Reserve	11/01/02	Jiangsu	78,000 ha
	Dalai Lake National Nature Reserve, Inner Mongolia	11/01/02	Inner Mongolia	740,000 ha
	Dalian National Spotted Seal (*Phoca vitulina*) Nature Reserve	11/01/02	Liaoning	11,700 ha
	Dashanbao	07/12/04	Yunnan	5,958 ha
	Dongdongtinghu	31/03/92	Hunan	190,000 ha
	Dongzhaigang	31/03/92	Hainan	5,400 ha
	Eerduosi National Nature Reserve	11/01/02	Inner Mongolia	7,680 ha
	Eling Lake	07/12/04	Qinghai	65,907 ha
	Fujian Zhangjiangkou National Mangrove Nature Reserve	02/02/08	Fujian	2,358 ha
	Guangdong Haifeng Wetlands	02/02/08	Guangdong	11,591 ha
	Guangxi Beilun Estuary National Nature Reserve	02/02/08	Guangxi	3,000 ha
	Honghe National Nature Reserve	11/01/02	Heilongjiang	21,836 ha
	Hubei Honghu Wetlands	02/02/08	Hubei	43,450 ha
	Huidong Harbor Sea Turtle National Nature Reserve	11/01/02	Guangdong	400 ha
	Lashihai Wetland	07/12/04	Yunnan	3,560 ha
	Mai Po Marshes & Inner Deep Bay	04/09/95	New Territories, Hong Kong	1,540 ha
	Maidika	07/12/04	Tibet Autonomous Region	43,496 ha
	Mapangyong Cuo	07/12/04	Tibet Autonomous Region	73,782 ha
	Nan Dongting Wetland & Waterfowl Reserve	11/01/02	Hunan	168,000 ha
	Napahai Wetland	07/12/04	Yunnan	2,083 ha
	Niaodao ("Bird Island")	31/03/92	Qinghai	53,600 ha
	Poyanghu	31/03/92	Jiangxi	22,400 ha
	San Jiang National Nature Reserve	11/01/02	Heilongjiang	164,400 ha
	Shanghai Yangtze Estuarine Wetland Nature Reserve for Chinese Sturgeon	02/02/08	Shanghai	3,760 ha

	Shankou Mangrove Nature Reserve	11/01/02	Guangxi	4,000 ha
	Shuangtai Estuary	07/12/04	Liaoning	128,000 ha
	Sichuan Ruoergai Wetland National Nature Reserve	02/02/08	Sichuan	166,570 ha
	Xi Dongting Lake (Mupinghu) Nature Reserve	11/01/02	Hunan	35,000 ha
	Xingkai Lake National Nature Reserve	11/01/02	Heilongjiang	222,488 ha
	Xianghai	31/03/92	Jilin	105,467 ha
	Yancheng National Nature Reserve	11/01/02	Jiangsu	453,000 ha
	Zhaling Lake	07/12/04	Qinghai	64,920 ha
	Zhalong	31/03/92	Heilongjiang	210,000 ha
	Zhanjiang Mangrove National Nature Reserve	11/01/02	Guangdong	20,279 ha
	Berbak	08/04/92	Jambi	162,700 ha
Indonesia (3 Ramsar sites, 656,510 ha)	Danau Sentarum	30/08/94	Kalimantan Barat	80,000 ha
	Wasur National Park	16/03/06	Irian Jaya	413,810 ha
	Kuching Wetlands National Park	08/11/05	Sarawak	6,610 ha
Malaysia (6 Ramsar sites, 134,158 ha)	Lower Kinabatangan-Segama Wetland	28/10/08	Sabah	78,803 ha
	Pulau Kukup	31/01/03	Johor	647 ha
	Sungai Pulai	31/01/03	Johor	9,126 ha
	Tanjung Piai	31/01/03	Johor	526 ha
	Tasek Bera	10/11/94	Pahang	38,446 ha
	Agusan Marsh Wildlife Sanctuary	12/11/99	Mindanao	14,836 ha
Philippines (4 Ramsar sites, 68,404 ha)	Naujan Lake National Park	12/11/99	Oriental Mindoro	14,568 ha
	Olango Island Wildlife Sanctuary	01/07/94	Cebu	5,800 ha
	Tubbataha Reefs National Marine Park	12/11/99	Sulu Sea	33,200 ha
Vietnam (2 Ramsar sites, 25,759 ha)	Bau Sau (Crocodile Lake) Wetlands and Seasonal Floodplains	04/08/05	Dong Nai	13,759 ha
	Xuan Thuy Natural Wetland Reserve	20/09/88	Nam Ha	12,000 ha

Source: Ramsar Convention Web site, available at http://www.ramsar.org/ (accessed 25 September 2009).

Convention.[48] For the most part, SCS states have designated sites for cultural values. Of the relatively few sites designated for their natural value in the SCS, only a handful are located in the coastal marine environment; namely, in Indonesia, the Philippines, and Vietnam.[49] This suggests that SCS states are not maximizing opportunities to designate coastal and marine natural sites as World Heritage sites for their natural value and, thereby, achieve international recognition and support that comes from inclusion in the World Heritage List.

Under the auspices of the United Nations Educational, Cultural and Scientific Organization (UNESCO) through the Man and the Biosphere (MAB) Programme, biosphere reserves can be designated that cover internationally recognized terrestrial and coastal marine ecosystems.[50] These reserves have similar conservation purposes to World Heritage and Ramsar Convention sites. SCS states that are members of UNESCO are also members of the MAB Programme.[51] The biosphere reserves are "designed to promote and demonstrate a balanced relationship between people and nature."[52] Although not designated under an international convention, biosphere reserves are nominated by governments and designated by the International Coordinating Council of the MAB Programme to form part of a global network that involves cooperative research, monitoring, and exchange. Nominating states retain full sovereignty over the areas concerned and participation in the network remains voluntary. Five SCS states have biosphere reserves: Cambodia (1), China (28), Indonesia (7), Malaysia (1), the Philippines (3), and Vietnam (8).[53] As in the case of Ramsar Convention sites, the majority of these are not located in the SCS coastal region. However, the existence of biosphere reserves demonstrates a commitment by these states to promote conservation while pursuing development. As in the case of the paucity of World Heritage sites, SCS states are underutilizing biosphere reserves as a tool to further marine ecosystem protection.

All SCS states are parties to CITES.[54] CITES promotes international cooperation in regulating and restricting the illegal trade in species listed as endangered. This instrument provides a powerful tool to achieve conservation objectives for species listed on three appendices: species that are endangered (Appendix 1); species which, while not threatened with extinction, may become so if their trade is left unregulated (Appendix 2); and species listed at the request of a state party that requires the cooperation of other states parties (Appendix 3). In the case of some species, CITES cooperation is consciously coordinated to support the objectives of the 1979 Convention on the Conservation of Migratory Species of Wild Animals,[55] such as in relation to the marine turtles of Southeast Asia (among others), the whale shark (*Rhincodon typus*) of South and Southeast Asia, and the great white shark (*Carcharodon carcharias*).[56]

The record of SCS states in relation to the Migratory Species Convention[57] is less impressive than for the conventions discussed above, considering the several migratory species on the Convention list that are to be found in the SCS. The Migratory Species Convention provides an international framework for transboundary and cooperative conservation and management of migratory species of wild animals, including listed marine species (e.g., cetaceans, dugong, seals, turtles) whose life cycles encompass more than one jurisdiction. Only the Philippines is a party to the Convention. The Migratory Species Convention is also a framework for species-specific agreements that may also involve states that are not party to the Convention, and two of these are important for species found in the SCS LME. The Philippines is the only SCS state party to the Memorandum of Understanding on the Conservation and Management of Dugongs and Their Habitats Throughout Their Range.[58] The record is different in the case of the Memorandum of Understanding

Concerning Conservation Measures for Marine Turtles and Their Habitats of the Indian Ocean and South-East Asia, 2001, which in addition to the Philippines includes Indonesia and Vietnam as parties.[59]

Lack of support of the Migratory Species Convention by SCS states is also echoed in relation to important fisheries conservation instruments which, although not central to the discussion in this article, are relevant because of the impact of fishing on the marine environment and the challenge of effective fisheries enforcement. In this respect, none of the SCS states are party to the 1995 Agreement for the Implementation of the Provisions of the United Nations Convention on the Law of the Sea of 10 December 1982 Relating to the Conservation and Management of Straddling Fish Stocks and Highly Migratory Fish Stocks (UN Fish Stocks Agreement)[60] or the 1993 Agreement to Promote Compliance with International Conservation and Management Measures by Fishing Vessels on the High Seas (FAO Compliance Agreement).[61] This is not encouraging in a region where both coastal and industrial fishing are important. On the other hand, it appears that SCS states are increasingly embracing the Food and Agriculture Organization of the United Nations (FAO) Code of Conduct for Responsible Fisheries.[62] Several regional states support the voluntary Regional Plan of Action (RPOA) to Promote Responsible Fishing Practices (including Combating [illegal, unreported, and unregulated] IUU Fishing) in the Region,[63] which is based, among other instruments on the UN Fish Stocks Agreement, the FAO Compliance Agreement, and the FAO Code of Conduct.

Regional Framework

There is no one marine environmental regime focused on the SCS. Instead various regimes include the region for particular purposes. The first is the East Asian Seas Programme (EAP), a regional arrangement forming part of UNEP's Regional Seas Programme.[64] Its membership includes non-SCS states and Brunei Darussalam, an SCS coastal state, is not a member. The EAP provides a general contextual role for the encouragement of cooperation among SCS states engaged in the region's territorial disputes. The EAP has had a mixed record with successive action plans falling short of implementation.[65] The Coordinating Body of the Seas of East Asia (COBSEA) recently adopted the "New Strategic Direction for COBSEA (2008–2012)."[66]

A significant COBSEA accomplishment for the purposes of this article is a project supported by UNEP and the Global Environment Facility (GEF) entitled "Reversing Environmental Trends in the South China Sea and Gulf of Thailand," commenced in 2002 at the request of COBSEA and terminating in 2008 with the adoption of the important Strategic Action Programme for the South China Sea (SAP).[67] The SAP consists of a framework for strategic priority actions to conserve mangroves, coral reefs, sea grass meadows, coastal wetlands, fish and habitat, and fish stocks. This is a major initiative that was undertaken on the basis of consultation with all SCS (and Gulf of Thailand) states and which was followed by the adoption of national programs of action. It is hoped that this will make a significant difference in SCS environmental cooperation. It should be underscored, however, that implementation of the SAP is voluntary and it remains to be seen how much commitment SCS states will provide given that the EAP is a regional agreement that includes non-SCS states. Implementation will rely on whatever resources regional governments are willing to commit. Past experience has shown that pledged contributions do not necessarily materialize.[68] Another concern is the lack of apparent networking of the various national actions encouraged by the SAP. Networking is important because collective action is needed to enhance the status of the SCS LME and, for effectiveness, it is important that the choice of areas under protection are conceived with larger LME functions in mind, irrespective of geographical location.

As in the case of marine environment protection, the SCS does not have a dedicated regional fisheries management organization (RFMO). Rather, the SCS falls within the larger geographical mandate of the Asia-Pacific Fishery Commission,[69] which includes most SCS states among its membership; namely, China, Indonesia, Malaysia, the Philippines, and Vietnam. With a mandate that is essentially facilitative, and providing a framework for information generation and exchange and capacity building, this body has not played a significant conservation role. Its current orientation appears to be directed more at development and management than conservation.[70] Because of its contemporary orientation toward sustainable fisheries management, the Commission has the potential of playing an important role in advocating conservation measures among its membership. As noted earlier, the 2008 RPOA is an initiative of the Commission,[71] although its voluntary nature means that Commission member states cannot be compelled to take measures, even when measures may be necessary in the interests of good management, conservation, and compliance.

ASEAN is another regional forum for functional cooperation, but is obviously limited to its membership, which in the region includes: Brunei Darussalam, Indonesia, Malaysia, the Philippines, Singapore, and Vietnam. ASEAN has not been especially active in marine conservation, but particular actions should be mentioned. For example, the ASEAN Declaration on Heritage Parks establishes a list of ASEAN Heritage Parks to which sites may be added periodically.[72] The Declaration recognizes that

> common cooperation is necessary to conserve and manage ASEAN Heritage Parks for the development and implementation of regional conservation and management action plans as well as regional mechanisms complementary to and supportive of national efforts to implement conservation measures.[73]

As in the case of Ramsar sites, World Heritage sites, and biosphere reserves, there is scope for designating MPAs as ASEAN Heritage Parks to enhance their conservation status and recognition at the regional level.

A more pointed initiative for MPA networking is IUCN's Regional Action Plan to Strengthen a Resilient Network of Effective Marine Protected Areas in Southeast Asia: 2002–2012, developed in recognition of the need for greater action for effective conservation.[74] Adopted after a broad consultative process in the region, the plan aims, among other things, to "co-ordinate, guide and implement existing and new plans of action related to the strengthening and networking of representative Marine Protected Areas (MPAs) in Southeast Asia."[75] It remains to be seen to what extent such an initiative by a highly respected international nongovernmental organization (NGO), which has had significant success in other marine regions, will be able to achieve effective and cooperative marine conservation in the SCS.[76]

National MPA Action

The World Database on Marine Protected Areas, although not exhaustive in its coverage, provides useful insights into the MPA practices of SCS states.[77] Table 3 summarizes these practices and divides them into exclusively marine areas and areas that are both terrestrial and marine (terrestrial-marine MPAs). The first impression provided is that the SCS states have a substantial number of MPAs, with 739 classified across the full spectrum of IUCN categories.[78] However, the figure includes all MPAs of SCS states, both within the SCS and outside. Only Brunei Darussalam, Singapore, and Vietnam have coastal frontage that is exclusively or preponderantly in the SCS. The extensive practice of other states, in particular China, Indonesia, Malaysia, and the Philippines, includes MPAs in adjacent ecosystems. Further, a closer look at the total figure shows that 70% of the MPAs consist of terrestrial ecosystems with a marine annex and, consequently, they do not generally extend far beyond inshore waters. A more in-depth look at the MPA practices of those states whose coastal frontage is totally or preponderantly in the SCS (i.e., Brunei Darussalam, Singapore and Vietnam) shows far fewer MPAs and only a fraction of which consist of fully marine MPAs. Clearly, the terrestrial-marine MPAs perform valuable functions because they tend to protect particularly sensitive coastal systems such as forests (including mangroves) and wetlands as well as the related wildlife therein. They are essential tools for adaptation to the impacts of climate change. Accordingly, the terrestrial-marine MPAs tend to be parks or reserves (nature, game, or both).

In effect, only 30% of MPAs are exclusively marine (and many are small and for fish sanctuary purposes and coral reefs), suggesting that the vast SCS LME offshore hydrospace and its numerous ecosystems are not receiving as much protective attention through MPAs as are terrestrial-marine ecosystems. The Philippines is the only SCS state whose MPA practice is preponderantly marine, rather than terrestrial-marine. While taking into consideration that the MPAs include the SCS LME and the South Celebes LME, the remarkable emphasis on marine space reflects the archipelagic nature of the country, the extensive dependence of rural communities on fishery resources, and the authority given by the Local Government Code to local governments, especially to coastal municipalities.[79] This has enabled coastal municipalities and communities, aided by NGOs, to play an important role in local and frequently community-based marine resource management. Indonesia, which is comparable to the Philippines in many respects, places a preponderant emphasis on terrestrial-marine MPAs.

The marine MPAs are also located primarily in coastal or inshore waters. Many protect coral reef systems. In the Philippines, there are numerous fish sanctuaries, mostly in coastal regions. The MPAs located offshore are few and tend to be associated with a neighboring

Table 3
Marine protected area (MPA) practices

SCS state	Exclusively marine (approx.)	Terrestrial and marine (approx.)	Total number of MPAs (approx.)
Brunei Darussalam	2	7	9
PR China	2	29	31
Indonesia	24	216	240
Malaysia	11	155	166
Philippines	174	47	221
Singapore	0	3	3
Taiwan	5	15	20
Vietnam	6	43	49
Total	224/30%	515/70%	739

Source: Data extracted from the World Database on Marine Protected Areas (4 July 2009), available at http://www.wdpa.org/Default.aspx (accessed 25 September 2009).

island. Further, it is unclear how much of the contemporary SCS MPA practice meets the effectiveness criterion for the CBD COP VII target. The practice of evaluating MPA effectiveness is relatively recent, and studies undertaken to date for other regions have suggested a low level of effectiveness, partly because of poor design, weak governance, and insufficient resources.[80] At this time, the World Database for Marine Protected Areas does not contain comprehensive information on effectiveness. There is evidence that protective action in the region might not be as effective as might be desirable. There appear to be significant gaps that the SCS states of Indonesia, Malaysia, the Philippines, and Vietnam need to address, including through the strengthening of MPAs.[81] A similar, but more extensive, study that looked at a broader range of MPAs in Southeast Asia estimated that only 10% to 20% of the MPAs were "effectively managed and as such, MPA management remains inadequate."[82]

MPA Networks: A Modern Approach to Ecosystem-Based Management

The relative lack of conservation attention to the offshore waters of the SCS LME should be cause for concern. Such concern needs to be addressed with a careful use of the MPA tool to increase the number of marine areas under protection and, in doing so, to ensure that the selected areas are truly representative of essential components and functions of the LME. The protected areas should be networked so that they perform protective functions collectively to generate critical conservation mass. This is not the current practice, although the IUCN project mentioned above[83] aims to network MPAs. For the most part, the SCS MPA practice consists of protection zones for various purposes and to different extents that are not configured to achieve macroecosystemic purposes and functions, whether with respect to ecosystemic components within national jurisdiction or even more significantly with reference to the SCS LME. The Global International Waters Assessment (GIWA) Regional Assessment for the SCS has recommended "functional, integrated networks of marine protected areas founded on ... research and with strong co-management focus."[84]

This is precisely where the concept of an MPA network, and in the regional LME case, a transboundary MPA network comes in. An *MPA network* is understood as being "a collection of individual MPAs or reserves operating cooperatively and synergistically, at various spatial scales, and with a range of protection levels that are designed to meet objectives that a single reserve cannot achieve."[85] Simply stated, the network concept can be considered at three levels:

- at a minimum, more than one MPA;
- more usefully, a collection of MPAs either as representative networks or with some degree of connectivity that could be ecological or social, including sharing of governance resources;
- ideally, a synergistic system of MPAs with the "whole greater than the sum of the parts" relative to objectives.[86]

In the SCS, this would mean a system of MPAs spread throughout the regional sea. The areas included would cover both disputed and undisputed areas. The system should be designed to address the particular structure, functions, and processes of the SCS LME as they may be defined in spatial and ecosystemic terms. An MPA network for the SCS LME would require coordination at the regional level.

Layering Additional International Protection for an SCS MPA Network

MPA designation is essentially a domestic process and, in general, has to take into consideration the international community's right of innocent passage, archipelagic sea-lanes passage, transit passage through straits used for international navigation, and freedom of high seas navigation (which also applies in the exclusive economic zone [EEZ]). Even when MPAs are established through regional cooperation, as in the case of a hypothetical SCS LME MPA network, there will be constraints on the regional states' abilities to exercise jurisdiction and control over international shipping activities that may have an adverse impact on SCS LME components. The major international maritime trade routes through the SCS produce impacts on fragile ecosystems through discharges of operational vessel source pollution, ship groundings, ship strikes of marine mammals, anchoring in sensitive areas, and accidental pollution. These threats are not theoretical.[87] Ships have grounded on the coral reef fringe of Taiwan's Dongsha Marine National Park, a unique atoll, and continue to lie there as wrecks.[88] The LOS Convention and international maritime law instruments empower the IMO to provide assistance to member states that request the raising of standards for international shipping in relation to Particularly Sensitive Sea Areas (PSSAs). There are numerous examples of domestic MPAs in other regions provided with an additional layer of protection through IMO routeing measures.[89] The advantage of such measures is the empowerment of the coastal state concerned to apply those higher standards in relation to international shipping, when they would not otherwise have jurisdiction to do so if they proceeded outside of the IMO.

MARPOL Special Area Status?

Surprisingly although many marine regions have been designated as special areas under the Convention on Prevention of Pollution from Ships, 1973/78 (MARPOL)[90] or as PSSAs within which appropriate protective measures are applied, the SCS has not. This is surprising because the SCS compares well to the Caribbean, Mediterranean, Red, Baltic, and North Seas, which have all received such protection.[91] In those regions, the discharge standard for ship waste is higher than the general norm, both in terms of type of waste that may be discharged and the rate of discharge at a certain distance from the nearest land. On the other hand, the SCS is subject to the general rules that do permit the discharge of certain wastes in certain amounts at a prescribed distance from the nearest land.

The SCS merits protection from special area status as designated by the IMO and would likely qualify under all three criteria (i.e., oceanographic, ecological, and ship traffic conditions).[92] The semienclosed geography of the SCS "may cause the concentration of harmful substances in the waters or sediments of the area."[93] As seen earlier, the SCS LME has numerous sensitive ecosystems and species that need to be protected. The coastal communities of the SCS are heavily dependent on their coastal and marine resource economies that may be affected by heavy shipping traffic. The SCS would also satisfy the requirement that

> the sea area is used by ships to an extent that the discharge of harmful substances by ships when operating in accordance with the requirements of MARPOL 73/78 for areas other than special areas would be unacceptable in the light of the existing oceanographic and ecological conditions in the area.[94]

MARPOL, Annexes I (oil), II (noxious substances), and V (garbage) and the Guidelines define a *special area* as "a sea area where for recognized technical reasons in relation to its oceanographical and ecological conditions and to the particular character of its traffic, the adoption of special mandatory methods for the prevention of sea pollution by oil, noxious liquid substances, or garbage, as applicable, is required."[95] Annex VI (atmospheric emissions) provides for the designation of emission control areas. The effect of special area designation is a higher standard for discharges, which could be at a zero discharge requirement. The designation of the SCS as a special area under any of the MARPOL annexes entails an amendment to the relevant MARPOL 73/78 annex at the request of the SCS states. SCS states would be expected to provide reception facilities in their ports. Thus, if the SCS is designated as a MARPOL special area under Annex I, the SCS states would be expected to "ensure that all oil loading terminal and repair ports within the special area are provided with facilities adequate for the reception and treatment of all the dirty ballast water and tank washing water from oil tankers" and for those ports to "be provided with reception facilities for other residues and oily mixtures from ships" without unnecessary delay.[96] Moreover, SCS states would be able to apply the higher standard through port state control inspection and through the framework of the Asia-Pacific Memorandum on Port State Control, in which their national maritime authorities are members.[97]

Strategic PSSA Designation?

As in the case of MARPOL special areas, there are no PSSAs in the SCS region, although there are routeing measures in areas of dense marine traffic.[98] A *PSSA* is defined as a marine area "that needs special protection through action by IMO because of its significance for recognized ecological, socio-economic, or scientific attributes where such attributes may be vulnerable to damage by international shipping activities."[99] The designation is spatially defined and the actual protective measures are routeing and other measures that may be obtained through the IMO. In the various PSSAs designated to date, protective measures have consisted of areas to be avoided, traffic rerouteing and separation schemes, mandatory ship reporting, and prohibited discharges.[100] These measures may be voluntary or mandatory in application. The LOS Convention further provides for the adoption of special mandatory measures through the IMO.[101]

PSSAs designated to date include: the Great Barrier Reef (the first PSSA to be designated), the Torres Strait, the Sabana-Camaguey archipelago (a fringing reef along the north coast of Cuba), the Florida Keys, Malpelo Island (Colombia), Paracas National Reserve (Peru), and the Galapagos archipelago (Ecuador), among others.[102] These PSSA designations are relevant for MPAs in the SCS because they all concern marine spaces that are also designated as domestic MPAs. The eligibility criteria are: ecological; social, cultural, and economic; and scientific and educational, with only one criterion necessary to be satisfied. The PSSA and related measures, although proposed by the coastal state(s) concerned, are designated by the IMO on the basis of the area's environmental conditions, the area's demonstrated vulnerability to international shipping, and the IMO's competence to provide measures.[103] Although the IMO has approved several routeing measures in the SCS, the numerous coral reefs of the SCS would likely benefit from buffer zones consisting of areas to be avoided and higher discharge waste standards for international shipping.

Assessment

At the current rate of MPA-making practice, SCS states have a major challenge to meet in increasing the area under protection from the current 0.31% to 10% of the over 3 million square kilometers of their LME to meet the CBD COP VII target. Also, for those areas ostensibly already under protection, it is likely that many do not meet the requirement of effective protection. This will not be unique to the SCS; most regions will likely have a similar record by 2012. There is much to be done to protect the SCS LME and, in doing so, to protect the interests of SCS states and their coastal communities. SCS states must not lose sight of the long-term goal of adaptation to climate change and mitigating impacts. Conserving coastal and marine ecosystems is a vital step in that direction.

At present, most of the marine areas under protection fall within undisputed waters. What is missing is a networking of existing MPAs as well as cooperation to pursue the common conservation interest in disputed waters. Although there are some MPAs designated in disputed areas, unilateral designation in those areas is not particularly helpful because it does not necessarily reflect a regionally endorsed common conservation interest. Although the region's territorial disputes appear as stumbling blocks to cooperation, the bleak ecological outlook for the region should be a trigger to work around them.

Clearly, a regional strategy to identify a course of action is needed. It should be premised on the understanding reached in the Declaration on the Conduct of Parties in the South China Sea.[104] Modern marine conservation suggests that ecosystem-based management should occur within the larger architecture of the SCS LME. This requires cooperation at the SCS regional level because multiple MPAs will need to be designated across the SCS, including in disputed and undisputed waters. There will be a need of a regional Memorandum of Understanding (MOU) developed on the basis of consensus. Its status should be voluntary because treaty-based regional environmental regimes appear to generate antipathy in the region. The lack of a regional arrangement dedicated to the SCS necessitates the development of a framework that is consistent with the region's international relations culture: consensual, informal (i.e., a "soft" rather than a "hard" structure and process as a treaty), and ensuring that the regional states drive the agenda.

An MOU could provide a general framework to enable existing national MPAs to be "functionally linked" as a network, to the extent that they represent essential components and functions in the SCS LME. Clearly, the responsibility remains with each state. As key components and functions are spatially defined, SCS states should consider attaining regional and international recognition of several sites. For some sites, there should be consideration of taking additional measures to protect them from international shipping, to the extent necessary. SCS states could approach the IMO to achieve PSSA designations as needed, and indeed there is no spatial restriction on the size of the PSSA that can be designated as long as the protection requested can be justified.[105] SCS states should, in any case, approach the IMO to increase the standards for ship-generated waste in the region to achieve a comparable level of protection to that extent in other particularly sensitive areas. As part of this strategy, SCS states should also consider providing targeted protection for more marine species, perhaps similar to the MOU for the protection of turtles under the Migratory Species Convention.[106] Indeed, there is much to be gained for SCS states to join the Philippines in becoming parties to the Migratory Species Convention.

For such a strategy to be developed, it will be necessary for SCS states to look beyond the differences engendered by sovereignty and maritime boundary disputes and to develop the political will and readiness to act on the marine conservation imperative. There is a need for a larger perspective, one that builds on a regional approach while understanding the role this has in a global context. There is a need to pursue conservation objectives at the ecosystem, species, and genetic levels, and the pursuit of these in situ and ex situ. The voluntary SAP is an important step in this direction.[107] The states would need to provide direction and purpose for governmental efforts from a high level of decision making while rationalizing intergovernmental and multiagency efforts.

The commonly shared obstacles identified by the SAP will need to be overcome by the SCS states.[108] In a region that has developed as rapidly as the SCS, there should not be financial constraints and problems of continued long-term financing. The region should take greater ownership of initiatives to protect its common ecosystemic heritage and commit the necessary financial and administrative resources. International organizations may play important facilitative roles, but those roles will necessarily be catalytic and the ultimate responsibility to make marine conservation work rests on the regional states.

The wide knowledge gaps need to be filled. For example, the continuing lack of understanding of the root causes of regional marine environmental problems should challenge the region's substantial research establishment to address these needs. This lack of knowledge is accompanied by a lack of consideration of long-term impacts and capacity to predict the impacts of future threats. For the research establishment to be usefully mobilized, there is a need for decision makers to provide greater recognition and opportunity to regional expertise. Science and management need to cross paths. There is an important role to be played by the region's marine science establishments that form an essential epistemic network. MPAs must have a strong research basis and draw on local and indigenous knowledge.

Conclusion

The urgency of accelerating marine conservation in the SCS can hardly be overstated. The ecological and economic losses sustained to date are likely to worsen. SCS states share an indivisible LME. The interdependence highlights the imperative of conservation cooperation. By cooperating through an ambitious MPA network program, the states will be acting in their own individual and collective long-term interests to adapt to climate change impacts from weakened marine and coastal ecosystems and, thereby, protect their coastal communities. Good LME stewardship can only benefit the region's future generations.

Notes

1. See Hasjim Djalal, "South China Sea Island Disputes," *Raffles Bulletin of Zoology* 8 (2000): 9–21. Djalal describes the various working groups established to facilitate dialogue and the various initiatives that were proposed since the Fourth Workshop in Surabaya, Indonesia, in 1993. See also Hasjim Djalal, "Managing Potential Conflicts in the South China Sea: Lessons Learned," in *Maritime Regime-Building: Lessons Learned and Their Relevance for Northeast Asia*, ed. Mark J. Valencia (The Hague: Nijhoff, 2001), 87–92 (hereafter, Djalal, "Lessons Learned"). See further Douglas M. Johnston, "Southeast Asia Lessons Learned," in *Maritime Regime-Building: Lessons Learned and Their Relevance for Northeast Asia*, ed. Mark J. Valencia (The Hague: Nijhoff, 2001), 73–86.

2. For example, the 2004 Tripartite Agreement for Joint Marine Seismic Undertaking in the Agreement Area in the South China Sea, "China, Philippines, Vietnam Begin Oil Research in S. China Sea," Chinese Embassy to Pakistan, 26 August 2005, available at www.fmprc.gov.cn/ce/cepk/eng/xnyfgk/t209366.htm (accessed 25 September 2009).

3. Intergovernmental Panel on Climate Change (IPCC), *First Assessment Report*, 1990, available at www.ipcc.ch/publications_and_data/publications_and_data_reports.htm#1 (accessed 25 September 2009).

4. This is so because of the high human density and extensive infrastructures in many low-lying coastal areas. The main threats will be posed by large tidal variations, increased frequency of tropical cyclones, potential increase in regional precipitation, sea-level rise, and increase in sea surface temperature. These factors will likely lead to flooding, coastal erosion, movement of salinity boundaries, and loss of sensitive ecosystems and species, among other impacts. In the event of a sea-level rise of 1 meter, it is anticipated that millions of people will be displaced. The cost of responding could amount to many millions of dollars per year. IPCC, *Fourth Assessment Report*,

2007, available at www.ipcc.ch/ (accessed 25 September 2009). See also "The Global Mechanism: United Nations Convention to Combat Desertification—Climate Change Impacts: South East Asia," available at www.ifad.org/events/apr09/impact/se_asia.pdf (accessed 25 September 2009).

5. IPCC, *Fourth Assessment Report*, supra note 4.

6. See Chapter 10 of the *Fourth Assessment Report*, supra note 4, and published as M. L. Parry, O. F. Canziani, J. P. Palutikof, P. J. van der Linden, and C. E. Hanson, eds., *Contribution of Working Group II to the Fourth Assessment Report of the Intergovernmental Panel on Climate Change* (Cambridge: Cambridge University Press, 2007), 484, available at www.ipcc.ch/pdf/assessment-report/ar4/wg2/ar4-wg2-chapter10.pdf (accessed 25 September 2009):

> Projected sea-level rise could flood the residence of millions of people living in the low lying areas of South, South-East and East Asia such as in Vietnam, Bangladesh, India and China (Wassmann et al., 2004; Stern, 2007). Even under the most conservative scenario, sea level will be about 40 cm higher than today by the end of 21st century and this is projected to increase the annual number of people flooded in coastal populations from 13 million to 94 million . . . [a]bout 20% will occur in South-East Asia, specifically from Thailand to Vietnam including Indonesia and the Philippines (Wassmann et al., 2004).

A recent authoritative report noted that: "[I]n 2005, the estimated population living within 100 km of the coast reached about 452 million people, equivalent to about 79% of the total population. Most of these people depend on coastal and marine resources for their livelihoods." Asian Development Bank, *The Economics of Climate Change in Southeast Asia: A Regional Review* (Mandaluyong City, the Philippines: Asian Development Bank, 2009), 48. A 2% demographic growth rate is projected for the region. See C. Wilkinson et al., *Global International Waters Assessment: South China Sea GIWA Regional Assessment* (Kalmar, Sweden: University of Kalmar on behalf of UNEP, 2005), 9, available at www.unep.org/dewa/giwa/areas/reports/r54/giwa_regional_assessment_54.pdf (accessed 25 September 2009) (hereafter, *GIWA Assessment*).

7. Asian Development Bank, supra note 6, at 48–53.

8. Convention on Biological Diversity, 5 June 1992, 1760 *U.N.T.S.* 79.

9. Convention on Biological Diversity, Seventh Conference of the Parties (2004), Decision VII/28, "Protected Areas," para. 18.

10. K. Sherman and G. Hempel, eds., *The Large Marine Ecosystem Report: A Perspective on Changing Conditions in LMEs of the World's Regional Seas*, UNEP Regional Seas Reports and Studies No. 182 (Nairobi, Kenya: UNEP, 2009), 297.

11. A *marine protected area* (MPA) is defined by IUCN (The World Conservation Union) as: "Any area of intertidal or subtidal terrain, together with its overlying water and associated flora, fauna, historical and cultural features, which has been reserved by law or other effective means to protect part or all of the enclosed environment." See G. Kelleher, *Guidelines for Marine Protected Areas* (Gland, Switzerland: IUCN, 1999), xviii (hereafter, IUCN, *MPA Guidelines*). An MPA may include terrestrial areas, but is considered marine to the extent that the marine area exceeds the terrestrial portion.

12. "Plan of Implementation of the World Summit on Sustainable Development," in *Report of the World Summit on Sustainable Development*, Johannesburg, South Africa, 26 August–4 September 2002, UN Doc. A/CONF.199/20 (2002), para. 32(c), creation of a representative network of MPAs by the year 2012.

13. United Nations Millennium Declaration, UN General Assembly Resolution, UN Doc. A/RES/55/2, 18 September 2000. See, in particular, Target 7.6, MDG Monitor, available at www.mdgmonitor.org/ (accessed 25 September 2009).

14. Vth World Parks Congress, Durban, South Africa, 8–17 September 2003, WPC Recommendation V. 22 (Building a Global System of Marine and Coastal Protected Area Networks), available at www.iucn.org/about/union/commissions/wcpa/wcpa_work/wcpa_wpc/ (accessed 25 September 2009).

15. "Coral Triangle Leaders Adopt Plan to Manage Coastal and Marine Resources," Asian Development Bank Press Release, 15 May 2009, available at www.adb.org/Media/Articles/2009/12893-coral-triangle-management/ (accessed 25 September 2009).

16. Sherman and Hempel, supra note 10, at 273.

17. *Ibid.*, at 298.

18. *Ibid.*, at 297.

19. *Ibid.*, at 304.

20. *Ibid.*, at 304.

21. *Ibid.*, at 304–305.

22. Parry et al., supra note 6, at 485.

23. *Ibid.*, at 481.

24. Sherman and Hempel, supra note 10, at 301.

25. *Ibid.*, at 302–303. See also GESAMP, *A Sea of Troubles* (Nairobi, Kenya: UNEP, 2001), 14, available at unesdoc.unesco.org/images/0012/001229/122986e.pdf (accessed 25 September 2009).

26. GESAMP, supra note 25, at 1. Overfishing appears to have a more far-reaching impact than coastal activities.

27. Sherman and Hempel, supra note 10, at 303–304.

28. *Ibid.*, at 304.

29. Peter K. L. Ng and K. S. Tan, "The State of Marine Biodiversity in the South China Sea," *Raffles Bulletin of Zoology*, Suppl. 8 (2000): 3–7, available at http://www.southchinasea.org/docs/Ng%20&%20Tan,%20SCS%20Marne%20Biodiversity.htm.

30. *Ibid.*

31. *Ibid.*

32. IUCN, *World Commission on Protected Areas—Southeast Asia*, available at www.wcpasea.org/?q=node/95 (accessed 25 September 2009).

33. See Ben Boer, Ross Ramsay, and Donald Rothwell, *International Environmental Law in the Asia-Pacific* (Leiden, the Netherlands: Kluwer Law, 1998), 196.

34. Convention on Wetlands of International Importance Especially as Waterfowl Habitat, 2 February 1971, 996 *U.N.T.S.* 245.

35. Convention Concerning the Protection of the World Cultural and Natural Heritage, 16 November 1972, 1037 *U.N.T.S.* 151.

36. Convention on International Trade in Endangered Species of Wild Fauna and Flora, 3 March 1973, 993 *U.N.T.S.* 243.

37. United Nations Convention on the Law of the Sea, 10 December 1982, 1833 *U.N.T.S.* 396.

38. *Ibid.*, in particular, Parts V, IX, and XII.

39. Declaration on the Conduct of Parties in the South China Sea, adopted at Phnom Penh, 4 November 2002, available at www.aseansec.org/13163.htm (accessed 25 September 2009). During a 2009 state visit of Malaysian prime minister Najib Tun Razak to China, Chinese premier Wen Jiabao was quoted as stating that the Declaration should be strictly followed. "China Calls for Dialogue, Cooperation over South China Sea," *People's Daily Online*, 4 June 2009, available at english.peopledaily.com.cn/90001/90776/90883/6671212.htm (accessed 25 September 2009).

40. Declaration on the Conduct of Parties, supra note 39, para. 7.

41. Convention on Biological Diversity, supra note 8, arts. 8–9.

42. Ramsar Convention, supra note 34.

43. World Heritage Convention, supra note 35.

44. Ger Bergkamp and Bret Orlando, "Exploring Collaboration Between the Convention on Wetlands (Ramsar, Iran, 1971) and the UN Framework Convention on Climate Change" (IUCN, October 1999), available at 195.143.117.139/key_unfccc_bkgd.htm (accessed 25 September 2009).

45. For the Montreux List, visit the Ramsar Convention site, available at www.ramsar.org.

46. Hwey-Lian Hsieh, Chang-Po Chen, and Yaw-Yuan Lin, "Strategic Planning for a Wetlands Conservation Greenway Along the West Coast of Taiwan," *Ocean and Coastal Management Journal* 47 (2004): 257–272.

47. World Heritage Convention, supra note 35, art. 4.

48. *Ibid.*, art. 11. The World Heritage List is available at whc.unesco.org/en/list (accessed 25 September 2009).

49. Indonesia: Komodo National Park, Ujung Kulon National Park, Lorentz National Park; the Philippines: Tubbataha Reefs Natural Park, Puerto-Princesa Subterranean River National Park; Vietnam: Ha Long Bay. World Heritage List (as of 3 July 2009), supra note 48.

50. UNESCO, "The Statutory Framework of the World Network of Biosphere Reserves," available at www.sovereignty.net/tline/statutory-framework.htm (accessed 25 September 2009). The objectives are set at a regional scale, and specifically in Article 3 as follows, for

> (i) conservation—contribute to the conservation of landscapes, ecosystems, species and genetic variation; (ii) development—foster economic and human development which is socio-culturally and ecologically sustainable; (iii) logistic support—support for demonstration projects, environmental education and training, research and monitoring related to local, regional, national and global issues of conservation and sustainable development.

51. UNESCO, Man and the Biosphere Programme (MAB), Asia-Pacific, available at portal.unesco.org/science/en/ev.php-URL_ID=5821&URL_DO=DO_TOPIC&URL_SECTION=201.html> (accessed 25 September 2009).

52. UNESCO, "Statutory Framework," supra note 50, Introduction.

53. UNESCO, "Biosphere Reserves World Network" (Paris: UNESCO, May 2009), available at www.unesco.org/mab/doc/brs/BRList2009.pdf (accessed 25 September 2009). See also the Asia-Pacific region where additional sites appear under each country link (e.g., Cambodia and China), available at portal.unesco.org/science/en/ev.php-URL_ID=5821&URL_DO=DO_TOPIC&URL_SECTION=201.html (accessed 25 September 2009).

54. CITES, supra note 36.

55. Convention on the Conservation of Migratory Species of Wild Animals, 23 June 1979, 1651 *U.N.T.S.* 355.

56. CITES, Conf. 13.3, "Cooperation and Synergy with the Convention on the Conservation of Migratory Species of Wild Animals (CMS)," available at www.cites.org/eng/res/13/13-03.shtml (accessed 25 September 2009).

57. Migratory Species Convention, supra note 55.

58. Memorandum of Understanding on the Conservation and Management of Dugongs and Their Habitats Throughout Their Range, 31 October 2007, available at www.cms.int/species/dugong/index.htm.

59. Memorandum of Understanding Concerning Conservation Measures for Marine Turtles and Their Habitats of the Indian Ocean and South-East Asia, 1 September 2001, available at www.cms.int/species/iosea/IOSEAturtle_mou.htm.

60. Agreement for the Implementation of the Provisions of the United Nations Convention on the Law of the Sea of 10 December 1982 Relating to the Conservation and Management of Straddling Fish Stocks and Highly Migratory Fish Stocks, 4 December 1995, 2167 *U.N.T.S.* 3.

61. Agreement to Promote Compliance with International Conservation and Management Measures by Fishing Vessels on the High Seas, 24 November 1993, 2221 *U.N.T.S.* 120.

62. Code of Conduct for Responsible Fisheries (Rome: FAO, 1995), available at www.fao.org/docrep/005/v9878e/v9878e00.htm (accessed 25 September 2009).

63. Regional Plan of Action (RPOA) to Promote Responsible Fishing Practices (including Combating IUU Fishing) in the Region, Asia-Pacific Fishery Commission, 10 June 2008, available at www.apfic.org/modules/wiwimod/index.php?page=Regional%20Plan%20of%20Action%20for%20%20Responsible%20Fishing (accessed 25 September 2009).

64. See United Nations Environment Programme: Regional Seas Programme East Asian Seas, available at www.unep.ch/regionalseas/regions/eas/easint.htm. The Action Plan for the Protection and Development of the Marine Environment and Coastal Areas of the East Asian Seas Region was

adopted in 1981, was revised in 1994, and is available at www.cobsea.org/documents/action_plan/ActionPlan1994.pdf.

65. Johnston, supra note 1, at 76.

66. "New Strategic Direction for COBSEA (2008–2012)," available at www.cobsea.org/aboutcobsea/newtrategicdirection.html (accessed 25 September 2009).

67. *Strategic Action Programme for the South China Sea*, UNEP/GEF/SCS Technical Publication No. 16 (Bangkok, Thailand: UNEP, 2008), available at www.unepscs.org/SCS_Documents/startdown/1965.html (accessed 25 September 2009) (hereafter, SAP).

68. *Ibid*, at 5.

69. Established as the Indo-Pacific Fisheries Council in 1948, it was renamed in 1976 as the Indo-Pacific Fisheries Commission, and renamed again with its current title in 1994. The Commission was established by an international agreement under the auspices of the Food and Agricultural Organization of the United Nations (FAO). See Agreement for the Establishment of the Asia-Pacific Fishery Commission, last amended by the Commission in 1996 and approved by the FAO Council in 1997, available at ftp.fao.org/FI/DOCUMENT/apfic/apfic_convention.pdf.

70. For an overview of the history and future directions, see Deb Menasveta, "APFIC: Its Evolution, Achievements and Future Direction," RAP Publication: 1998/15, available at www.fao.org/DOCREP/003/X6942E/x6942e00.htm#Contents/ (accessed 25 September 2009).

71. Regional Plan of Action, supra note 63.

72. ASEAN Declaration on Heritage Parks, adopted at Yangon, Myanmar, 18 December 2003, available at www.aseansec.org/15524.htm (accessed 25 September 2009). This Declaration succeeds and replaces the ASEAN Declaration on Heritage Parks and Reserves, 29 November 1984.

73. *Ibid*.

74. "Regional Action Plan to Strengthen a Resilient Network of Effective Marine Protected Areas in Southeast Asia: 2002–2012," IUCN/World Commission on Protected Area—Southeast Asia, available at www.wcpasea.org/?q=node/85 (accessed 25 September 2009).

75. *Ibid*.

76. For example, the SAP, while allowing for an invitation to a limited number of observers from regional and international organizations, is clearly grounded in the regional political reality that a management framework: "[R]estricts the membership of the policy/decision making body to government representatives only." SAP, supra note 67, at 64.

77. World Database on Marine Protected Areas, available at www.wdpa.org/Default.aspx (accessed 25 September 2009). The database is the most authoritative list of terrestrial and marine protected areas. It was established by UNEP and the World Commission on Protected Areas of the World Conservation Union (WCU/IUCN). The database is maintained with the cooperation of governments and nongovernmental organizations.

78. IUCN, *MPA Guidelines*, supra note 11, at xviii, create the following categories of MPAs:

I(a): "Strict Nature Reserve: protected area managed mainly for science;"
I(b): "Wilderness Area: protected area managed mainly for wilderness protection;"
II: "National Park: protected area managed mainly for ecosystem protection and recreation;"
III: "Natural Monument: protected area managed mainly for conservation of specific natural features;"
IV: "Habitat/Species Management Area: protected area managed mainly for conservation through management intervention;"
V: "Protected Landscape/Seascape: protected area managed mainly for landscape/seascape conservation and recreation;"
VI: "Managed Resource Protected Area: protected area managed mainly for the sustainable use of natural ecosystems."

79. See Local Government Code of the Philippines, available at www.lga.gov.ph/downloads/downloadables/LGC%20Code%20Book%20III.pdf (accessed 25 September 2009). Coastal municipalities have 15 kilometers of jurisdiction over adjacent marine resources.

80. See Kevern L. Cochrane, "Marine Protected Areas as Management Measures: Tools or Toys?" in *Law, Science and Ocean Management*, eds. Myron H. Nordquist, Ronán Long, Tomas H. Heidar and John Norton Moore (Leiden, the Netherlands: Nijhoff, 2007), 701–737, especially at 705 et seq.

81. UNEP, ed., *The Status of Coral Reef Management in Southeast Asia: A Gap Analysis*, report prepared by Heidi Schuttenberg and David Bizot (Bangkok, Thailand: UNEP, 2002), in particular at 17, available at www.cobsea.org/documents/report_coral_reef/Status_Coral_Reef_Management_in_SEA.pdf (accessed 25 September 2009).

82. *Marine Protected Areas in Southeast Asia* (Los Baños, the Philippines: ASEAN Regional Centre for Biodiversity Conservation, Department of Environment and Natural Resources, 2002), available at www.southchinasea.org/docs/marine%20protected%20areas_in_South%20East%20Asia.pdf (accessed 25 September 2009)

83. "Regional Action Plan to Strengthen MPAs in Southeast Asia," supra note 74.

84. *GIWA Assessment*, supra note 6, at 10.

85. IUCN World Commission on Protected Areas, *Establishing Marine Protected Area Networks—Making It Happen* (Washington, DC: IUCN-WCPA, National Oceanic and Atmospheric Administration and the Nature Conservancy, 2008), 11.

86. FAO, Report and Documentation of the Expert Workshop on Marine Protected Areas and Fisheries Management: Review of Issues and Considerations, Rome, 12–14 June 2006, FAO Fisheries Report No. 825 (Rome: Food and Agriculture Organization, 2006), 5.

87. For example, claims for cleanup and compensation (including fishing losses) to the 1992 International Oil Pollution Compensation Fund included: *Mary Anne*, the Philippines (US$2.5 million and PHP 1.8 million); *Natuna Sea*, Indonesia (US$2.8 million), Malaysia (RM 2.2 million), and Singapore (US$8.4 million); *Solar I*, the Philippines (PHP 957.5 million). IOPCF, available at www.iopcfund.org/npdf/AR08_E.pdf#page=202 (accessed 25 September 2009).

88. "Dongsha Atoll and Marine National Park, Research Data," available at dongsha.cpami.gov.tw/en/emain4_1_1.aspx?study_id=10 (accessed 25 September 2009).

89. The protection consists of a Particularly Sensitive Sea Area (PSSA) designation and accompanying routing measures, which are published regularly in IMO, *Ships' Routeing*, 9th ed. (London: IMO, 2008). See also Aldo Chircop, "The Designation of Particularly Sensitive Sea Areas: A New Layer in the Regime for Marine Environmental Protection from International Shipping," in *The Future of Ocean Regime-Building: Essays in Tribute to Douglas M. Johnston*, Aldo Chircop, Ted L. McDorman, and Susan J. Rolston (Leiden, the Netherlands: Nijhoff, 2009), 573–608.

90. International Convention for the Prevention of Pollution from Ships, 1973, as modified by the Protocol of 1978 relating thereto, 17 February 1978, 1340 *U.N.T.S.* 61. A consolidated version of the amended text is available in *MARPOL* (Consolidated Edition, 2006) (London: IMO, 2007).

91. See Chircop, supra note 89.

92. Guidelines for the Designation of Special Areas Under MARPOL 73/78, IMO Doc. A 22/Res. 927, 15 January 2002, available at www.imo.org/includes/blastDataOnly.asp/data_id%3D10469/927.pdf.

93. *Ibid.*, para. 2.4.

94. *Ibid.*, para. 2.6.

95. *Ibid.*, para. 2.1.

96. MARPOL 1973/78, supra note 90, Annex I, Reg. 10 (7)(a)(i) and Reg. 12.

97. Memorandum of Understanding on Port State Control in the Asia-Pacific Region, Tokyo, December 1993, available www.tokyo-mou.org (accessed 25 September 2009).

98. See IMO, *Ship's Routeing*, supra note 89.

99. Guidelines for the Identification and Designation of Particularly Sensitive Sea Areas, IMO Doc. A.982(24), 1 December 2005 (hereafter, PSSA Guidelines), available at www.imo.org/includes/blastDataOnly.asp/data_id%3D14373/982.pdf.

100. See Chircop, supra note 89, at 602 et seq.

101. LOS Convention, supra note 37, art. 211(6).

102. See, generally, Chircop, supra note 89, at 594 et seq.

103. PSSA Guidelines, supra note 99.
104. Declaration on the Conduct of Parties, supra note 39.
105. Australia's Great Barrier Reef is a good example. Stretching over 344,400 square kilometers, the entire system is covered by a PSSA. "Protection of the Great Barrier Reef Region," MEPC Resolution, IMO Doc. MEPC.45(30), 16 November 1990. See Great Barrier Marine Park Authority, available at www.gbrmpa.gov.au/ (accessed 25 September 2009).
106. MOU Concerning Conservation Measures for Marine Turtles, supra note 59.
107. SAP, supra note 67.
108. *Ibid.*, at 62.

Toward Establishing a Spratly Islands International Marine Peace Park: Ecological Importance and Supportive Collaborative Activities with an Emphasis on the Role of Taiwan

JOHN W. MCMANUS

Marine Biology and Fisheries and National Center for Coral Reef Research
Rosenstiel School of Marine and Atmospheric Science
University of Miami
Miami, Florida, USA

KWANG-TSAO SHAO
SZU-YIN LIN

Biodiversity Research Center
Academia Sinica
Taipei, Taiwan, Republic of China

The Spratly Islands constitute one of the earth's most ecologically significant areas, hosting a high diversity of marine species, providing critical habitats for endangered species, and providing marine larvae to reestablish depleted stocks among the heavily overfished and degraded coastal ecosystems of the South China Sea. Territorial disputes have led to the establishment of environmentally destructive, socially and economically costly military outposts on many of the islands. Given the rapid proliferation of international peace parks around the world, it is time to take positive steps toward the establishment of a Spratly Islands Marine Peace Park. Its purpose would be to manage the area's natural resources and alleviate regional tensions via a freeze on claims and claim supportive actions.

Geographical Features and Legal Aspects of the Spratly Islands

The South China Sea is a marginal sea partially enclosed by the lands of the People's Republic of China, the Republic of China (referred to as Taiwan), the Philippines, Malaysia, Brunei, Indonesia, Singapore, and Vietnam. Covering an area of 800,000 square kilometers and containing more than 200 identified islands, islets, reefs, shoals, sand cays, and banks, four major archipelagos named the Pratas Islands (Dongsha 東沙), Paracel Islands (Xisha

西沙), Macclesfield Bank (Chungsha 中沙), and Spratly Islands (Nansha 南沙) are distributed from north to south.

The Spratly Islands are scattered between 12° and 6° north, and 109° and 117° east in the southern part of South China Sea. The water area of the Spratly Islands is substantial, encompassing approximately 160,000–360,000 square kilometers, depending on how limits are chosen. There are approximately 150 named landforms, and innumerable unnamed spits of land. The majority of these are rocks, reefs, sandbanks, or other types of partially submerged landforms. They rest primarily on partially submerged coral reef atolls, ranging in length up to approximately 40 kilometers. The largest island in the Spratly group is called Taiping Island (太平島) or Itu Aba by others. Taiping Island and six other reefs form a lagoon-shaped Tizard Bank or Zhenghe Reefs (鄭合群礁) near the center of the South China Sea. The island itself has an elliptical shape, 1,289 meters in length and 365 meters in width, with 0.49 square kilometers of area. The altitude is less than 5 meters. The geographical distance between Taiping Island and Kaohsiung (Taiwan) is about 850 nautical miles; to Hainan (China) 550 nautical miles; Ho Chi Minh City (Vietnam) 330 nautical miles; Palawan (the Philippines) 220 nautical miles. Taiping Island has been under control of Taiwan since 1956.

The Spratly archipelago is the focus of complex sovereignty disputes. There are competing claims to island territories, exclusive economic zones (EEZs), and continental shelf by Taiwan, China, Malaysia, the Philippines, Vietnam, and Brunei. Though these countries claim the sovereignty of part or all of the Spratly Islands, each major island is controlled and governed by only one country that, in many cases, has installed military facilities. The eight largest islands and the controlling nations are listed accordingly: Taiping Island (Taiwan), Thitu Island (the Philippines), West York (the Philippines), Spratly Island (Vietnam), Northwest Cay (the Philippines), Southwest Cay (Vietnam), Grierson Cay (Vietnam), and Swallow Reef (Malaysia). Mainland China controls several reefs and emergent features scattered throughout the area, including Mischief Reef.

Ecological Significance of the Spratly Islands

The Spratly Islands are subject to a tropical climate. The average annual temperature is 27°C. During summer, from May to August, the high temperature is approximately 30°C while, in winter, the average temperature is about 25°C. The Spratlies experience a 7-month dry season and a 5-month rainy season, with an annual average rainfall of 1,800 to 2,200 millimeters. Southeast monsoon winds blow from March to April, and then shift to a southwest monsoon wind from May to November. Few of the islands have surface freshwater. However, on some, wells were successfully dug that, over the years, have provided a source of water to troops, tourists, and visiting fishermen. Thirteen islands, including Taiping Island, have terrestrial vegetation that indicates a significant degree of soil formation.[1]

Due to the remote distance and limited accessibility to the Spratly Islands, only a few surveys have been conducted during the past few decades. The earliest Taiwanese ecological inventory in Taiping Island was led by K. H. Chang with a group of experts from the Institute of Zoology, Academia Sinica (中央研究院) in 1980. They recorded 33 families and 173 species of fish within an 800-square-meter sea area south of Taiping Island. They published a fish guide book[2] and a fish checklist in a scientific journal.[3] In 1994, a group led by the National Museum of Marine Biology and Aquarium recorded 399 reef fish species from 49 families, 190 coral species from 69 genera from 25 families, 99 mollusk species,

91 invertebrate species from 72 genera, 27 crustacean species, 14 polychaete species, 4 echinoderm species, and 109 terrestrial vascular plant species. There were also 59 bird species observed, which indicates that Taiping Island is a major stop for migratory birds in East Asia.[4] According to BirdLife International (2001), the species mainly included streaked shearwater (*Calonectris leucomelas*), brown booby (*Sula leucogaster*), red-footed booby (*S. sula*), great crested tern (*Sterna bergii*), and white tern (*Gygis alba*).[5] Both the green turtle (*Chelonia mydas*) and the hawksbill turtle (*Eretmochelys imbricata*) were often reported to be nesting even on islands inhabited by military personnel in the Pratas and Spratly Islands, though their numbers have gradually declined.[6] The richness of marine biodiversity, spectacular coral reefs, and threatened species such as the crested tern and green turtle together add considerable value to Taiping Island as a future conditional ecotourism reserve.

The Spratly Islands hosts a high diversity of marine organisms. White included the islands as a priority area for marine conservation and management in 1983.[7] However, the importance of the island group to regional fisheries was identified in the early 1990s based on studies of water circulation relative to the presettlement pelagic times of coral reef fish.

Currently, there is a project evaluating whether Taiping Island should be established as a marine park, similar to the Pratas Islands (Dungsha) Group, which was successfully established as a Taiwanese National Marine Park in 2007.[8] In their expedition in June 2009, the project personnel added more records of terrestrial and marine species in Taiping Island.[9] For example, there were 40 newly recorded terrestrial invertebrate species, 3 newly recorded bird species, and 66 newly recorded fish species. However, they also noticed that many coral-eating crown-of-thorns starfish (*Acanthaster planci*) occurred in one station.

Along the coasts of the South China Sea, many of the coral reef fisheries are heavily overfished, especially along southern mainland China, Vietnam, Malaysia, and the Philippines. Harvests of adult fish are in decline. Coastal fish populations are periodically renewed via influxes of presettlement pelagic juveniles. Wyrtki determined that a cyclonic (counterclockwise) circulation predominates across the basin in the winter and an anticyclonic circulation (clockwise) caused by the annual shift in monsoon starting from the south in summer.[10] Various recent studies have confirmed that this general pattern does indeed exist, although a number of smaller subgyres and vortices also occur periodically.[11] Using the circulation charts of Wyrtki and a 24-day pelagic time determined from a compilation of published studies of various reef fish species, McManus determined that the seasonally shifting currents of the South China Sea could disperse presettlement fish from the Spratly Islands throughout the coasts of the South China Sea.[12] Some coasts could be reached within 24 days, while others could be reached in a process in which fish from the Spratly Islands settle on intermediate reefs and then pass in a second generation to the coast. This finding indicates the importance of the water area of Spratly Islands for conservation.

During the period 2000 to 2002, the WorldFish Center, along with Academia Sinica Taiwan and institutional partners from other neighboring countries, organized a collaborative project to examine interreef connectivity patterns by analyzing genetic groupings among marine organisms. The results showed that each genetic subgroup may include portions of the Spratly area.[13] This was consistent with the idea that juvenile pelagic fish could be transported from the Spratlies to rejuvenate dwindling populations around the region, including the reefs of Taiwan.

There have been many reports emanating from other investigations of the South China Sea, but few have focused on the Spratly Islands or specifically on Taiping Island. Thus, it is also difficult to sort out the species of marine animals or plants from which collections were made. The *Raffles Bulletin of Zoology* from Singapore has devoted two issues to the South China Sea biomes and biodiversity.[14] They included comprehensive species checklists of marine fauna and flora as well as papers with newly recorded species.

Types and Severity of Threats

The South China Sea is the site of major fishing operations. According to the Global International Waters Assessment (GIWA), "Regional Assessment 54 South China Sea," the South China Sea ranks fourth among the world's 19 fishing zones with regard to total annual marine production.[15] However, unsustainable exploitation of fish has led to difficulty in finding adult fish of heavily exploited species in the region. China estimated that the total fishery production in the Spratly Islands was less than 7000 tons each year, about 0.3 tons per square kilometer.[16]

Between 1980 and 1990, the Taiwan Fisheries Research Institute collected harvests from experimental and commercial fishing vessels, and published reports on the fisheries potential and the situation in the Spratlies. For example, Wu investigated the marine environment, biological resources, and fishery resources around Taiping Island.[17] Chi and Huang both inventoried the fisheries of the Spratly Islands with the records of 20 families (72 species) and 45 families (245 species) of fishes.[18]

Since 1985, China, Vietnam, and the Philippines have upgraded their fisheries in the Spratly Islands to include large-scale explosive and cyanide fishing operations that have depleted the resources at a high speed. Additionally, the El Niño conditions in 1998–1999 and 2007–2008 caused short-term increases in water temperature, resulting in widespread coral bleaching and subsequent mortality. The combination of destructive fishing and coral bleaching has created a serious threat to the reef resources of the area.

Being bordered by some of the world's most rapidly industrializing countries, as well as being located amid some of the world's busiest shipping lanes, has proven detrimental to the island ecosystems in many ways. Concerns with political disputes, maximizing economic growth, and ensuring adequate energy supplies have taken precedence over the preservation of the bordering nations' common maritime environment. Although it is effectively the oceanic hub of Asia's industrial revolution, the Spratlies and other South China Sea islands have been and are being degraded by physical disruption of native flora and fauna, by overexploitation of natural resources such as guano and turtles, and by severe environmental pollution.

Marine Protected Area Development and Regional Cooperation

The Convention on Biological Diversity targets the establishment of 10% of marine protected area coverage throughout the world by 2012.[19] With regard to the Spratlies, transboundary protected area arrangements have often been proposed. There is a well-established precedent for these, although they are primarily in the form of parks on land. In 1988, the Commission on National Parks and Protected Areas of the International Union for the Conservation of Nature (IUCN) listed 70 protected areas in 65 countries that straddle national borders.[20] In 2007, there were 227 complexes surveyed by the United Nations Environment Programme (UNEP), including both terrestrial and marine.[21]

The conflicting territorial claims over parts of the South China Sea have not totally dampened cooperation among the claimant countries. Cooperative activities in the fields of marine scientific research, environmental protection, and defense are regularly carried out on bilateral or multilateral bases. These have included two major expeditions in 2002 and 2004 under the auspices of the South China Sea Workshop series[22] and a joint scientific expedition between Vietnam and the Philippines in 2006. These and other studies are believed to have contributed to a certain degree of stability in the area as "confidence-building exercises," and gathered valuable information on the area's natural resources. The important question, however, is whether the present level of cooperation can be enhanced and extended to ensure natural resource stability in the South China Sea.

One option for regional cooperation that has often been proposed is the initiation of a Large Marine Ecosystem (LME) study. The LME concept was developed by the U.S. National Oceanic and Atmospheric Administration (NOAA) to agglomerate consensus, and to monitor and assess the changing of the world's coastal ecosystems. It is widely recognized that such an international cooperative study would improve international relationships and facilitate knowledge-based management of the South China Sea, although no such study has yet been initiated in the region.

Examples of Regional Joint Programs

The Philippines-Vietnam Joint Research in the South China Sea, 1996–2007

In 1994, the Presidents of the Philippines and Vietnam signed a bilateral agreement to conduct a Joint Oceanographic and Marine Scientific Research Expedition in the South China Sea (JOMSRE-SCS). After 11 years of research, the findings on marine biodiversity showed that the Spratly Islands could be a source of coral propagules for destroyed reef areas in the southern and western Philippines. However, the densities of marine species associated with offshore coral reefs were found to have been drastically reduced, particularly in shallow waters where blast and poison fishing are common. The biomasses of target fish species in 2007 had been reduced to approximately one-third of their levels in the late 1990s. This project not only provided strong evidence that heavy exploitation of the fishery resources has occurred in the South China Sea, but also demonstrated a cooperative governance mechanism for larger-scale research, safety navigation, and conservation.[23]

UNEP/GEF South China Sea Project, 2002–2008

The UNEP/Global Environment Facility (GEF) funded the project Reversing Environmental Degradation Trends in the South China Sea and Gulf of Thailand, which involved a partnership of seven countries bordering the South China Sea (Cambodia, China, Indonesia, Malaysia, the Philippines, Thailand, and Vietnam). The project consisted of 59 organizations as a "networked institution," plus around 100 subcontracted institutions and more than 400 institutions involved through individual participation. An important by-product of this project is an interactive project Web site that serves as an information portal for 1,800 relevant documents and a metadatabase containing 1,428 entries.[24]

Coral Triangle Initiative

The Coral Triangle Initiative is an intergovernmental, multiply-sponsored, coordinated effort to improve the management of coral reefs and related resources.[25] It covers a triangular area previously determined to be high in coral diversity, encompassing Indonesia, the Philippines, Timor Leste, Papua New Guinea, and the Solomon Islands. The total area is approximately 18,000 square kilometers and includes, for many groups of organisms, the richest species diversity in the world. This area hosts more than 600 species of coral, over 3,000 species of fish, and the world's largest mangrove forests.

The objective of the initiative is to protect the region's marine resources for future generations. In May 2009, six heads of State from the region met in Manado, North Sulawesi, Indonesia and signed a declaration approving the Coral Triangle Initiative.[26] Although there is no legal enforcement power, the whole process is based on strong political will among neighboring countries.

The Spratly Islands is located at the border of the Coral Triangle Initiative area as presently defined. Because of the demonstrated potential influence of the Spratly Island reefs on coral reef ecosystems within the initiative area, it would be rational to extend initiative resources to improve their protection. However, the sovereignty complexity and lack of research data might be an obstacle preventing this important archipelago from being included in the initiative's activities.

The Proposed Spratly Islands Marine Peace Park

The term *peace park* does not necessarily imply that it is sited within an area in conflict, although the term does indicate a propensity for this kind of protected area to reduce violent conflict and bring more harmony to a region.

The IUCN defined *parks for peace* as: "Transboundary protected areas that are formally dedicated to the protection and maintenance of biological diversity, and of natural and associated cultural resources, and to the promotion of peace and cooperation."[27]

During the past century, many peace parks have been established around the world. The first was established between Canada and the United States in 1932, and named the Waterton-Glacier International Peace Park. Another milestone was the Red Sea Marine Peace Park, one of the most well-known examples of a marine peace park. The term refers to an area in the northern Gulf of Aqaba in which Israel and Jordan have developed a binational partnership to share natural resources and confront ecological pressure together. Some aspects of this park are under further development, including an extension into Egypt.[28]

In the South China Sea, the Spratly archipelago is characterized not only by territorial claimant disputes, but also by the multifaceted importance of waterways, fisheries, tourist value, and possible deposits of hydrocarbons. The process of gathering consensus among claimant countries is troublesome. Valencia et al. summarized the political situation and proposed various scenarios of international cooperation in the area.[29] They expressed the concern that making the whole area a marine park might be difficult because of, in addition to strategic military concerns, the strong interest in exploiting oil in the area. However, Townshend-Gault, summarizing the results of an international workshop on the South China Sea, pointed out that there was little evidence that substantial, economically extractable oil actually exists in the area, and reemphasized that the protection of the natural resources of the Spratly Islands was vital to maintaining fisheries and economically important ecosystems throughout the coastlines of the entire South China Sea.[30] Valencia and van Dyke replied, clarifying the view expressed in a 1997 book that the concerns about exploitation of oil were secondary to sovereignty and the strategic significance of the Spratlies in general.[31]

Strategic concerns and vague possibilities of hydrocarbon deposits have led each country in the region to station troops in the area, resulting in occasional violent confrontations and environmental stress. The feasibility of establishing a Marine Peace Park when originally proposed was enhanced by the high cost of military maintenance in the area. As suggested by Valencia et al., confidence-building activities are important and could lead to a lessening of regional tension and to increased regional support for the marine park.[32] Scientific collaboration and the further development of economic trade would be helpful. In some cases, it might be easier to set up informal international activities by sponsoring participation in scientific and conservation activities by nongovernmental organizations (NGOs), rather than to concentrate efforts solely on sponsoring participation by representatives of governmental agencies. A concept for a full-area Spratly Island Marine Peace Park, which may have sounded unrealistic in 1994, gained substantial credibility by 2009 in a world that had come to understand the value of this approach.[33]

Following up on suggestions from previous investigators, McManus suggested that a treaty for the Spratlies might follow the leads of the 1959 Antarctic Treaty[34] and the 1978 Torres Strait Treaty[35] for raising the flag of truce and freezing ownership claims for a definite period, such as 50 years, with an option for review and indefinite renewal.[36] A possible management strategy might include five elements: (1) an international board of directors, (2) a contracted research and management institution, (3) a private ranger/air-sea rescue force, (4) tourism facilities, and (5) research facilities and programs.

The engaged countries would provide representatives and form a board of directors. A scientific research group with the extra function of planning for international collaboration on research programs in the area would be a good first step. Park management would involve monitoring activities in order to head off possible deterioration from such things as regional oil spills from tanker incidents, or diminishing supplies of larvae from other areas. An international organization might be contracted to oversee management and conduct activities such as air-sea rescue, charting, channel marking, and antipiracy enforcement. These suggestions are generally in keeping with the multiuse cooperation scenario presented in Valencia et al.,[37] with the exception of replacing their suggested "managed multi-use approach" with the more natural resource and regional fisheries protection oriented and tourism industry supportive full-area marine peace park.

Taiwan's Role in Working Toward a Spartly Island International Marine Peace Park

Taiwan's policy toward the South China Sea sovereignty was considered self-restrained and moderate from the 1970s to 1990s. In 2000, jurisdiction of the islands of the South China Sea shifted from the Ministry of National Defense to the newly established Coast Guard Administration, which is considered a law enforcement agency under the administration of the Executive Yuan. In 2007, Tungsha (the Pratas Islands) National Marine Park became the seventh national park in Taiwan. In 2008, former President Chen Shui-bian announced the Spratly Initiative at the opening ceremony for the airstrip on Taiping Island.[38] He was Taiwan's first President to set foot on Taiping Island. The Spratly Initiative is an ecofriendly invitation toward surrounding countries to cooperate in regional environmental protection and sustainable development.[39] President Ma also announced a marine policy to gradually open the South China Sea and cooperate with international conservation organizations for a Marine Peace Park in order to enhance positive interaction with neighboring countries, and to conserve ecosystem and cultural heritages.[40]

Neither a member of the United Nations nor of the Association of Southeast Asian Nations (ASEAN), Taiwan cannot join the Convention on Biological Diversity (CBD),[41] the Law of the Sea Convention,[42] and any other major political international organizations, except APEC and the International Council for Science (ICSU). This diplomatic impediment has limited Taiwan's participation in many international collaborations. However,

Beckman highlighted the importance of Taiwan's participation in regional cooperation because Taiwan occupies the largest island and is a major fishing entity in the South China Sea.[43] Recently, the relationship between Taiwan and China has greatly improved. In 2002, China and the ASEAN countries signed the breakthrough Declaration on the Conduct of Parties in the South China Sea,[44] which has helped to make the South China Sea relatively calm and peaceful. The signing in 2010 of the Economic Cooperation Framework Agreement (ECFA) between Taiwan and China[45] may give Taiwan a better chance to promote the Spratlies as an international Marine Peace Park.

Given Taiwan's significant capacity for biodiversity research, the following priorities are recommended for further activities.

1. Creating a taxonomy and compilation of fauna and flora of the South China Sea.
2. Establishing a long-term ecological research and monitoring program, including a centralized information portal that will make all data widely accessible in a Geographic Information System (GIS) format with real-time remote sensing data, links to onsite sensors and video systems, and the ability for users to explore scientific hypotheses and management action scenarios via online simulation systems.
3. Undertaking ecological community studies of both terrestrial and marine organisms as well as their metapopulation relationships such as the dependence of one reef system on the larvae washed in from a downstream reef (connectivity).
4. Conducting phylogeographical studies on selected groups of organisms (e.g., the relationships among taxonomic groups and their spatial distributions).
5. Undertaking population studies for certain important species in South China Sea.
6. Engaging in fishery resource analyses and simulations to guide sustainable use and conservation biology.
7. Ensuring other database integration, including links to the Catalog of Life (COL), Barcode of Life (BOL), Encyclopedia of Life (EOL), Tree of Life (TOL), ReefBase, FishBase, and expert's name lists.
8. Studying the effect of climate change on marine biodiversity, ecological connectivity and fisheries in the South China Sea.

The establishment of state-of-the-art marine stations at several islets would greatly facilitate the long-term research needed to unravel the complexities of South China Sea ecology. Sufficient research facilities and equipment including dry and wet labs, living accommodations, diving boats, and wireless Internet access will be essential to support this research. The research at these stations would benefit greatly by being open to international visiting scientists. As with the scientific exchange provisions of the Antarctic Treaty, a system for freely exchanging specimens, physical oceanographic observations, and ecological distribution data should be established based on agreements among collaborating countries. Gradually, opposing military installations could be supplanted with collaborating scientific research laboratories. Military and political disputes should be supplanted with scientific debates and jointly agreed, effective, natural resource management. Ultimately, it is envisioned that, under the guidance of an international natural resource management authority, any scientist or tourist would be able to enter any part of the Spratly Islands, passing in freely on vessels and aircraft from any international destination, and then move on to any other destination with no more difficulty than is found in traveling among the nations of the European Union.

Conclusion

The Spratly Islands have considerable ecological and biodiversity value, both intrinsically, and as the source of larvae for coastal ecosystems throughout the South China Sea. Sovereignty disputes have limited the implementation of effective measures to protect these resources from overexploitation and destructive fishing. Recently, strong support from some, including the Government of Taiwan, has spurred renewed interest in the incorporation of the islands and surrounding waters into an international Marine Peace Park. Agreements associated with this park would include a freeze on claims and claim-supportive activities for a specified but renewable period of time, thus easing tensions and facilitating collaborative research and resource management activities. Whether it is achieved via a single agreement, or via the accumulation of nationally declared parks into a coordinated network, a Spratly Islands International Peace Park would be an achievement of considerable regional and global significance.

Notes

1. See, generally, T. W. Chao, *Physical Geography of Nansha Islands, Report of the Multidisciplinary Oceanographic Expedition Team of Academia Sinica to the Nansha Islands* (1996).

2. K. H. Chang, R. Q. Jan, and C. S. Hua, *Fishes of Itu Aba Island in South China Sea* (Taipei, Taiwan: Encyclopedia Sinica Inc., 1982).

3. K. H. Chang, R. Q. Jan, and C. S. Hua, "Scientific Note on Inshore Fishes at Tai-pin Island (South China Sea)," *Bulletin of the Institute of Zoology, Academica Sinica* 20 (1981): 87–93.

4. L. S. Fang and J. C. Lee, *Terminal Report for Ecological Environmental Studies in South China Sea* (Council of Agriculture, 1994), 471.

5. BirdLife International, "Truong Sa Proposed Marine Protected Area. Sourcebook of Existing and Proposed Protected Areas in Vietnam," 2001, available at www.biology.hcmuns.edu.vn/store/elib/pub/IBA/Cddata/source_book/sb_pdf/Truong_Sa.pdf (accessed 15 August, 2009).

6. I. Jiunn Cheng, "Sea Turtles at Dungsha Tao, South China Sea," *Marine Turtle Newsletter* 70 (1995): 13–14, available at www.seaturtle.org/mtn/archives/mtn70/mtn70p13.shtml (accessed 17 August, 2009).

7. A. White, "Priority Areas for Marine Resource Management," in *Atlas for Marine Policy in Southeast Asian Seas*, eds. Joseph Morgan and Mark J. Valencia (Berkeley: University of California Press, 1984), 141.

8. The official name of the park is Dongsha Marine National Park (東沙海洋國家公園) or Dongsha Atoll National Park (東沙環礁國家公園). The park is to be first of several marine parks in the marine national parks system under the Marine National Park Headquarters (海洋國家公園管理處). Other proposed sites, such as Taiping Island, are currently undergoing internal study and assessment. The official Web site of the Dongsha Marine National Park is available at dongsha.cpami.gov.tw/en/e_main.aspx (accessed 29 March 2010).

9. K. T. Shao, et al., "Evaluating the Possibility of Setting Taiping Islands as a National Marine Park" (2010), an unpublished report in Chinese.

10. K. Wyrtki, "Physical Oceanography of the South East Asian Waters," *NAGA Report*, Vol. 2 (1961).

11. S. Jilan, "Overview of the South China Sea Circulation and Its influence on the Coastal Physical Oceanography Outside the Pearl River Estuary," *Continental Shelf Research* 24 (2004): 1745–1760; J. Gan, H. Li, E. N. Curchitser, and D. B. Haidvogel, "Modeling South China Sea Circulation: Response to Seasonal Forcing Regimes," *Journal of Geophysical Research* 3 (2006): C06034.

12. J. W. McManus, "The Spratly Islands: A Marine Park?" *Ambio* 32, no. 3 (1994): 181–186.

13. M. C. A. Ablan, J. W. McManus, and K. Viswanathan, "Indicators for Management of Coral Reefs and Their Applications to Marine Protected Areas," *NAGA: WorldFish Center Quarterly* 27, nos. 1–2 (2004): 31–39.

14. See, specifically, P. K. L. Ng and K. S. Tan, "The State of Marine Biodiversity in the South China Sea," *Raffles Bulletin of Zoology*, Supplement Series No. 8 (2000): 3–7; and S. H. Tan and L. S. Chen, "Aquatic Biodiversity of the South China Sea," *Raffles Bulletin of Zoology*, Supplement Series No. 19 (2008): 292.

15. C. Wilkinson, L. DeVantier, L. Talaue-McManus, D. Lawrence, and D. Souter, "South China Sea," Global International Waters Assessment (GIWA) Regional Assessment 54, University of Kalmar, Kalmar, Sweden, on behalf of the UN Environment Programme (UNEP) (2005).

16. Y. Z. Lee, G. B. Chen, and W. W. Yuan, "The Status and Capacity of Fishery Resources Development in the Spratly Islands," *Journal of Tropical Oceanography* 23, no. 1 (2004): 69–75 (in Chinese).

17. C. C. Wu, "Marine Environment and Biological Resources Studies at Spratly Island," Part I, *Bulletin of Taiwan Fisheries Research Institute* 33 (1981): 195–229.

18. T. S. Chi, "Investigation of Fishery Resources in Spratly Islands," *Bulletin of Taiwan Fisheries Research Institute* 46 (1989): 53–69; S. C. Huang, "Investigation of Whole Spratly Island," Taiwan Fishery Research Institute Report (1988).

19. Convention on Biological Diversity, Seventh Conference of the Parties (2004), Decision VII/28, "Protected Areas," para. 18.

20. D. Zbicz, "Global List of Complexes of Internationally Adjoining Protected Areas: Transboundary Protected Areas for Peace and Co-operation," IUCN/WCPA, Best Practice Protected Area Guidelines Series No. 7 (2001).

21. "Transboundary Protected Areas Inventory 2007," UNEP-WCMC, available at www.tbpa.net/tpa_inventory.html (accessed 22 February 2010).

22. See, generally, Yann-huei Song, "The South China Sea Workshop Process and Taiwan's Participation," in this Special Issue.

23. A. C. Alcala, "The Philippines-Vietnam Joint Research in the South China Sea, 1996–2007," *Manila Bulletin*, 27 April 2008, available at www.articlearchives.com/environment-natural-resources/ecology-environmental/173704-1.html (accessed 10 July 2009).

24. The interactive project Web site is at www.unepscs.org. See J. C. Pernetta, "Terminal Report of the UNEP/GEF South China Sea Project," UNEP/GEF (2009), available at www.unepscs.org/SCS_Documents/startdown/2228.html (accessed 10 July 2009).

25. See the Web site of the Coral Triangle Initiative, available at www.cti-secretariat.net (accessed 7 April 2010).

26. "Coral Triangle Declaration Signed," Antara News, 15 May 2009, available at www.antara.co.id/en/arc/2009/5/15/coral-triangle-declaration-signed/ (accessed 20 May 2010).

27. "Marine Peace Parks: Establishing Transboundary MPAs to Improve International Relations and Conservation," *MPA News* 9, no. 9 (April 2008): 1, available at depts.washington.edu/mpanews/MPA95.pdf (accessed 31 March 2010).

28. See, generally, M. P. Crosby et al., "The Red Sea Marine Peace Park: Early Lessons Learned from a Unique Trans-boundary Cooperative Research, Monitoring and Management Program," in *Proceedings of IUCN/WCPA-EA-4 Taipei Conference*, 18–23 March 2002, Taipei, Taiwan, available at pdf.usaid.gov/pdf_docs/PCAAB748.pdf (accessed 31 March 2010).

29. M. J. Valencia, J. M. van Dyke, and N. A. Ludwig, *Sharing the Resources of the South China Sea* (Honolulu: University of Hawaii Press, 1999), 187–222.

30. I. Townsend-Gault, "Preventive Diplomacy and Proactivity in the South China Sea," *Contemporary Southeast Asia* 20 (1998): 171–190.

31. M. J. Valencia and J. M. van Dyke, "Oil and the Lack of It in the South China Sea (Includes Reply) (Response to Article by Ian Townsend-Gault)," *Contemporary Southeast Asia* 21 (1999): 153.

32. Valencia et al., supra note 29, at 171–190.

33. J. W. McManus and L. A. B. Menez, "Potential Effects of a Spratly Island Marine Park," *Proceeding of the International Coral Reef Symposium*, Vol. 2 (1997), 1943–1948.

34. Antarctic Treaty, 402 U.N.T.S. 71.

35. Treaty Between Australia and Papua New Guinea Concerning Sovereignty and Maritime Boundaries in the Area Known as Torres Strait, International Legal Materials 18 (1979): 291.

36. McManus and Menez, supra note 33, at 1943–1948.

37. Valencia et al., supra note 29, at 171–190.

38. See, generally, Song, supra note 22.

39. E. Hsiao, "Chen Urges Cooperation with 'Spratly Initiative,'" Taiwan Today, available at www.taiwantoday.tw/ct.asp?xItem=29848&CtNode=427 (accessed 1 March 2010).

40. See Song, supra note 22.

41. Convention on Biological Diversity, 1760 U.N.T.S. 79.

42. U.N. Convention on the Law of the Sea, 1833 U.N.T.S. 397.

43. R. Beckman, "Territorial Disputes in the South China Sea: A New Model of Cooperation," Straits Times, 4 June 2007, available at law.nus.edu.sg/news/archive/2007/ST040607.pdf (accessed 20 March 2010).

44. Declaration on the Conduct of Parties in the South China Sea, 4 November 2002, available at the Web site of ASEAN at www.aseansec.org/13163.htm (accessed 19 July 2009).

45. "Excerpts of Ma in the ECFA Debate," Worldpress.org, 29 April 2010, available at www.worldpress.org/Asia/3536.cfm (accessed 20 May 2010).

Semi-enclosed Troubled Waters: A New Thinking on the Application of the 1982 UNCLOS Article 123 to the South China Sea

NIEN-TSU ALFRED HU

The Center for Marine Policy Studies
and College of Social Sciences
National Sun Yat-sen University
Kaohsiung City, Taiwan, Republic of China
and
National Cheng Kung University
Tainan City, Taiwan, Republic of China

Part IX of the 1982 United Nations Convention on the Law of the Sea deals with one particular kind of "special maritime situations and features"—"enclosed or semi-enclosed seas." There are only two articles within Part IX. Article 122 provides a descriptive definition of these maritime features. Article 123 stipulates cooperation among States bordering an enclosed or semi-enclosed sea as a treaty obligation while putting forward three substantive "spheres" in which bordering States can coordinate among themselves to perform such a treaty obligation. The South China Sea fits this wording and is in need of a cooperative mechanism in order to reduce the potential tension and conflicts in the region. By examining the practices of cooperation among bordering States in two other semi-enclosed seas, the Mediterranean Sea and the Caribbean Sea respectively, this article draws certain lessons for the bordering States of the South China Sea to consider for their potential application of Article 123.

Introduction

Part IX of the 1982 United Nations Convention on the Law of the Sea (UNCLOS)[1] deals with a particular kind of "special maritime situations and features"—the "enclosed or semi-enclosed seas"—with two articles, Article 122, Definition, and Article 123, Co-operation of States Bordering Enclosed or Semi-enclosed Seas.[2] The inclusion in the UNCLOS of this Part reflects the recognition of the drafters and negotiators of the special geographical situation of such seas as well as the relationship that can be envisaged between or among bordering States in managing activities and quality of the environment in such seas.[3]

The geographical reality of the South China Sea, the long-standing tension among the bordering States of the South China Sea, and the continual seeking of regional cooperation in the South China Sea all accentuate the importance of the provisions of this Part. The question of how to approach the issues of South China Sea, especially the issues of peace and development, deserves examination with a new view not simply from within the region or based on realpolitik, but from the lessons learned from other similar regions.

This article will first briefly present the provisions of Part IX, followed by a detailed examination on the practice of States pursuant to this Part, especially Article 123 as it is the substantive and operative provision, in two similar semi-enclosed sea regions, the Mediterranean Sea and the Caribbean Sea. The purpose is to extract lessons from these two semi-enclosed sea regions that may have application in the South China Sea. The article then turns to the current practice of Article 123 in the South China Sea and concludes by providing some new thinking on future cooperation in the South China Sea.

The Definition and Requirements of the UNCLOS With Respect to Enclosed or Semi-enclosed Seas

Article 122 of the UNCLOS defines a "enclosed or semi-enclosed sea" as follows:

> For the purposes of this Convention, "enclosed or semi-enclosed sea" means a gulf, basin or sea surrounded by two or more States and connected to another sea or the ocean by a narrow outlet or consisting entirely or primarily of the territorial seas and exclusive economic zones of two or more coastal States.

Without doubt, the South China Sea (traditionally referred to in Chinese and by Chinese as the South Sea) geographically fits this definition and is a semi-enclosed sea.[4] Similarly, the Mediterranean Sea and the Caribbean Sea fall into this definition.

An enclosed or semi-enclosed sea inevitably entails a situation in which the bordering States are competing for marine space and resources. From a marine space perspective, the bordering States may encounter difficulty of claiming a full 200-nautical-mile exclusive economic zone (EEZ) and continental shelf, or even a full 12-nautical-mile territorial sea, without the occurrence of overlapping claims with neighboring opposite or adjacent States. From a resources perspective, the bordering States share the same water body for land-based effluent discharge and the same marine resource base, both living and nonliving, for their livelihood and economic development. Thus, States bordering enclosed or semi-enclosed seas can be said to be "geographically disadvantaged States."[5]

The geographical reality or limitation of enclosed or semi-enclosed seas requires the bordering States to develop "intraregional" mechanisms to reduce, mitigate, or eliminate competition and conflicts. The mechanism envisaged by the UNCLOS is described in Article 123.

> States bordering an enclosed or semi-enclosed sea should cooperate with each other in the exercise of their rights and in the performance of their duties under this Convention. To this end they shall endeavor, directly or through an appropriate regional organization:
>
> (a) to coordinate the management, conservation, exploration and exploitation of the living resources of the sea;

(b) to coordinate the implementation of their rights and duties with respect to the protection and preservation of the marine environment;
(c) to coordinate their scientific research policies and undertake where appropriate joint programmes of scientific research in the area;
(d) to invite, as appropriate, other interested States or international organizations to cooperate with them in furtherance of the provisions of this article.

The prescription of Article 123, with its wording "should cooperate with each other" and "shall endeavor to coordinate," requires States bordering an enclosed or semi-enclosed sea to cooperate directly or through an appropriate "regional organization" in order to coordinate among themselves in three substantive spheres:

(1) the management, conservation, exploration and exploitation of the living resources of the sea;
(2) the protection and preservation of the marine environment; and
(3) the scientific research policies and undertaking joint scientific research programs.

Subparagraph (d) envisages the involvement of "extra-regional" States or "international organizations" in the cooperation with enclosed or semi-enclosed sea States. These "extra-regional States" may well be user States in the enclosed or semi-enclosed seas while the international organizations may well be those having regional or global competence in the affairs or the spheres as set out in Article 123(a), (b), or (c).[6]

The Practice of Article 123 in the Mediterranean Sea Region: An Overview

The Mediterranean Sea is bordered by 21 countries of southern Europe, western Asia or the Arabian Peninsula, and northern Africa,[7] three of which are highly industrialized countries on its northwestern coast, a few with limited industrial development located in the northern eastern part, and a number of developing countries on its eastern and southern coast.[8] Through the Strait of Gibraltar, it connects with the Atlantic Ocean to the west. And through the Aegean Sea, Strait of Dardanelle, Sea of Marmara, and Strait of Bosporus, it connects with the Black Sea, a nearly closed sea to its east.[9] The Mediterranean covers an area of about 2.5 million square kilometers with a coastline of 46,000 kilometers and constitutes 0.7% of the global water surface. The existence of diversity in terms of economic development, let alone the other factors, has a significant impact on the efficacy of regional cooperation (see Figure 1).

The very narrow and only outlet of the Strait of Gibraltar to the Atlantic Ocean generates an oceanographically unique situation in the Mediterranean Sea in that it has a negative water balance, or with evaporation greatly exceeding precipitation and river runoff. High population growth, industrialization and urbanization, and active tourism in the region all create pressure on the protection of marine environment and living marine resources in the Mediterranean Sea.

Management of Marine Living Resources

Long before the 1982 UNCLOS or even prior to the 1958 four Geneva Conventions on the Law of the Sea,[10] the Agreement for the Establishment of the General Fisheries Council for the Mediterranean (the GFCM Agreement) was approved by the United Nations Food and Agriculture Organization (FAO) Conference, under the provisions of Article XIV of the FAO Constitution,[11] on 24 September 1949 and entered into force on 20 February 1952.[12]

Figure 1. The Mediterranean Sea. (*Source:* Taken from http://www.answers.com/topic/mediterranean-sea, accessed 8 August 2009.)

The GFCM Agreement underwent several amendments in 1963, 1976, and 1997, respectively.[13] The GFCM adopted two sets of amendments in 1997 that were approved by the FAO Council. One set of amendments concerned changes, inter alia, to allow for regional economic integration organizations that are members of FAO to become members of GFCM and to change the name of General Fisheries Council for the Mediterranean to the General Fisheries Commission for the Mediterranean. These amendments came into force upon the approval of the FAO Council. The second set of amendments concerned an autonomous budget for the functioning of the Commission, or a "budgetary de-link from the FAO," involving new obligations for the Contracting Parties. This amendment came into force in 2004 upon acceptance by two-thirds of the members of the Commission.[14]

Article 1, paragraph 2 of the 1997 GFCM Agreement stipulates that the membership of the Commission is open to members and associate members of the FAO and nonmember States that are members of the United Nations, any of its Specialized Agencies or the International Atomic Energy Agency (IAEA), that are coastal States situated wholly or partly within the Mediterranean Region, or whose vessels engage in fishing in the Region for stocks covered by the Agreement, or regional economic integration organizations of which any State is a member that is either a coastal State of the region or a fishing State in the Region and to which that State has transferred competence over matters within the purview of this Agreement. The GFCM currently has 24 members, including 22 Mediterranean and Black Sea coastal States,[15] 1 non-Mediterranean State (i.e., Japan), and the European Community.

The Region in the GFCM Agreement is defined in Article IV: "The Commission shall carry out the functions and responsibilities set forth in Article III in the Region as referred to in the Preamble" with the Preamble indicating the Mediterranean and the Black Sea and connecting waters.

Article III, paragraph 1 of the GFCM Agreement stipulates the purpose of the GFCM is "to promote the development, conservation, rational management and best utilization of living marine resources, as well as the sustainable development of aquaculture in the Region." ... In order to fulfill these purposes, the Commission has the functions and responsibilities as stipulated in Article III, paragraph 1(a) to (h).[16]

It is worth noting that Article III, paragraph 2 stresses the application of the precautionary approach to conservation and management decisions as well as the taking into account of the best scientific evidence available while, at the same time, it also highlights "the need to promote the development and proper utilization of the marine living resources." This paragraph intends to strike a balance between conservation and the development and proper utilization of the marine living resources.

In order for the GFCM to discharge its functions, the Commission has established several subsidiary bodies, including: the Scientific Advisory Committee (SAC, established in 1997); the Committee on Aquaculture (CAQ, established in 1995); the Compliance Committee (CoC, established in 2006); and their respective subsidiaries along with a Secretariat based in Rome.[17] As explained by a GFCM leaflet, the GFCM "enjoys the support of cooperative projects executed by FAO at sub-regional and regional level which enhance, in particular, scientific fishery cooperation and capacity building in participating countries in line with GFCM priorities and strategies" and "other cooperative projects in the field of aquaculture are executed by the Secretariat."[18] The cooperative projects include: Scientific Cooperation to Support Responsible Fisheries in the Adriatic Sea (ADRIAMED), Advice, Technical Support and Establishment of Cooperation Networks to Facilitate Coordination to Support Fisheries Management in the Western and Central Mediterranean (COPEMED), Assessment and Monitoring of the Fishery Resources and the Ecosystems in the Straits of Sicily (MEDSUDMED), and Mediterranean Fishery Statistics and Information System (MEDFISIS).[19]

Cooperation between GFCM and other regional fisheries management organizations (RFMOs) also occurs. At its twentieth session in 1994, GFCM endorsed the recommendations of the second GFCM/ICCAT (International Commission for the Conservation of Atlantic Tunas[20]) Expert Consultations to establish the Joint GFCM/ICCAT *Ad Hoc* Working Group on Large Pelagic Species. The Working Group held its first meeting in September 1994 in Fuengirola, Spain. The GFCM Secretariat was entrusted with the administrative work while the ICCAT provided the technical secretariat. The eighth session of the Joint GFCM/ICCAT Working Group on Large Pelagic Species was held in Malaga, Spain, 5–9 May 2008.[21]

The bordering States of the Mediterranean Sea have demonstrated a mutual interest in the development and proper utilization of the marine living resources in the region, and have cooperated by drawing up a multilateral regional treaty and establishing a regional intergovernmental organization for such purpose. Through time, the number of Parties to the GFCM Agreement has increased. These Parties have tried to embody the developments in the major international fisheries instruments, such as the 1982 UNCLOS, Agenda 21 adopted by the 1992 United Nations Conference on Environment and Development (or the Rio Earth Summit),[22] and the Code of Conduct for Responsible Fisheries adopted by the FAO Conference in 1995,[23] by incorporating concepts such as the precautionary approach and the best scientific evidence available into the GFCM Agreement and by including fishing nations from outside the region, such as Japan, into the GFCM regime.

Protection of the Marine Environment

Preceding the adoption of the 1982 UNCLOS, countries of the Mediterranean region began to deal with the marine pollution problems by adopting the Mediterranean Action Plan

(MAP) in 1975 under the auspice of the United Nations Environment Program (UNEP).[24] This Action Plan was the first plan adopted as a Regional Seas Programme (RSP) under UNEP's umbrella.[25]

Early Phase of the Mediterranean Action Plan. The Action Plan to protect the Mediterranean from marine pollution was considered and adopted at the Intergovernmental Meeting on the Protection of the Mediterranean, convened by the Executive Director of the UNEP in Barcelona from 28 January to 4 February 1975.[26] As indicated in the Introduction texts of the Report of this Intergovernmental Meeting, the Meeting was convened as a response to decisions made by the UNEP Governing Council in 1974.[27] The Intergovernmental Meeting was clearly initiated as a part of an effort made by the UNEP. The Mediterranean countries were fortunate to have the support and endorsement of the UN system. This may not be the case in other semi-enclosed sea regions, although the involvement of the UN system does not necessarily guarantee the success of such a regional effort.

The 1975 Intergovernmental Meeting was attended by representatives of 16 Mediterranean States,[28] with extraregional States (i.e., the Union of Soviet Socialist Republics, the United Kingdom, and the United States) attending as observers.

During discussion, "[i]t was emphasized that the protection of resources should not be viewed as an obstacle to socio-economic development and examples of development projects which was perfectly compatible with the protection of the environment were given."[29] In view of the environmental diversities in the region and the differing national developmental priorities, the concept of "unity in diversity," or that "the Mediterranean eco-system was a common heritage and one of the most important assets of the Mediterranean eco-region," was stressed.[30] "The ecological and economic interdependence of the Mediterranean eco-system, defined as *the Mediterranean Sea with a narrow coastline*, and the rest of the Mediterranean eco-region" was also stressed (emphasis added).[31] The concept of sea use corresponding to the concept of land use based on the characteristics and dynamics of the ecosystem was introduced in the elaboration of a plan covering the Mediterranean ecosystem. The plan would deal with: "(a) the optimum distribution of activities in the Mediterranean ecosystem; (b) the rational utilization and development of resources; and (c) *the classification into zones* assigned to exclusive activities (routes for oil and cargo ships) or to activities compatible with their environment, and also zones not subject to further degradation or pollution (emphasis added)."[32]

As early as 1975, the Mediterranean countries used the concept of integrated development as a basis for discussion in pursuing a balanced approach to the protection of the marine environment and resources and the development of national economies.[33] It is clear that their discussion and the subjects included in the MAP prognosticated the concepts of "ecosystem-based management" and "ocean zoning."

A major achievement of the 1975 Intergovernmental Meeting was the preparation of regional legal instruments designed to "provide a legal basis for international co-operation to protect the marine environment in the Mediterranean."[34] Before Committee II were three draft legal instruments:

1. a draft framework convention for the protection of the marine environment against pollution in the Mediterranean prepared under the auspices of the FAO;
2. a draft protocol on cooperation in combating pollution of the Mediterranean by oil and other harmful substance prepared by a consultant from the Intergovernmental Maritime Consultative Organization (IMCO); and

3. a draft protocol for the prevention of pollution of the Mediterranean Sea by dumping from ships and aircraft prepared by the Spanish delegation.[35]

It was decided that a Plenipotentiary Conference would be held in Barcelona in February 1976 for the adoption of these legal instruments and that a meeting of intergovernmental legal and technical experts would be convened in Geneva in April 1975 to consider the framework convention, protocols, and annexes.[36]

The 1975 Intergovernmental Meeting not only adopted the MAP, but also substantively prepared for the soon-to-be adopted regional framework convention and its protocols for the protection of marine environment against pollution in the Mediterranean.

The Adoption of the Framework Convention and Protocols. A Conference of Plenipotentiaries of the Coastal States of the Mediterranean Region on the Protection of the Mediterranean Sea was convened by the Executive Director of the UNEP in Barcelona in 1976.[37] Eighteen Mediterranean coastal States were invited and 16 participated.[38] Again, the Soviet Union, United Kingdom, and the United States attended as observers. On 13 February 1976, the Conference adopted, along with 10 resolutions,[39] the Convention for the Protection of the Marine Environment Against Pollution in the Mediterranean (the Barcelona Convention)[40] and two protocols, the Protocol for the Prevention of Pollution of the Mediterranean Sea by Dumping from Ships and Aircraft[41] and the Protocol on Co-operation in Combating Pollution of the Mediterranean Sea by Oil and Other Harmful Substances in Cases of Emergency.[42]

The Convention and its two Protocols provided the legal basis for marine environment protection for the coastal States of the Mediterranean. Through the resolutions adopted, institutional arrangements were made. For example, the UNEP was assigned the secretariat functions for the three regional treaties,[43] a committee of experts was established to study the possibility of establishing an Interstate Guarantee Fund for the Mediterranean Sea Area,[44] a regional oil-combating center and subregional oil combating centers for the Mediterranean were established,[45] and an Intergovernmental Meeting was planned for 1977 to review the progress of the MAP.[46]

The 1976 Barcelona Convention characterized the marine environment and the economic, social, health, and cultural value of the Mediterranean Sea Area as the "common heritage" that should be preserved for the benefit and enjoyment of present and future generations.[47] Article 1 defined the Mediterranean Sea Area as "the maritime waters of the Mediterranean Sea proper, including its gulfs and seas bounded to the west by the meridian passing through Cape Spartel lighthouse, at the entrance of the Straits of Gibraltar, and to the East by the southern limits of the Straits of the Dardanelles between Mehmetcik and Kumkale lighthouses" and as not including the internal waters of the Contracting Parties. The internal waters of the Contracting Parties as well as the Sea of Marmara and the Black Sea were excluded from the area of application of the Convention due to sovereignty and geographical considerations.

Article 4, "General Undertakings" of the Convention, obliged the Contracting Parties to:

> individually or jointly take all appropriate measures in accordance with the provisions of this Convention and those protocols in force to which they are Party, to prevent, abate and combat pollution of the Mediterranean Sea Area and to protect and enhance the marine environment in that Area;

co-operate in the formulation and adoption of protocols, in addition to the protocols opened for signature at the same time as this Convention, prescribing agreed measures, procedures and standards for the implementation of this Convention", while further pledge themselves to promote, within the international bodies considered to be competent by the Contracting Parties, measures concerning the protection of the marine environment in the Mediterranean Sea Area from all types and sources of pollution.

This Article required the Parties not only to cooperate among themselves to prevent, abate, and combat marine pollution in the Mediterranean Sea Area, but also to promote the same within other international bodies measures that would be instrumental in the protection of the marine environment of the Mediterranean Sea Area. The provision, along with Article 15, "Adoption of additional protocols," envisaged the formulation and adoption of additional Convention protocols for other marine environment protection purposes.

Developments After the Adoption of the 1976 Barcelona Convention. Article 14 of the 1976 Barcelona Convention establishes Meetings of the Contracting Parties (MoCP) and bestows such meetings with the function of keeping under review the implementation of the Convention and its protocols. This function includes, inter alia: "to adopt, review and amend as required the annexes to this Convention and to the protocols;" "to make recommendations regarding the adoption of any additional protocols or any amendments to this Convention or the protocols;" and "to consider and undertake any additional action that may be required for the achievement of the purposed of this Convention and the protocols."

Spurred by the 1992 UN Conference on Environment and Development (UNCED or the Earth Summit), a Conference of Plenipotentiaries adopted texts of four instruments along with five resolutions on 10 June 1995:[48]

1. amendments to the Barcelona Convention;[49]
2. amendments to the Dumping Protocol;[50]
3. the Protocol concerning Specially Protected Areas and Biological Diversity in the Mediterranean[51] (to replace the 1982 Protocol concerning Mediterranean Specially Protected Areas[52]); and
4. the Barcelona Resolution on the Environment and Sustainable Development in the Mediterranean Basin.[53]

The title of the Barcelona Convention was amended to be the "Convention for the Protection of the Marine Environment and the Coastal Region of the Mediterranean," which reflects the extension of the application of the Convention and protocols "to coastal areas as defined by each Contracting Party within its own territory."[54] Several new articles were added concerning: conservation of biological diversity (Article 10), pollution resulting from the transboundary movements of hazardous wastes (Article 11), environmental legislation (Article 14), public information and participation (Article 15), the establishment of the Bureau (Article 19), and observers (Article 20).

The MAP Phase II was also adopted as Appendix I contained in the Annex to the "Barcelona Resolution on the Environment and Sustainable Development in the Mediterranean Basin" of Resolution I "Adoption of the Barcelona Resolution on the Environment and Sustainable Development in the Mediterranean Basin."[55] Quite different from the original MAP, which was presented in 5 pages, the MAP Phase II is 31 pages and has a complicated structure.

Through time, the Barcelona Convention has given rise to seven Protocols addressing specific aspects of Mediterranean environment conservation.[56]

The MAP and its Phase II, as well as the Barcelona Convention and its associated Protocols, have created a complicated scheme for the protection of marine environment of the Mediterranean. The scheme consists of various programs, such as the scientific component of the MAP, the Long-Term Program for Pollution Monitoring and Research in the Mediterranean (MED POL), the MAP's socioeconomic component, the Blue Plan as well as the Coastal Area Management Program (CAMP), the Global Program of Action (GPA) for the Protection of the Marine Environment from Land-Based Activities, the Strategic Action Program (SAP), the Priority Actions Program (PAP), and various Regional Activity Centers (RACs) to facilitate or implement the various programs.[57]

In 1975, the MAP was initiated by the UNEP as the first plan adopted as an RSP. The UNEP has continued to be deeply involved in the development and evolution of the regional legislation and legal framework in the Mediterranean. The MAP and framework Convention and its associated Protocols have widened their mandate to include integrated coastal zone planning and management, but also have created a complicated institution.

The Practice of Article 123 in the Caribbean Sea Region: An Overview

Caribbean Sea is another often-cited example of semi-enclosed sea. It is an arm of the Atlantic Ocean and washes upon: the South American countries of Venezuela and Colombia to the south; the Central American countries of Panama to the southwest; Costa Rica, Nicaragua, Honduras, Guatemala, Belize, and Mexico to the west; the Greater Antilles (Cuba, Jamaica, Hispaniola, and Puerto Rico) to the north; and the Lesser Antilles to the east. The Caribbean Sea is one of the largest saltwater seas with an area of about 2,754,000 square kilometers (1,063,000 square miles) (Figure 2).[58] Most of the countries bordering the Caribbean Sea are small-sized developing economies or small island developing countries. With limited human, institutional, and financial resources, it would be difficult for many of these States to deal easily with the issues of sustainable fisheries development and management and marine environment protection.

In the Caribbean Sea region, there is a political entity, the Caribbean Community (CARICOM), and an economic entity, the Caribbean Common Market, both established by the 1973 Treaty of Chaguaramas.[59] CARICOM currently has 15 member States (Antigua and Barbuda, the Bahamas, Barbados, Belize, Dominica, Grenada, Guyana, Haiti, Jamaica, Montserrat, Saint Lucia, St. Kitts and Nevis, St. Vincent and the Grenadines, Suriname, Trinidad and Tobago) and 5 associate members (Anguilla, Bermuda, the British Virgin Islands, the Cayman Islands, and Turks and Caicos Islands).

Management of Marine Living Resources

With the support of Canadian Government, the CARICOM Governments in January 1991 launched the CARICOM Fisheries Resource Assessment and Management Programme (CFRAMP) to promote the sustainable use and conservation of the fisheries resources of CARICOM member States.[60] After a decade of operation, CFRAMP was superseded by the Caribbean Regional Fisheries Mechanism (CRFM) in 2003 through the signing of the Agreement Establishing the CRFM on 4 February 2002.[61]

Figure 2. The Caribbean Sea. (*Source:* Taken from http://www.answers.com/topic/caribbean-sea, accessed 8 August 2009.)

The CRFM is a regional body exclusively for the Caribbean countries as Article 3, paragraph 1 stipulates that the "Membership of the Mechanism shall be open to Member States and Associate Members of CARICOM." The CRFM has 18 member States: Anguilla, Antigua and Barbuda, the Bahamas, Barbados, Belize, the British Virgin Islands, Dominica, Grenade, Guyana, Haiti, Jamaica, Montserrat, St. Kitts and Nevis, St. Lucia, St. Vincent and the Grenadines, Suriname, Trinidad and Tobago, and Turks and Caicos Islands.

The objectives of the Mechanism are defined in Article 4 of the 2002 Agreement:

(a) the efficient management and sustainable development of marine and other aquatic resources within the jurisdictions of Member States;
(b) the promotion and establishment of co-operative arrangements among interested States for the efficient management of shared, straddling or highly migratory marine and other aquatic resources;
(c) the provision of technical advisory and consultative services to fisheries divisions of Member States in the development, management and conservation of their marine and other aquatic resources.

In order to achieve these objectives, Article 6 sets up three organs within the Mechanism:

(a) the Ministerial Council;
(b) the Caribbean Fisheries Forum (the Forum); and
(c) the Technical Unit.

The Ministerial Council, composed of the ministers of fisheries of each member of the Mechanism, determines the policy of the Mechanism[62] while the Forum, composed of representatives of each member of the Mechanism and representatives of all interest bodies, organizations, or groups (or stakeholders), determines the technical and scientific work of the Mechanism.[63] The Forum has an Executive Committee and can establish subcommittees as necessary.[64] The Technical Unit functions as the Secretariat[65] with the Director of the Technical Unit being the chief executive officer of the Mechanism and "shall exercise full responsibility for all aspects of the work of the Mechanism."[66] The Technical Unit is, inter alia, to "provide technical, consultative and advisory services to Member States in the development, assessment, management and conservation of marine and other aquatic resources and, on request, in the discharge of any obligations arising from bilateral and other international instruments."[67]

Worth noting is that, through Article 20, the Agreement accords "full juridical personality" and "full capacity" to the Mechanism so that it can contract, acquire, and dispose of movable and immovable property, institute legal proceedings, and enter into agreements with member States, third States, and other international organizations for the achievement of its objectives. Article 19 and Articles 21 to 27 accord the Mechanism and its personnel varying privileges, immunities, and exemptions.

The CRFM is thus a multilateral, regional, intergovernmental fisheries organization without being named an "organization" but, more importantly, without a decisionmaking function on the management of fisheries. In addition, CRFM differs from most other regional RFMOs by having the Forum that engages various stakeholders in the decisionmaking process of the Mechanism. The operation of the Mechanism and the interaction among its three organs is set out in Figure 3.

Protection of the Marine Environment

The Adoption of the Action Plan for the Caribbean Environment Programme. As in the Mediterranean, the UNEP was deeply involved in the development and formulation of a regional environment program in the Caribbean.[68] UNEP convened the 1981 Intergovernmental Meeting on the Action Plan for the Caribbean Environment Programme in cooperation with the UN Economic Commission for Latin America (ECLA). The representatives from 22 States of the region adopted the Action Plan for the Caribbean Environment

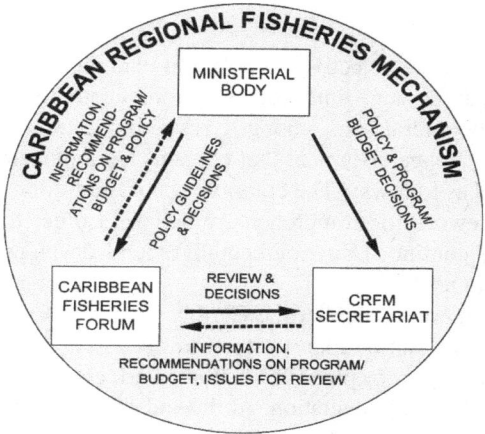

Figure 3. The operation of the Caribbean Regional Fisheries Mechanism (CRFM). (*Source:* Reprinted from *Marine Policy* 28, Figure 3 of Milton O. Haughton et al., "Establishment of the Caribbean Regional Fisheries Mechanism," 351–359, at 356, Copyright (2004), with permission from Elsevier.)

Programme and a resolution dealing with: (a) program implementation, (b) institutional arrangements, and (c) financial arrangements related to the implementation of the Action Plan and the program priorities for the Action Plan.[69]

The geographic region covered by this Action Plan is termed the "Wider Caribbean," which comprises "the insular and coastal States and Territories of the Caribbean Sea and the Gulf of Mexico, including Bahamas, Guyana, Suriname and the French Department of Guiana, as well as the waters of the Atlantic Ocean adjacent to these States and Territories."[70] The Action Plan is open to other countries as noted in paragraph 2 of the Preamble: "Other countries may participate in the Action Plan if they so desire, and, in accordance with United Nations procedures, they will be classified in terms of the nature of their participation."

The Action Plan was formulated recognizing the diversities within the region. "The region is a geographical entity made up of States and Territories with diverse economic and political structures, natural resources, social systems, environmental characteristics and potential development capabilities. These diversities have been recognized in the formulation of this Action Plan."[71] The participating countries also recognized that: "[t]he island countries of the region have special needs owing to the fragility of their ecosystems and their particularly limited carrying capacities. These were specifically recognized in the Action Plan."[72]

Paragraph 4 of the Preamble of the Action Plan stated the objectives of the Action Plan:

> The principle objectives of the Action Plan are to assist the Governments of the region in minimizing environmental problems in the Wider Caribbean through assessment of the state of the environment and development activities in environment management. Furthermore, the Action Plan will establish a framework for activities requiring regional co-operation in order to strengthen the capacity of the States and Territories of the Wider Caribbean region for implementing sound environmental management practices and thus achieve the development of the region on a sustainable basis.

In order to achieve these objectives, the Action Plan required a process of assessment and management and, at the same time, concentration of activities on the coastal areas with special reference to the interactions among terrestrial, coastal, and marine ecosystems.[73] The Action Plan is a 12-page document that contains a complicated structure and various components described as follows: "The components of the Action Plan are interdependent and constitute a framework for comprehensive action in order to contribute both to the protection and to the continued environmentally sound development of the region. No component is an end in itself."[74]

Unlike the MAP, however, neither the Caribbean Action Plan nor the 1981 Intergovernmental Meeting on the Action Plan for the Caribbean Environment Programme took a strong approach in calling for or preparing a framework convention and associated protocols as the legal basis for implementation. At the end of the Caribbean Action Plan, under the section of "Regional legal agreement," it is stated that: "The Action Plan should be supported by a flexible and general Regional Agreement."[75] The Resolution on the Action Plan for the Caribbean Environment Programme requested the Executive Director of the UNEP to convene, in early 1983, another intergovernmental meeting of the Caribbean States participating in the Action Plan to review the progress achieved in the implementation of the Action Plan, to adopt the work plan and budget for the 1984–1985 biennium, and to consider the adoption of a regional legal agreement.[76]

The Adoption of the Framework Convention and Protocol. With the mandate set forth by the 1981 Resolution on the Action Plan, the 1983 Conference of Plenipotentiaries on the Protection and Development of the Marine Environment of the Wider Caribbean Region adopted two instruments:[77] the Convention for the Protection and Development of the Marine Environment of the Wider Caribbean Region (the Cartegena Convention);[78] and the Protocol Concerning Co-operation in Combating Oil Spills in the Wider Caribbean Region.[79] Both entered into force in 1986. Among the resolutions adopted was one concerning "pollution from land-based sources," which requested UNEP to convene a working group of experts nominated by the Contracting Parties and Signatories to prepare a draft protocol on land-based sources of marine pollution and another resolution concerning "specially protected area and wildlife in the Wider Caribbean Region," which requested UNEP to convene a working group of experts nominated by the Contracting Parties and Signatories to prepare a draft protocol on specially protected areas and wildlife in the Wider Caribbean Region.[80]

The Cartegena Convention, is characterized by the UNEP Caribbean Environment Programme (CEP) as "a comprehensive, umbrella agreement for the protection and development of the marine environment" that "provides the legal framework for cooperative regional and national actions in the WCR (Wider Caribbean Region)."[81] The UNEP CEP indicates that "[t]he Cartegena Convention is not the only Multilateral Environmental Agreement applicable in the region" since "[o]ther applicable agreements include the Convention on Biological Diversity, MARPOL 73/78, the Basel Convention and others"[82] also apply to their respective Contracting Parties in the Caribbean region. It is its regional area of application that makes the 1983 Cartegena Convention an important complement to the other agreements.

In the Cartegena Convention, the "Wider Caribbean" region referred to in the Action Plan for the CEP was further defined as "the Convention Area," which means "the marine environment of the Gulf of Mexico, the Caribbean Sea and the areas of the Atlantic Ocean adjacent thereto, south of 30 deg north latitude and within 200 nautical miles of the Atlantic coasts of the States referred to in article 25 of the Convention" but does "not include internal waters of the Contracting Parties."[83] The Cartegena Convention dealt with five different sources of marine pollution from: ships (Article 5), dumping (Article 6), land-based sources (Article 7), seabed activities (Article 8), and airborne (Article 9). However, other than calling for the Contracting Parties to "take all appropriate measures to prevent, reduce and control pollution" from these different pollution sources, the Convention did not lay down substantive requirements or rules, except referring to "applicable international rules and standards." This makes the Convention an umbrella agreement. The Convention does oblige its Contracting Parties to "individually, or jointly, take all appropriate measures to protect and preserve rare or fragile ecosystems, as well as the habitat of depleted, threatened or endangered species, in the Convention Area" by endeavoring to establish protected areas.[84]

While the UNEP CEP characterizes the Cartegena Convention as an umbrella treaty, Article 4, paragraph 3 and Article 17 of the Convention together also make the Convention a framework convention since the former requires that: "The Contracting Parties shall co-operate in the formulation and adoption of protocols or other agreements to facilitate the effective implementation of this Convention" and the latter stipulates that: "The Contracting Parties, at a conference of plenipotentiaries, may adopt additional protocols to this Convention pursuant to paragraph 3 of article 4." Pursuant to these clauses, two protocols

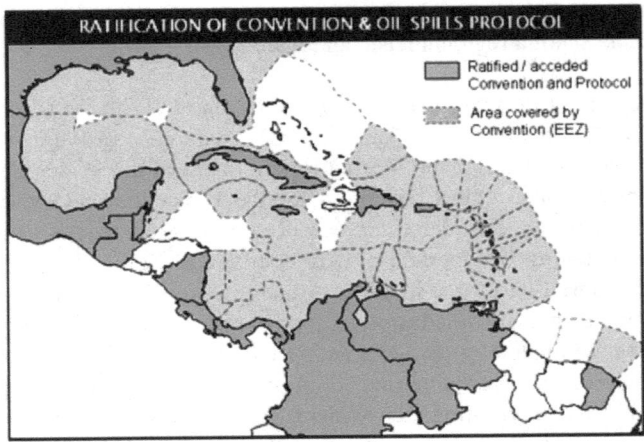

Figure 4. The Convention Area of the Cartagena Convention and its ratifiers. (*Source:* Taken from Web site of UNEP CEP at http://www.cep.unep.org/cartagena-convention/convention-and-oil-spills.png/view, accessed 11 August 2009.)

have been adopted: the Protocol Concerning Specially Protected Areas and Wildlife (SPAW) in the Wider Caribbean Region (adopted on 18 January 1990 and entered into force on 18 June 2000)[85] and the Protocol Concerning Pollution from Land-Based Sources and Activities (LBS Protocol) (adopted on 6 October 1999 and not yet in force).[86] There are 22 Parties to the 1983 Cartagena Convention and the Oil Spills Protocol.[87] Figure 4 shows the Convention Area of the Cartagena Convention and its ratifiers.

Lessons Drawn from the Mediterranean and Caribbean Sea Regions

After a detailed examination of the practice of Article 123 of the 1982 UNCLOS in the Mediterranean Sea and the Caribbean Sea, this section draws a number of lessons from the two cases based on academic assessments of the success and failure of the relevant outputs (Action Plans, conventions and associated protocols, mechanisms, and organization, etc.) and outcomes (i.e., things that have or have not changed) in the two case study areas. Such lessons may shed some light on the discussion of issues concerning regional cooperation in the South China Sea, especially from the perspective of the application of Article 123 of the UNCLOS in the region.

UNEP Regional Seas Programme and Marine Environment Protection

UNEP has been active and involved in shaping the mechanisms of marine environment protection in the Mediterranean Sea and Caribbean Sea regions, through its RSP. As indicated at the Web site of the UNEP RSP, the RSPs have several common elements:

> The process of establishing a regional programme usually begins with the development of an Action Plan outlining the strategy and substance of a regionally coordinated programme, aimed at the protection of the common body of water. The Action Plan is based on the region's particular environmental concerns and challenges as well as its socio-economic and political situation.

It may cover issues ranging from chemical wastes and coastal development to oil spill preparedness and response and the conservation of marine species and ecosystems.[88]

A typical Regional Seas Action Plan consists of the following chapters: Environmental Assessment, Environmental Management, Environmental Legislation, Institutional Arrangements, and Financial Arrangements.[89]

In some cases, the role and value of the RSP has been praised highly. Peter Hulm has written that:

> It is hard to think of another international forum where Libya will sit down with Israel, the US with Cuba or Iran with Iraq, and agree on a common solution to their collective problems. It is, in effect, an effort to beat the clock without beating ourselves: to preserve the marine environment without putting a stranglehold on economic and social development.[90]

Hulm also noted a remark made by Lorne Clark, Director of the Canadian Department of External Affairs' Legal Operations Division that the "Regional Seas is the jewel in UNEP's crown."[91] However, Hulm also indicated that financing has been the number one problem of UNEP since it could do no more than its budget permitted.[92]

The similar approach taken by the UNEP in developing RSPs in various regions does not guarantee the same results and expected effectiveness of marine environment protection. UNEP has noted that "[s]ome of these regional instruments have proven extraordinarily effective" and that "the Cartagena Convention for the Caribbean and the Barcelona Convention for the Mediterranean have always been extremely active and visible."[93] Academic studies or assessments have often indicated the opposite.

An academic study assessing the environmental effectiveness of the Barcelona Convention after nearly 30 years concluded that:

> From the data available it is not possible to measure if the Mediterranean Sea is cleaner than prior to the Convention. Even if it could be proved that it is cleaner, it is ambiguous whether this change can be attributed to the Convention or to other factors such as physical processes, introduction of cleaner technologies, etc.[94]

This assessment argued that, although the "[o]rigins of the Barcelona Convention lie in the concern expressed by the scientific 'epistemic community' over pollution in the Mediterranean Sea," the availability of reliable scientific data is still in question and these data "can be neglected if they do not correspond with politically acceptable goals," and that the data, information, or assessments taken into account to produce National Diagnostic Analyses, National Baseline Budgets and National Action Plans "were not directly taken from the monitoring activities, but rather from other scientific assessments."[95] The 2008 assessment also argued that "institutional, rather than scientific, dimensions are driving the operation of MAP" and "there is no established mechanism in the Barcelona Convention for a science-policy interaction, ... Even though legal texts of the Barcelona Convention and its related Protocols are highly technical in that they set scientific targets and do not directly address socio-economic issues, it is difficult to estimate the overall environmental effectiveness of the Convention."[96]

In another assessment on the effectiveness of the Barcelona Convention and its related protocols, the Land-Based Sources Protocol[97] in particular, found that

> Generally, due to lack of implementation, the Barcelona Convention has failed to combat increasing pollution and prevent further degradation of the Mediterranean ecosystem. As the system operates currently, it is apparent that the polluting processes that have been proven to cause severe environmental and health impacts are still flourishing in industrialized countries, and unhygienic methods of sewage disposal are still ongoing in developing countries. These issues bring into question the effectiveness of the implementation process of the LBS protocol, Barcelona convention as well as the MAP.[98]

Moreover, "the LBS protocol which was designed to control the most significant cause of pollution would probably be categorized the least effective considering that most of the measures required to make the protocol operational have not been implemented."[99]

This assessment attributed the failure of the Barcelona Convention and its associated protocols to the lack of financial resources and technical expertise in some of the Mediterranean countries.[100] This situation may be shown further by the uneven distribution of designated marine protected areas in the Mediterranean Sea region. (See Figure 5.)

Studies on the Wider Caribbean Region have also shown that similar problems exist. For example, Marian Miller pointed out eight "challenges" that the Caribbean Environment

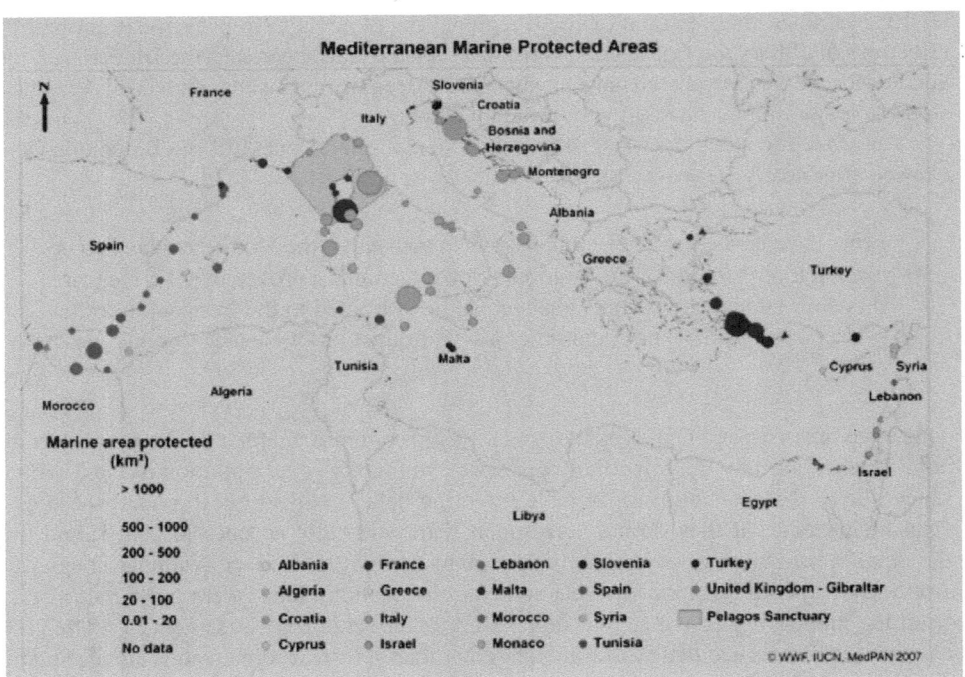

Figure 5. Distribution of Mediterranean Marine Protected Areas. (*Source:* Taken from Figure 2 in IUCN and WWF, *Status of Marine Protected Areas in the Mediterranean Sea: A Collaborative Study by IUCN, WWF and MedPAN* (2008), 39, available at http://www.medpan.org/_upload/1120.pdf, accessed 7 August 2009.)

Programme (CEB) was facing.[101] Miller first indicated that "[a]lthough regional institution-building can count as a Programme achievement, its translation to the national level will be a major challenge for the Action Plan."[102] And then she indicated that "environment is not yet a first-order concern for many of these States and territories"; "[l]imited financial resources continued to challenge the Action Plan, impeding progress at both the national and regional level"; "[c]ounterpart contributions and contributions from other organizations . . . sometimes have to be targeted to satisfy the interests of the donor rather than the immediate concerns of the Caribbean Environment Programme"; and that the financial crisis of the United Nations also is adversely affecting the Programme.[103]

In another paper written by Benedict Sheehy, in which he examined the success of the International Convention for the Prevention of Pollution from Ships (MARPOL Convention)[104] and the Cartagena Convention, the grade that he gave to the achievements and effectiveness of Cartagena Convention was an "F."[105] A few passages can be cited from his paper.

> Article 7 [of the Cartagena Convention] deals with land-based sources of pollution.
>
> By 1993, sewage had been identified as by far the most significant pollutant. As noted in the RSP report, "the main problem affecting the Caribbean Sea are domestic sewage and solid waste." The WCR [Wider Caribbean Region] sewage problem is caused by the large number of people living along the coast, tourism, industry and ship wastes. . . . Despite knowledge of the problem in the 1980s, the situation appears no different in 2003.
>
> The WCR is one of the world's leading oil producing regions. . . . Even basic monitoring responsibilities, created under the Cartagena Convention's oil spill protocol of 1983, are not being fulfilled.
>
> Article 8 of the Convention deals with sea-bed exploitation. . . . WCR seems to have had little success in dealing with its oil pollution problems whether caused by the industry itself or by ship related activities.
>
> Article 10 requires the Parties to create specially protected areas. . . . Many of the parks created under SPAW are no more than "paper parks."
>
> Article 11 requires the development of contingency plans. This obligation was created in 1983. It has yet to occur.
>
> Article 12 requires international consultation with respect to major development projects . . . no evidence of such consultations having occurred was uncovered in the course of researching this paper.
>
> Article 14 requires the development of laws to address liability and compensation in the event of pollution damage. To date, this has not occurred.
>
> Article 15 requires institutional development and integration. Such development and integration has not yet occurred to a significant extent.
>
> Overall, as to the actual condition of the environment, there is little evidence that the situation today is different than it was twenty years ago when the Cartagena Convention was first ratified.[106]

Sheehy's concluding assessment is like the ones made regarding the Barcelona Convention and its associated protocols in the Mediterranean.

Sheehy attributed the failure in the Wider Caribbean Region to several causes: poverty leading to a lack of resources, unsustainable consumption patterns and financing problems, failed efforts to management economic development, legislative gaps, corruption, and lack of political will to deal with the issues.[107]

The UNEP RSP in the Mediterranean and Caribbean Sea regions has not yet achieved the goals or delivered the results that the RSPs and regional legal frameworks had envisaged.

The UNEP RSPs may have good intentions; however, the regions that each RSP intends to take care of seem too large, the issues that each RSP is designed to deal with seem too many, and the manner of operation seems too complicated. As indicated above, each RSP starts with a regional action plan (a soft law type of international instrument), followed by the establishment of a framework or umbrella convention and associated protocols (legally binding international instruments), and the creation of numerous coordinating units for each individual subprogram or activity. A typical organizational chart of an RSP is shown in Figure 6. This demonstrates the complexity of their operation and the associated costs.

The diversity among participating States in a UNEP RSP can further compromise its effectiveness. As has been observed: "[i]t became evident that large-scale monitoring, and the capacity thereof, did not yield desired results of immediate practical value to decision-makers."[108] Put another way, the policy intention and the mechanism design of UNEP RSPs can overwhelm the capacity of at least some participating States. In addition, some participating States, especially those developing countries, might have too high an expectation on the UNEP for financial assistance.

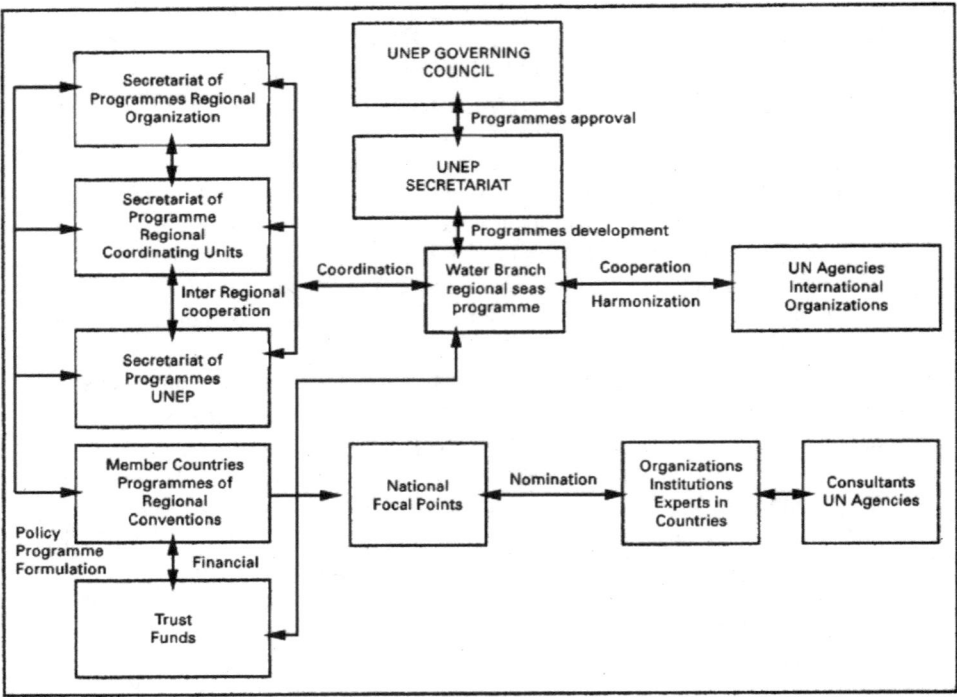

Figure 6. A typical organizational chart of a United Nations Environment Programme Regional Seas Programme (UNEP RSP). (*Source:* Reprinted from *Marine Policy* 22, no. 3, P. Akiwumi and T. Melvasalo, "UNEP's Regional Seas Programme: Approach, Experience and Future Plans," 229–234, at 232, Copyright (1998), with permission from Elsevier.)

FAO Regional Fishery Bodies and Fisheries Conservation and Management

With respect to marine living resources conservation and management, collective effort through regional cooperation is vital in a semi-enclosed sea. Similar to the marine environment protection, a regional mechanism is necessary, but too many such mechanisms are not helpful.

As stated in Article 4 of the CRFM Agreement,[109] the aim of the CRFM is to efficiently manage and sustainably develop shared, straddling or highly migratory marine and other aquatic resources. In other words, the CRFM is intended to deal with the management and sustainable development of a full spectrum of marine living resources. However, there are other regional bodies that have similar functions to the CRFM or overlapping competence over fisheries management and development in the same geographical area, such as the International Commission for the Conservation of Atlantic Tunas (ICCAT)[110] and the Western Central Atlantic Fishery Commission (WECAFC).[111] Bisessar Chakalall et al. have indicated that ICCAT is a "full" RFMO covering the entire Wider Caribbean Region and beyond, but only for tunas and tuna-like species and focusing primarily on the large commercial species. And the WECAFC provides coordination of development, information gathering, and analysis for all the countries of the Wider Caribbean, but had no management decision-making function.[112] Chakalall et al. observed that the existence of overlapping and competing arrangements for various aspects of marine governance do not provide a coherent governance framework and that this situation is unlikely to lead to the emergence of a rational, integrated governance framework.[113] Chakalall et al. termed this overlapping situation as an "institutional maze" and a figure in their paper (see Figure 7) vividly describes this "maze."

Similarly, in the Mediterranean Sea region, while the GFCM possesses a decisionmaking function with respect to the conservation and management of marine living resources, ICCAT's competence area also covers the GFCM region, even though ICCAT only deals with tunas and tuna-like species. The overlapping functions and membership between GFCM and ICCAT will inevitably create certain degree of confusion in terms of the "development, conservation, rational management and best utilization of living marine resources as well as the sustainable development of aquaculture in the Region."[114] This situation shows that the problem of institutional maze also exists in the Mediterranean Sea region regarding fisheries.

The Application of Part IX in the South China Sea

To the Chinese people and in Chinese language, the "South China Sea" is "Nan-Hai" or literally "South Sea" or "Southern Sea" since it is situated to the south of China.[115] However, there is no official geographical definition for the South Sea.[116]

A book by Fu Chün (符駿) entitled *Nan-Hai Ssu-Sha Ch'un-Tao* (南海四沙群島 *The Four Sands Islands of the South Sea*) defined the South Sea as "starting from the south mouth of the Taiwan Strait to the north, then all the way to the south until the equator, a north-east to south-west oblique rectangle."[117] Yu Kuan-Tss (俞寬賜) defined the South Sea in his book entitled *Nan-Hai Chu-Tao Ling-T'u Cheng-Tuan chih Ching-Wei yu Fa-Li* (南海諸島領土爭端之經緯與法理 *The Warp and the Woof, or the Main Points, as well as the Legal Theory of the Territorial Disputes of the South Sea Islands*) as "situating within from three degree south latitude to twenty-five degree north latitude and from one hundred degree east longitude to one hundred twenty degree east longitude."[118] The former Director-General of the Department of Land Administration of the Ministry of the Interior,

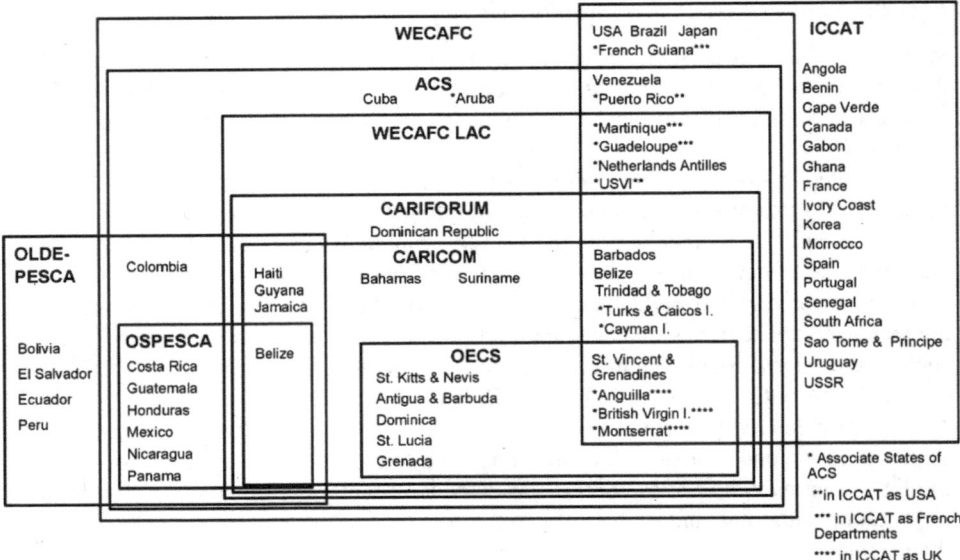

Figure 7. The membership of regional and international organizations with responsibility for fisheries management and development in the Wider Caribbean. Acronyms: WECAFC, FAO West Central Atlantic Fishery Commission; ACS, Association of Caribbean States; CARICOM, Caribbean Community and Common Market; OECS, Organization of Eastern Caribbean States; LAC, Lesser Antilles Committee; OLDEPESCA, Latin American Organization for Fishery Development; OSPESCA, Organizaci'on del Sector Pesquero y Acu'ıcola del Istmo Centroamericano; ICCAT, International Commission for the Conservation of Atlantic Tunas. (*Source:* Reprinted from *Fisheries Research* 87, Chakalall et al., "Governance of fisheries and other living marine research in the Wider Caribbean" 92–99, at 94, Copyright (2007), with permission from Elsevier.)

Chang Wei-I (張維一) offered another definition for the South Sea in his book entitled *Nan-Hai Tsu-Yuan K'ai-Fa yu Chu-Ch'uan Wei-Hu* (南海資源開發與主權維護 *The Resources Exploitaiton and Sovereignty Protection of the South Sea*):

> starting from the east along 117°50′E, or the easternmost Seahorse (or Routh) Bank (海馬灘) of the Nan-Sha (Spratly) Islands, to the west along 109°30′E, or the westernmost Vanguard Bank (萬安灘); south to 3°40′N, or the southernmost James Shoal (曾母暗沙), and north to 21°58′N (Yu Kuan-Tss' writing suggesting 21°04′N), or the North Verker Bank (北衛灘) of the Tung-Sha (Pratas) Islands. The north-south length reaches about 1,800 and some km, and the east-west span is more than 900 km, with an area of more than 3,600 thousand square km.[119]

Due to his former in-charge position in the government, Chang's definition may be the most authoritative. And, more importantly, Chang's definition is close to the general geographical understanding or perception of Chinese people over the location and extend of the South Sea. It is also roughly similar to the geographical description of South China Sea (area 6.1) given by the International Hydrographical Organization for the limits and names of subdivisions of the oceans and seas.[120] In other words, to the Chinese people and in the Chinese language, South Sea is more or less the waters surrounded by nowadays Taiwan, mainland China, Vietnam, Malaysia, and the Philippines, including the Gulf of Tonkin (東京灣或北部灣), but excluding the Gulf of Thailand (or Gulf of Siam) (泰國灣或暹羅灣).

Furthermore, a map entitled "The Location Map of the Islands in the South Sea" (南海諸島位置圖), carrying the issuance date on its left upper corner, "December of the Thirty-fifth Year of the Republic of China" (namely, December 1946), and the name of the agency that made this map on its left lower corner, "Made by the Department of Territories and Boundaries of the Ministry of the Interior" (內政部方域司製), shows the "famous" U-shaped 11 discontinued (or broken) lines with the named islands, islets, reefs, banks, and shoals within these lines and the bordering States as well.[121] See this map in Nien-Tsu Alfred Hu, "South China Sea: Troubled Waters or a Sea of Opportunity?", Figure 2, in this Special Issue. Worth noting is that the legend applied to the U-shaped lines is exactly the same as the national boundaries on land between China and Vietnam. The waters within these U-shaped lines and their adjacent waters also fit the mental image of the Chinese people on the geographical extend of the South Sea.

The South Sea fits the definition of a semi-enclosed sea as defined by Article 122 of the UNCLOS, although it possesses more than "a narrow outlet" to the seas and oceans. Like other semi-enclosed sea regions, the bordering States of the South Sea are also faced with the common problems of marine living resources conservation and management, protection of the marine environment, and joint efforts in marine scientific research. However, the problems existing in the South China Sea are further complicated by a different context from some other semi-enclosed sea regions. The South Sea has been characterized by many as a potential "flash point" due to the complexity of territorial and maritime disputes over the maritime features like islands, islets, banks, shoals, or submerged reefs. In addition, the Republic of China (or Taiwan), as one of the bordering States of the South Sea, and the one that has made early claims over all the maritime features within the U-shaped lines[122] and that has long occupied the largest island, the Tai-Ping Island (太平島 in Chinese or Itu Aba Island in English), in the Spratly Islands of the South Sea, has been excluded from almost all intergovernmental fora or mechanisms that deal with the South Sea problems over the past four decades.[123]

This section will briefly touch on the status quo in the South China Sea with respect to the efforts in relation to marine living resources conservation and management and the protection of the marine environment, followed by a discussion of new thinking on the potential to apply Article 123 of the UNCLOS in the region based on the lessons drawn from the Mediterranean and Caribbean Sea regions.

Management of Marine Living Resources

In the South China Sea region, there is no RFMO that deals with fisheries resources. The Asia-Pacific Fishery Commission (APFIC), a regional fishery body established in 1948 under the auspices of the FAO, has a wide "area of competence" that includes the "Asia Pacific Area" and covers both marine and inland aquatic resources of the Asia-Pacific area.[124] Its membership includes, inter alia, the People's Republic of China, Malaysia, the Philippines, and Vietnam.[125] Since APFIC is an FAO body, Taiwan is excluded.[126]

The APFIC Web site characterizes itself as a body designed "to improve understanding, awareness and cooperation in fisheries issues in the Asia-Pacific region."[127] The Preamble of the Agreement for the Establishment of the Asia-Pacific Fishery Commission states the original intent was that: "The contracting Governments having a mutual interest in the development and proper utilization of the living aquatic resources of the Asia-Pacific area and desiring to further the attainment of these end through international cooperation by establishment of an Asia-Pacific Fishery Commission." However, other than the functions laid down in Article IV, the Agreement does not provide for resource management decision making. The APFIC is mainly a consultative and advisory body with no competence over the management of living marine resources in the South China Sea region.

The Western and Central Pacific Fisheries Commission (WCPFC), established by the Convention for the Conservation and Management of Highly Migratory Fish Stocks in the Western and Central Pacific Ocean (WCPFC Convention)[128] which is not an FAO agreement, was specifically created for the conservation and management of highly migratory fish stocks in the western and central Pacific region. Due to difficulties in negotiating the Convention, the RFMO has an undefined western boundary of its Convention Area[129] where the conservation and management measures adopted "shall be applied throughout the range of the stocks, or to specific areas within the Convention Area, as determined by the Commission."[130] Theoretically, the WCPFC covers the South China Sea region if the regulated or targeted stocks migrate into this region; nevertheless, it deals only with the conservation and management of highly migratory species. The WCPFC was established after the adoption of the 1995 United Nations Fish Stocks Agreement;[131] thus, its legal framework allows Taiwan to participate as a member in the capacity of "fishing entity" and under the designation of Chinese Taipei.[132]

Protection of the Marine Environment

The UNEP RSP comes to the western Pacific under the East Asian Seas Programme. The UNEP has described the East Asia Seas as follows:

> East Asia's astonishing variety of political, economic and social systems is matched by its environment: ship-crowded straits, island groups, wide gulfs, shallow estuaries and some of the most heavily populated countries in the world, where millions rely on fish for much of their protein.
>
> The threats to the region are just as varied, including erosion and siltation from land development, logging and mining, blast fishing in coral reefs, conversion of mangroves, overfishing, unimpeded coastal development and disposal of untreated wastes.

Seven areas of focus were identified for the region:

- Develop and maintain a regional database (later changed to a regional metadata base).
- Promote, improve, network and maintain marine protected areas in the region.
- Implement activities to restore marine habitats.
- Assist with State of Environment reporting for agencies preparing such reports and marine and coastal assessment.
- Implement activities to reduce land-based sources of pollution.
- Encourage monitoring and environmental assessment including mapping in the region.
- Encourage and implement projects to build capacity in the member countries to counter environmental degradation and to educate all members of the community in caring for the marine resources of the region.[133]

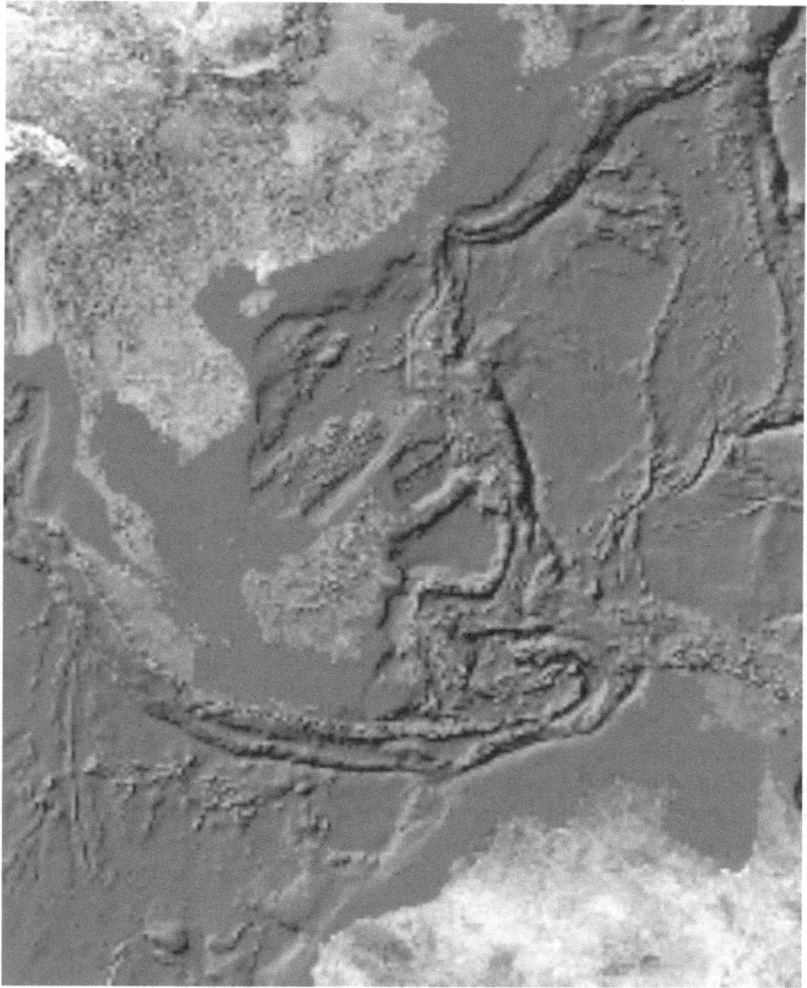

Figure 8. The area covered by the United Nations Environment Programme Regional Seas Programme (UNEP RSP) in the East Asian Seas. (*Source:* UNEP RSP Web site, at http://www.unep.org/regionalseas/programmes/unpro/eastasian/default.asp, accessed on 2009/7/19.)

The RSP covers a large area, shown in Figure 8, and the South China Sea is a subregion in the Programme.

An Action Plan for the Protection and Development of the Marine Environment and Coastal Areas of the East Asian Seas Region (the East Asian Seas Action Plan)[134] was developed and approved in 1981 stimulated by concerns on the effects and sources of marine pollution. Initially, the Action Plan involved five countries (Indonesia, Malaysia, the Philippines, Singapore, and Thailand). In 1994, it was revised to involve another five countries (Australia, Cambodia, the People's Republic of China, the Republic of Korea, and Vietnam) and to date the Action Plan still has ten member countries.[135] Thus, all the bordering States of the South China Sea, except Taiwan and Brunei, are members of the East Asian Seas Action Plan. The main components of the East Asian Seas Action

Plan are: assessment of the effects of human activities on the marine environment; control of coastal pollution, protection of mangroves, sea grasses, and coral reefs; and waste management.[136]

Among the UNEP RSPs, East Asia has steered a unique course. There is no regional convention; instead, the Programme promotes compliance with existing environmental treaties and is based on member country's goodwill.[137]

The East Asian Seas Action Plan is steered by the Coordinating Body on the Seas of East Asia (COBSEA). The COBSEA Secretariat is the lead agency of the United Nations for marine environmental matters in East Asia, responsible for coordinating the activities of all governments, nongovernmental organizations (NGOs), UN and donor agencies, and individuals in caring for the region's marine environment.[138]

There is another marine environmental program for the East Asia Seas, the Partnerships in Environmental Management for the Seas of East Asia (PEMSEA) (1999–2004),[139] which was funded by the Global Environment Fund (GEF), implemented by UN Development Programme (UNDP) and executed by the International Maritime Organization (IMO). PEMSEA was designed to build partnerships of stakeholders at the local, national, and regional levels. The project built on the results of a pilot project called the Regional Programme for Marine Pollution Prevention and Management in the East Asian Seas Region (1994–1999).[140] PEMSEA involved demonstrating the application of an integrated approach to coastal area management at a series of sites. PEMSEA had 11 participating countries: Brunei Darussalam, Cambodia, the People's Republic of China, Indonesia, Malaysia, North Korea, the Philippines, Singapore, South Korea, Thailand, and Vietnam. The project facilitated the development and the signing of the UNEP Action Plan for the Seas of East Asia.[141] PEMSEA's geographic coverage included the six subregional seas of the East Asian region, including the Yellow Sea, East China Sea, South China Sea, Sulu-Sulawesi and Indonesian Sea as well as the Gulf of Thailand. They are all semi-enclosed with a total sea area of 7 million square kilometers, a coastline of 234,000 kilometers, and a total watershed area of about 8.6 million square kilometers. These seas are ecologically and economically important both regionally and globally.[142] Again, Taiwan has been excluded from participating in this project due to political reasons.

Other Mechanisms of Regional Cooperation in the South Sea Region

The potential for tension arising from territorial and maritime disputes over the insular features and the need for regional cooperation to deal with problems of common concern in the South China Sea region has given rise to the development of other regional mechanism. Tables 1 and 2 briefly describe some of the mechanisms, including nongovernmental (second track) and intergovernmental (first track) processes, that are relevant to but not directly focused on regional cooperation in marine living resources conservation and management, and marine environment protection.

New Thinking on the Future Cooperation in the South China Sea

Part IX of the 1982 UNCLOS, especially Article 123, was intended to provide an obligation of cooperation on Parties bordering an enclosed or semi-enclosed sea to manage the activities occurring in their shared and common marine environment and to deal with their interrelations. The bordering States of the South China Sea should apply this provision in managing this semi-enclosed sea. While certain things have been done and certain organizations or mechanisms have been established, the perspective of future cooperation in the

Table 1
Regional cooperation mechanism in the South China Sea: Nongovernmental

Second track	Date	Type	ROC	PRC	Vietnam	Malaysia	Philippines	Brunei	Other participating countries	Purpose
SEAPOL	1981 Defunct now	Nongov't network of scholars, gov't officials, and individuals	√	√	√	√	√		The work covers Southeast Asia and APEC marine affairs	Facilitate the exchange of information and ideas related to current ocean law, policy, and management in Southeast Asia and APEC
Workshop on Managing Political Conflicts in the South China Sea	1990	Nonofficial network	√	√	√	√	√	√	Informal working group composed of individuals from South China Sea countries	Sponsor a series of Workshops on Managing Potential Conflicts in the South China Sea
CSCAP	1993	Nongov't network of scholars, gov't officials, and individuals	√	√	√	√	√	√	16 Other members	To submit policy recommendations to governments in the region, particularly in the promotion of confidence building

Abbreviations: ROC, Republic of China; PRC, People's Republic of China; SEAPOL, Southeast Asian Programme in Ocean Laws, Policy and Management; APEC, Asia-Pacific Economic Cooperation; CSCAP, Council for Security Cooperation in Asia Pacific.
Source: Information taken and modified from Table 5 of UNEP, *Review of the Legal Aspects of Environmental Management in the South China Sea and Gulf of Thailand*, UNEP/GEF/SCS Technical Publication No. 9 (2007), 20.

Table 2
Regional cooperation mechanism in the South China Sea: Intergovernmental

First track	Date	Type	ROC	PRC	Vietnam	Malaysia	Philippines	Brunei	Other participating countries	Purpose
ASEAN	1978	Sub-regional intergov't organization				✓	✓	✓	6 Other members	ASEAN Environment Programme
PEMSEA	1994	Intergov't project		✓	✓	✓	✓	✓	6 Other members	ICM
UNEP/GEF South China Sea Project	2001	Intergov't project		✓	✓	✓	✓		3 Other members	Conservation of habitats; fisheries; land-based pollution
UNEP East Asian Seas Action Plan	1981	Intergov't programme		✓	✓	✓	✓		5 Other members	Coordinate the activities of governments, UN and donor agencies, and communities in marine environment of East Asian Seas
IOC-WESTPC	1979	Intergov't programme		✓	✓	✓	✓	✓	13 Other members	Marine scientific research; workshops; training, etc.
Plan of Action on Sustainable Fisheries	2001	Regional intergov't resolution			✓	✓	✓	✓	5 Other members	Sustainable/responsible fisheries
ADB	1986	Intergov't organization	✓	✓	✓	✓	✓		56 Other members	ADB Environment Programme

Abbreviations: ROC, Republic of China; PRC, People's Republic of China; ASEAN, Association of Southeast Asian Nations; PEMSEA, Partnerships in Environmental Management for the Seas of East Asia; UNEP, United Nations Environment Programme; GEF, Global Environment Fund; IOC-WESTPC, Intergovernmental Oceanographic Commission (of UNESCO) Subcommission for the Western Pacific; ADB, Asian Development Bank; ICM, integrated coastal management.

Source: Information taken and modified from Table 5 of UNEP, *Review of the Legal Aspects of Environmental Management in the South China Sea and Gulf of Thailand*, UNEP/GEF/SCS Technical Publication No. 9 (2007), 20.

South China Sea region is not very promising, especially following the recent rounds of refutation between or among the bordering States with respect to their individual claims of outer continental shelf to the UN Commission on the Limits of the Continental Shelf (CLCS) during 2009.[143] Nevertheless, what lessons can be drawn from the experiences of practice in the Mediterranean and Caribbean Sea regions that may have application in the South China Sea?

One is that the involvement of the UN system, be it UNEP or FAO, will not guarantee the success of regional cooperation. This is more true in the South China Sea region since Taiwan, a substantive actor, will be automatically excluded from any activity of the United Nations or any of its Specialized Agencies.

Another lesson is that a large geographical coverage, a great number of participating States, and a high degree of diversity among participating States can result in difficulties in the operation of any regional cooperation program. The number of bordering States in the South China Sea is much fewer than in the cases in the Mediterranean and Caribbean Sea regions. Although diversity exists among the boarding States of the South China Sea, a small club is conceivably more likely to be successful than a big club. The solution to the South Sea problems seems better left to these fewer States to find.

At the same time, whether it is better to invite or allow the involvement of other interested States or international organizations, as envisaged by Article 123, paragraph 3 of the UNCLOS, is also questionable. Miller's comment on the Action Plan for the Caribbean Environment Programme is worthy of note: "Counterpart contributions and contributions from other organizations . . . sometimes have to be targeted to satisfy the interests of the donor rather than the immediate concerns of the Caribbean Environment Programme."[144] Since some extraregional interested States or international organizations will have their own agenda when participating in a regional cooperation program or mechanism, either from a financing or political perspective, the regional countries may suffer from the pull of these extraregional actors.

Another lesson from the Mediterranean and Caribbean Sea regions shows that a complicated mechanism with too many agenda issues and too high of an expectation with respect to lofty goals can overwhelm the capacities and political will of participating countries. Article 123 envisages regional cooperation "directly or through an appropriate regional organization." Thus, bilateral cooperation and multilateral regional approaches should not be mutually exclusive. An appropriate regional organization supported by a multilateral institutional agreement for simple issues or a single purpose may be desirable in the South China Sea region. In the initial stage, the issues being targeted should not be too complicated and the goals not too lofty. It is advisable that the bordering States in the South China Sea region start with issues of low political sensitivity, simplicity in implementation, and with a common need, such as conservation and management of fisheries resources, protection of the marine environment, and joint efforts in marine scientific studies.

The key question left unsolved is the political will of other bordering States of the South China Sea to treat Taiwan as an equal partner in bilateral or multilateral engagement in the region. If the limited number of partners possess a genuine political will to cooperate among themselves for the common good of the region and disallow the territorial or maritime disputes to hamper their desire for cooperation on the nonterritorial issues laid out in Article 123 of the UNCLOS, such as marine living resources conservation and management, marine environment protection, and joint marine scientific research, then there is a hope for regional cooperation and development.

Notes

1. United Nations Convention on the Law of the Sea, 1833 *U.N.T.S.* 397.
2. Regarding the evolution of these provisions at the Third United Nations Conference on the Law of the Sea, see Satya N. Nandan and Shabtai Rosenne, eds., *United Nations Convention on the Law of the Sea 1982: A Commentary*, Vol. III (The Hague: Martinus Nijhoff, 1995), 343–368. For a discussion on the weakness and problems of this Part, especially during the earlier stage of negotiations, see Budislav Vukas, "Enclosed and Semi-enclosed Sea," in *The Law of the Sea: Selected Writings*, ed. Budislav Vukas (Leiden, the Netherlands: Martinus Nijhoff, 2004), 263–279.
3. Nandan and Rosenne, supra note 2, at 343.
4. Although Vukas, supra note 2, at 271, indicated that the Mediterranean Sea (and its parts: the Adriatic, Aegean, and Black Seas), the Caribbean Sea, the South China Sea, and several others were "most frequently cited as belonging to" the category of enclosed and semi-enclosed seas, the South China Sea has more than one outlet connecting to another sea or the ocean and, thus, may be said to be a deviate from the definition in Article 122.
5. Art. 70, para. 2 of the 1982 UNCLOS, supra note 1.
6. Budislav Vukas, "The Mediterranean: An Enclosed or Semi-enclosed Sea?" in Vukas, supra note 2, at 287, stated that "[t]he term 'other interested States' should be understood as meaning, in the first place, all other States users of an enclosed or semi-enclosed sea" and "as 'interested international organizations' competent universal as well as regional organizations should be considered."
7. The 21 States that have a coastline on the Mediterranean Sea are: Spain, France, Monaco, Italy, Malta, Slovenia, Croatia, Bosnia and Herzegovina, Montenegro, Albania, Greece, Turkey, Cyprus, Syria, Lebanon, Israel, Egypt, Libya, Tunisia, Algeria, and Morocco.
8. M. A. Massoud, M. D. Scrimshaw, and J. N. Lester, "Qualitative Assessment of the Effectiveness of the Mediterranean Action Plan: Wastewater Management in the Mediterranean Region," *Ocean and Coastal Management* 46 (2003): 875–899, at 876.
9. Whether the "secondary" seas, such as the Adriatic Sea, the Black Sea, and the Aegean Sea, should be considered as separate semi-enclosed seas or the constituent seas of the Mediterranean Sea is not pursued here. As noted by one author, "[a]lthough the Black Sea and its coastal States have been excluded from some forms of co-operation among the rest of the Mediterranean States (e.g. from the Mediterranean Action Plan), it is an undeniable fact that the Black Sea is only the most eastern part of the Mediterranean Sea." See Vukas, supra note 6, at 284, especially n. 10.
10. Continental Shelf Convention; 499 *U.N.T.S.* 311; Territorial Sea and Contiguous Zone Convention, 516 *U.N.T.S.* 205; High Seas Convention, 450 *U.N.T.S.* 11; and Fishing and Conservation of the Living Resources of the High Seas, 559 *U.N.T.S.* 285.
11. The Constitution of the FAO is available at the Web site of the FAO Legal Office at www.fao.org/Legal/treaties/treaty-e.htm. Regional fishery bodies established under the FAO Constitution are categorized by the FAO as being FAO statutory (regional fishery) bodies.
12. The text of Agreement for the Establishment of the General Fisheries Council for the Mediterranean (the 1949 GFCM Agreement), 126 *U.N.T.S.* 237. For the official record on the approval of the substantive provisions of the draft agreement for the establishment of GFCM, see *Report of the Conference of FAO, Fifth Session*, 21 November–6 December 1949, Washington, DC, available at www.fao.org/docrep/x5579E/x5579e0a.htm#vii, "VII. Constitutional, Administrative, and Financial Questions." The full report can be found at www.fao.org/docrep/x5579E/x5579e00.HTM (accessed 20 June 2009, downloaded 17 March 2010).
13. The 1963 revised version is available at eelink.net/~asilwildlife/medfish.html; the amendments of 1976 are available at untreaty.un.org/unts/1_60000/30/3/00058135.pdf; and the 1997 revised version of the Agreement of GFCM is available at ftp.fao.org/FI/DOCUMENT/gfcm/web/GFCM_Agreement.pdf (accessed 22 June 2009).
14. See "About GFCM," available at www.gfcm.org/gfcm/about/en; and under the item "status," available at www.gfcm.org/gfcm/about/4/en (accessed 20 June 2009).

For the prerevised version of the 1997 Agreement for the Establishment of the General Fisheries Council for the Mediterranean, see the *Report of the Twenty-second Session of the General Fisheries*

Council for the Mediterranean, Rome, 13–16 October 1997 (Rome: Food and Agriculture Organization of the United Nations, 1997), Appendix D: Agreement of GFCM, which can be downloaded as a pdf file available at the GFCM Web site at www.gfcm.org/gfcm/topic/16091/en (accessed 20 June 2009).

15. These 22 States are: Albania, Algeria, Bulgaria, Croatia, Cyprus, Egypt, France, Greece, Israel, Italy, Lebanon, Libya, Malta, Monaco, Montenegro, Morocco, Romania, Slovenia, Spain, Syria, Tunisia, and Turkey. See Web site of the GFCM at www.gfcm.org/gfcm/about/5/en (accessed 21 June 2009).

16. The 1997 GFCM Agreement, supra note 13, art. III, paras. 1 (a) to (h):
  (a) to keep under review the state of these resources, including their abundance and the level of their exploitation, as well as the state of the fisheries based thereon;
  (b) to formulate and recommend, in accordance with the provisions of Article V, appropriate measures:
    (i) for the conservation and rational management of living marine resources, including measures:
      — regulating fishing methods and fishing gear,
      — prescribing the minimum size for individuals of specified species,
      — establishing open and closed fishing seasons and areas,
      — regulating the amount of total catch and fishing effort and their allocation among Members,
    (ii) for the implementation of these recommendations;
  (c) to keep under review the economic and social aspects of the fishing industry and recommend any measures aimed at its development;
  (d) to encourage, recommend, coordinate and, as appropriate, undertake training and extension activities in all aspects of fisheries;
  (e) to encourage, recommend, coordinate and, as appropriate, undertake research and development activities, including cooperative projects in the areas of fisheries and the protection of living marine resources;
  (f) to assemble, publish or disseminate information regarding exploitable living marine resources and fisheries based on these resources;
  (g) to promote programmes for marine and brackish water aquaculture and coastal fisheries enhancement;
  (h) to carry out such other activities as may be necessary for the Commission to achieve its purpose as defined above.

17. For a more detailed description of the organization of the GFCM, see GFCM Web site, especially "Organigram," available at www.gfcm.org/gfcm/about/6/en.

18. The leaflet can be downloaded from the GFCM Web site at ftp.fao.org/FI/DOCUMENT/gfcm/web/GFCM_leaflet.pdf.

19. The regional projects of the GFCM are explained at the GFCM Web site at www.gfcm.org/gfcm/topic/16108/en.

20. See the IATTC Web site at www.iattc.org.

21. See GFCM, 33rd Session, Tunis, Tunisia, 23–27 March 2009, "Intersessional Activities," Doc. GFCM:XXXIII/2009/2, 2 and 3, available at 151.1.154.86/meetingdocs/2009/GFCM_33/pdf/GFCM33_2009_2_e.pdf (accessed 21 June 2009).

22. Agenda 21, adopted on 14 June 1992 by the UN Conference on Environment and Development, U.N. Doc. A/Conf.151/26, Vols. I–IV.

23. Code of Conduct for Responsible Fisheries, available at www.fao.org/docrep/005/v9878e/v9878eoo.htm.

24. The United Nations Environment Programme (UNEP) was established after the 1972 United Nations Conference on the Human Environment held at Stockholm from 5 to 16 June 1972 and through UN General Assembly Resolution 2997, adopted on 15 December 1972.

25. See the Web site of the UNEP Mediterranean Action Plan at www.unepmap.org/index.php, especially the entries of "About MAP" and "The Action Plan" (accessed 11 July 2009).

26. See *Report of the Intergovernmental Meeting on the Protection of the Mediterranean, Barcelona, 28 January to 4 February 1975*, Doc. UNEP/WG.2/5, 11 February 1975, available at 195.97.36.231/acrobatfiles/75WG2_5_Eng.pdf (accessed 11 July 2009). The 5-page Action Plan is an annex to this report. The style of the Annex looks like a combination of a resolution and a final act coming from an intergovernmental meeting.

27. The cited decisions are taken from the Decision 8(II), Approval of activities within the environment programme, in the light, inter alia of their implications for the Fund programme, Section A. I. Priority Subject Areas of the Programme, 4. Oceans, paragraphs (a), (b) and (c), especially (c) referring to the Mediterranean as the "high priority." See *United Nations Environment Programme Report of the Governing Council on the Work of Its Second Session 11–22 March 1974*, 63, available at www.unep.org/resources/gov/prev_docs/74_05_GC2_report_K7409625.pdf (accessed 10 August 2009).

28. These 16 States were: Algeria, Egypt, France, Greece, Israel, Italy, Lebanon, the Libyan Arab Republic, Malta, Monaco, Morocco, Spain, the Syrian Arab Republic, Tunisia, Turkey, and Yugoslavia.

29. *Report of the Intergovernmental Meeting on the Protection of the Mediterranean*, supra note 26, para. 21.

30. *Ibid.*, para. 22.

31. *Ibid.*, para. 23.

32. *Report of the Intergovernmental Meeting on the Protection of the Mediterranean*, supra note 26, para. 24.

33. *Ibid.*, para. 18.

34. The quoted phrase is taken from *ibid.*, Action Plan, sec. III, subsec. A, para. 1.

35. *Ibid.*, para. 49.

36. *Ibid.*, para. 78.

37. *Final Act of the Conference of Plenipotentiaries of the Coastal States of the Mediterranean Region for the Protection of the Mediterranean Sea 1976*, available at 195.97.36.231/acrobatfiles/76CONF1_Final_Act_Eng.pdf (accessed 12 July 2009).

38. The 16 participating countries were: Cyprus, Egypt, France, Greece, Israel, Italy, Lebanon, the Libyan Arab Republic, Malta, Monaco, Morocco, Spain, the Syrian Arab Republic, Tunisia, Turkey, and Yugoslavia. Albania and Algeria were absent.

39. See *Final Act of the Conference of Plenipotentiaries*, supra note 37, at 5–6.

40. Convention for the Protection of the Mediterranean Sea Against Pollution (1976 Barcelona Convention), *I.L.M.* 15 (1976) 290.

41. Protocol for the Prevention of Pollution of the Mediterranean Sea by Dumping from Ships and Aircraft, *I.L.M.* 15 (1976) 300.

42. Protocol on Co-operation in Combatting Pollution of the Mediterranean Sea by Oil and Other Harmful Substances in Cases of Emergency, *International Legal Materials*, 15 (1976) 306.

43. See Resolution 2 Concerning Interim Arrangements, *Final Act*, supra note 37.

44. *Ibid.*, Resolution 4 Concerning the Establishment of a Committee of Experts on an Inter-State Guarantee Fund for the Mediterranean Sea Area.

45. *Ibid.*, Resolutions 7 and 8.

46. *Ibid.*, Resolution 9.

47. Paragraphs 1 and 2 of the Preamble of the Barcelona Convention, supra note 40.

48. See *Final Act of the Conference of Plenipotentiaries on the Amend[e]ments to the Convention for the Protection of the Mediterranean Sea Against Pollution, to the Protocol for the Prevention of Pollution of the Mediterranean Sea by Dumping from Ships and Aircraft and on the Protocol Concerning Specially Protected Areas and Biological Diversity in the Mediterranean*, available at 195.97.36.231/dbases/webdocs/BCP/95IG6_7_Eng.pdf (accessed 12 July 2009).

49. The 1995 amended Barcelona Convention is available at www.unep.ch/regionalseas/regions/med/t_barcel.htm. The amended Barcelona Convention entered into force on 9 July 2004.

50. See Amendments to Dumping Protocol, available at the Web site of the UNEP Mediterranean Action Plan at www.unepmap.org/index.php?module:content2&catid=001001001. The amendments are not in force.

51. Protocol Concerning Specially Protected Areas and Biological Diversity in the Mediterranean, 2102 *U.N.T.S.* 203.

52. Protocol Concerning Mediterranean Specially Protected Areas, 1425 *U.N.T.S.* 160.

53. *Final Act*, supra note 48, at 13, para. 9, subpara. 6.

54. Article 1, para. 2 of the Barcelona Convention, supra note 49.

55. See MAP Phase II as Appendix I contained in the Annex to the Resolution I in the Final Act of the 1995 Conference of the Plenipotentiaries, supra note 48.

56. See the status of the Convention and the seven Protocols, available at www.unepmap.org/index.php?module=content2&catid=001001001 (accessed 19 July 2009).

57. See, generally, Massoud et al., supra note 8, at 882–884.

58. See the entry of "Caribbean," available at the Web site of answer.com at www.answers.com/topic/caribbean-sea (accessed 8 August 2009).

59. See the Web site of the Caribbean Community (CARICOM) Secretariat, available at www.caricom.org/jsp/community/original_treaty.jsp?menu=community (accessed 8 August 2009). The Treaty of Chaguaramas, 946 *U.N.T.S.* 17, was signed by Barbados, Guyana, Jamaica, and Trinidad and Tobago on 4 July 1973 and came into effect on 1 August 1973. The Caribbean Community and the Caribbean Common Market replaced the Caribbean Free Trade Association in May 1974.

The Treaty of Chaguaramas created the Caribbean Community as a separate legal entity from the Common Market. The legal separation of these two institutions was emphasized by two discrete legal instruments: the Treaty Establishing the Caribbean Community and the Agreement Establishing the Common Market (which was later annexed to the Treaty and designated the Common Market Annex). This institutional arrangement facilitated States joining the Community without becoming Parties to the Common Market regime.

In addition to economic issues, the Community instrument addressed issues of foreign policy coordination and functional cooperation. Issues of economic integration, particularly those related to trade arrangements, were addressed in the Common Market Annex. Because of this juridically separate identity of the regional common market, it was possible for the Bahamas to become a member of the Community in 1983 without joining the Common Market.

In 2001, the original Treaty was revised and designated as the "Revised Treaty of Chaguaramas Establishing the Caribbean Community Including the CARICOM Single Market and Economy" in order to deepen regional economic integration through the establishment of the CARICOM Single Market and Economy (CSME).

60. For a brief history of CFRAMP, see Milton O. Haughton, Robin Mahon, Patrick McConney, G. Andre Kong, and Anthony Mills, "Establishment of the Caribbean Regional Fisheries Mechanism," *Marine Policy* 28 (2004): 351–359, at 352–354.

61. The text of the Agreement Establishing the Caribbean Regional Fisheries Mechanism, 2002, is available at www.caricom-fisheries.com/website_content/main/agreement_establishing_the_crfm.pdf (accessed 8 August 2009).

62. *Ibid.*, art. 7, para. 3.

63. *Ibid.*, arts. 8 and 9.

64. *Ibid.*, arts. 10 and 11.

65. *Ibid.*, art. 12, para. 1.

66. *Ibid.*, art. 12, para. 3.

67. *Ibid.*, art. 13(a).

68. A short history about the UNEP's effort in initiating and formulating a regional environment program in the Caribbean is provided in UNEP, *Action Plan for the Caribbean Environment Programme*, UNEP Regional Seas Reports and Studies No. 26, 1983, Preface, i–ii, available at www.unep.org/regionalseas/Publications/Reports/RSRS/pdfs/rsrs026.pdf (accessed 12 July 2009).

69. *Ibid.*, the Action Plan is at 1–12, and the Resolution is at 13–16.

70. *Ibid.*, at 1, para. 2.

71. *Ibid.*, at 1, para. 1.
72. *Ibid.*, at 1, para. 3.
73. *Ibid.*, at 2, paras. 5 and 6.
74. *Ibid.*, at 2, para. 8. The components of the Caribbean Action Plan are as follows:

Introduction
Environmental Assessment and Management
General, Pollution control, Coastal areas, Fisheries, Watersheds, Natural disasters, Energy, Human settlements, Tourism, Environmental health
Education, Training and Development of Human Resources
Supporting Measures Institutional arrangements, Financial arrangements, Regional legal agreement

75. *Ibid.*, at 12, para. 76.
76. *Ibid.*, at 14, para. 5.
77. See the Final Act of the 1983 Conference of Plenipotentiaries on the Protection and Development of the Marine Environment of the Wider Caribbean Region, available at www.cep.unep.org/pubs/legislation/cart2.html (accessed 12 July 2009).
78. Convention for the Protection and Development of the Marine Environment of the Wider Caribbean Region (the 1983 Cartegena Convention), *I.L.M.* 22 (1983) 221.
79. Protocol Concerning Co-operation in Combatting Oil Spills in the Wider Caribbean Region, *I.L.M.* 22 (1983) 240.
80. See the Resolutions adopted by the Conference, supra note 77.
81. See "About the Cartagena Convention," available at the UNEPCEP Web site at www.cep.unep.org/cartagena-convention/ (accessed 12 July 2009).
82. *Ibid.*
83. Articles 1 and 2 of the Cartagena Convention, supra note 78.
84. *Ibid.*, art.10.
85. Protocol Concerning Specially Protected Areas and Wildlife (SPAW) in the Wider Caribbean Region, 2180 *U.N.T.S.* Reg. A-25974.
86. See Protocol Concerning Pollution from Land-Based sources and Activities (LBS Protocol), available at cep.unep.org/repcar/lbs-protocol-en.pdf.
87. The Web site of UNEP CEP states that "The Cartagena Convention has been ratified by 23 United Nations Member States in the Wider Caribbean Region." However, after a careful counting of the States that have ratified or acceded to the Cartagena Convention and the Oil Spills Protocol, based on the table of "Status of the Cartagena Convention and Protocols" at the Web site, there are only 22 States that have ratified or acceded to the Convention and the Oil Spills Protocol. The table is available at www.cep.unep.org/cartagena-convention/about-the-cartagena-convention#status (accessed 11 August 2009).
88. See the UNEP Web site at www.unep.org/regionalseas/programmes/actionplans/default.asp (accessed 20 July 2009).
89. *Ibid.*
90. Peter Hulm, "The Regional Seas Program: What Fate for UNEP's Crown Jewels?" *Ambio* 12, no. 1 (1983): 2–13, at 2.
91. *Ibid.*, at 5.
92. *Ibid.*
93. See the UNEP Web site, supra note 86.
94. Sofia Frantzi and Jon C. Lovett, "Is Science the Driving Force in the Operation of Environmental Regimes? A Case Study of the Mediterranean Action Plan," *Ocean and Coastal Management* 51 (2008): 229–245, at 243.
95. *Ibid.*, at 242–243.
96. *Ibid.*, at 244.
97. Protocol for the Protection of the Mediterranean Against Pollution from Land-Based Sources, 1328 *U.N.T.S.* 119. The Protocol was amended in 1996. The revised is available at www.unep.ch/regionalseas/main/med/mlbsprot.html.

98. M. A. Massoud et al., supra note 8, at 894.
99. *Ibid.*, at 895.
100. *Ibid.*
101. Marian A. L. Miller, "Protecting the Marine Environment of the Wider Caribbean Region: The Challenge of Institution-Building," *Green Globe Yearbook 1996*, 37–45, at 42–43.
102. *Ibid.*, at 42.
103. *Ibid.*, at 42–43.
104. International Convention for the Prevention of Pollution from Ships, 1973, and the Protocol of Amendment, 1978, 1340 *U.N.T.S.* 61.
105. Benedict Sheehy, "International Marine Environment Law: A Case Study in the Wider Caribbean Region," *Georgetown International Environmental Law Review* 16 (2004): 441–472.
106. *Ibid.*, at 457–461.
107. *Ibid.*, at 461–464.
108. P. Akiwumi and T. Melvasalo, "UNEP's Regional Seas Programme: Approach, Experience and Future Plans," *Marine Policy* 22 (1998): 229–234, at 232.
109. CRFM Agreement, supra note 61.
110. See the Web site of ICCAT at www.iccat.int/en/ for its competence and convention area.
111. See the Web site of the UN FAO "Regional Fishery Bodies Summary Description" for a description of the WECAFC, available at www.fao.org/fishery/rfb/wecafc/en (accessed 8 August 2009).
112. Bisessar Chakalall, Robin Mahon, Patrick McConney, Leonard Nurse, and Derrick Oderson, "Governance of Fisheries and Other Living Marine Resources in the Wider Caribbean," *Fisheries Research* 87 (2007): 92–99, at 95.
113. *Ibid.*, at 94.
114. The quoted phrase is the purpose of the GFCM on the FAO Web site, available at www.fao.org/fishery/org/gfcm_inst/en, or as provided for by Article III, paragraph 1 of the GFCM Agreement, supra note 13.
115. Similarly, the "East China Sea" is "Dung-Hai" or "East Sea" to the Chinese people and in the Chinese language.
116. In the remainder of this article, South Sea and South China Sea are used interchangeably.
117. Fu Chün (符駿), *Nan-Hai Ssu-Sha Ch'un-Tao* (南海四沙群島 *The Four Sands Islands of the South Sea*) (Taipei, Taiwan: San-Min Books, June 1982), 11.
118. Yu Kuan-Tss (俞寬賜), *Nan-Hai Chu-Tao Ling-T'u Cheng-Tuan chih Ching-Wei yu Fa-Li* (南海諸島領土爭端之經緯與法理 *The Warp and the Woof, or the Main Points, as well as the Legal Theory of the Territorial Disputes of the South Sea Islands*) (Taipei, Taiwan: National Institute for Compilation and Translation, 2000), 1.
119. Chang Wei-I (張維一), *Nan-Hai Tsu-Yuan K'ai-Fa yu Chu-Ch'uan Wei-Hu* (南海資源開發與主權維護 *The Resources Exploitation and Sovereignty Protection of the South Sea*) (Taipei County, Taiwan: P'an Shih Library, December 1994), 1.
120. See Chris Rahman and Martin Tsamenyi, "A Strategic Perspective on Security and Naval Issues in the South China Sea," in the next Special Issue II, for a more detailed description and related map.
121. With respect to the 1947 ROC South China Sea map, and the ROC's early claims over the South China sea, see Nien-Tsu A. Hu, "South China Sea: Troubled Waters or a Sea of Opportunity" in this Special Issue.
122. *Ibid.*
123. See, however, Yann-huei Song, "The South China Sea Workshop Process and Taiwan's Participation," in this Special Issue.
124. See a summary description of the APFIC available at the FAO Web site at www.fao.org/fishery/rfb/apfic/en (accessed 12 August 2009).
125. For all of the members, see *ibid.* Others include Australia, the People's Republic of Bangladesh, Cambodia, France, India, Indonesia, Japan, the Republic of Korea, Malaysia, Myanmar,

Nepal, New Zealand, Pakistan, Sri Lanka, the Kingdom of Thailand, the United Kingdom, and the United States.

126. Article 1, paragraph 2 of the Agreement for the Establishment of the Asia-Pacific Fishery Commission, 120 *U.N.T.S.* 59, states: "The Members of the Commission shall be such Member Nations and Associate Members of the Organization (note: here means the FAO) and such non-member States of the Organization as are Members of the United Nations, or any of its Specialized Agencies or the International Atomic Energy Agency that accept this Agreement in accordance with the provisions of Article X thereof."

127. APFIC Web site, available at www.apfic.org/ (accessed 13 August 2009).

128. The WCPFC Convention was adopted on 5 September 2000 and entered into force on 19 June 2004, *I.L.M.* 40 (2000) 278.

129. For the map of WCPFC Convention Area, see the WCPFC Web site at www.wcpfc.int/doc/convention-area-map (accessed 13 August 2009).

130. Article 3, paragraph 3 of the WCPFC Convention, supra note 126.

131. U.N. Fish Stocks Agreement, 2167 *U.N.T.S.* 3.

132. Regarding the legal concept and practice of the term "fishing entities," see *Ocean Development and International Law* 37, no. 2 (2006), Special Issue: The Concept of Fishing Entities in International Law: A Decade of Practice. For Taiwan's practice, see Nien-Tsu Alfred Hu, "Fishing Entities: Their Emergence, Evolution, and Practice from Taiwan's Perspective," in *ibid*., at 149–183, and other articles in the same issue.

133. 1. See a summary description of the East Asian Seas Programme at the UNEP RSP Web site at www.unep.org/regionalseas/programmes/unpro/eastasian/default.asp (accessed 19 July 2009).

134. See the 1981 Action Plan for the Protection and Development of the Marine and Coastal Areas of the East Asian Region at www.cobsea.org/documents/action_plan/ActionPlan1983.pdf (accessed 13 August 2009).

135. The revised Action Plan is designated as the "Action Plan for the Protection and Sustainable Development of the Marine and Coastal Areas of the East Asian Region," available at www.cobsea.org/documents/action_plan/ActionPlan1994.pdf (accessed 13 August 2009).

136. Information retrieved from www.cobsea.org/aboutcobsea/background.html (accessed 13 August 2009).

137. *Ibid*.

138. *Ibid*.

139. See the PEMSEA Web site at pemsea.org (accessed 13 August 2009).

140. UNEP, *Review of the Legal Aspects of Environmental Management in the South China Sea and Gulf of Thailand*, UNEP/GEF/SCS Technical Publication No. 9, 2007, 19. This publication is available at www.unepscs.org/SCS_Documents/showdown/1959.html (accessed 30 July 2009).

141. *Ibid*.

142. Information available at the PEMSEA Web site at the page "The Seas of East Asia and PEMSEA Sites," supra note 136.

143. See relevant submissions made to the CLCS by bordering States of the South China Sea and reacting communications delivered to the UN Secretary-General and the CLCS at the CLCS Web site at www.un.org/Depts/los/clcs_new/commission_submissions.htm. Since Taiwan does not have access to the UN system, Taiwan's Ministry of Foreign Affairs made statements on behalf of the ROC Government. See, for example, Statement by the ROC Ministry of Foreign Affairs Concerning Malaysia-Vietnam Joint Submission to the CLCS, 11 May 2009, and Declaration of the Republic of China on the Outer Limits of Its Continental Shelf, 12 May 2009, available at www.mofa.gov.tw. See also Nien-Tsu A. Hu, "South China Sea: Troubled Waters or a Sea of Opportunity," in this Special Issue.

144. Miller, supra note 101, at 43.

Post-2009: An Overview of Recent Developments Concerning the South China Sea

NIEN-TSU ALFRED HU

Director and Professor, The Center for Marine Policy Studies
Professor, College of Social Sciences
National Sun Yat-sen University
Kaohsiung City, Taiwan, Republic of China

and

TED L. McDORMAN

Professor, Faculty of Law
University of Victoria
Victoria, British Columbia
Canada

Introduction

There is no question that the conflicting claims to islands and ocean areas within the South China Sea has dominated almost all discussions and undermined most attempts at regional cooperation on marine matters in the South China Sea. The bases of the legal/political arguments for the claims of Brunei, China (People's Republic of China and the Republic of China), Malaysia, the Philippines and Vietnam over the islands and ocean areas within the South China Sea, whether it be historic usage, discovery, occupation, proximity or a combination of these and other arguments, are well-known.[1] The activities of the various actors respecting the islands and ocean areas have been extensively documented and analyzed.[2] It is widely acknowledged that the 2002 Declaration on the Conduct of the Parties in the South China Sea involving the Association of South East Asian Nations (ASEAN) and the People's Republic of China[3] has had a stabilizing effect on State actions within the South China Sea[4] without, however, yielding much beyond a maintenance of the *status quo* respecting the conflicting ocean and insular claims. Subsequent to the Declaration there have been activities and statements that have provoked protests over interference with sovereignty and that the activity/statement is straying from the principles in the Declaration.[5] The South China Sea situation is further complicated by the interactions between the "two Chinas" – the People's Republic of China (PRC) and the Republic of China (ROC or Taiwan). While there has been a congruence of position across the Taiwan Strait on South China Sea matters,[6] Taiwan is an actor in the South China Sea, if for no other reason, that it occupies the largest of the

Spratly Islands – Itu Aba or the Tai-Ping Island.[7] Since the commencement in 2008 of Ma Ying-Jeou's Presidency, there has been a generally amicable political atmosphere across the Taiwan Strait. This has led to the PRC and Taiwan engaging in unprecedented levels of cooperation on the South China Sea issues, such as, a jointly proposed program of activity in a regional, multilateral, second-track forum (namely, the Workshops on Managing Potential Conflicts in the South China Sea), a jointly published regional situation assessment report[8] through a bilateral mechanism, and confidence building measures informally proposed by various scholars from both sides.

Apart from the intra- and extra-regional State actors that have shaped the situation in the South China Sea region, a non-State body, the Commission on the Limits of the Continental Shelf (CLCS) has also influenced recent developments in the region. While States understand that the CLCS is not a forum to settle disputes involving maritime claims and/or delimitation between or among States, it is inevitable that in their submissions to the CLCS that States have asserted and accentuated claims that may overlap with claims of other States. This has happened in the South China Sea.

This chapter provides information on new developments as well as a legal and policy overview analysis regarding South China Sea issues that have arisen subsequent to the writing and publication of the other chapters in this collection which was published in the Special Issue of *Ocean Development and International Law* entitled "Issues in the South China Sea" in mid-2010.

2009

Submissions, Legislation and Official Communications

In 2009 the focus of attention on the South China Sea moved from the water to the United Nations and specifically to the CLCS, a body of geoscience experts established pursuant to the U.N. Convention on the Law of the Sea (the LOS Convention)[9] to provide assistance to States regarding the application of the complex criteria set out in Article 76 of the Convention for the establishment by States of their outer limits of the continental shelf beyond 200-n. miles. The LOS Convention indicates that a coastal State is to submit information supporting its proposed outer limits of its "legal" continental shelf to the Commission.[10] Annex II to the Convention provides that a coastal State intending to establish outer limits of the continental shelf "shall" submit information to the Commission "within 10 years of entry into force" of the Convention for the State.[11] The 10 year mark for States that were parties to the LOS Convention when it came into effect in 1994 was adjusted at the Eleventh Meeting of the State Parties to the LOS Convention to commence as of 13 May 1999.[12] Thus, 13 May 2009 became the newly adjusted ten-year time limit or the new date of submission deadline as understood by most States.[13] In June 2008, the Eighteenth Meeting of the State Parties decided that the ten year time frame could be met by States submitting "preliminary information indicative of the outer limits … and a description of the status of preparation and intended date for making a submission."[14] The preliminary information would not be acted upon by the Commission and would be without prejudice to a subsequent full submission. As all the littoral States of the South China Sea became parties to the LOS Convention prior to 1999 (except the Republic of China due to obvious political and diplomatic difficulties), the above explains both why 2009 was an active year for communications to the Commission and the differences in the types of communications sent to the Commission.

It is important to note that the Commission's mandate is one of technical examination of the submitted material. The mandate of the Commission is not to involve an examination or resolution of legal or political matters. Both the LOS Convention and the Rules of Procedure of the Commission make it clear that actions of the Commission are without prejudice to the delimitation between States of maritime boundaries.[15] For greater clarity and pursuant to Article 9 of Annex II to the LOS Convention, the Commission's Rules of Procedure provide that as regards a submission, "where a land or maritime dispute exists," the Commission will not proceed with the submission.[16] The Rules of Procedure further indicate that "the competence with respect to matters regarding disputes ... rests with States."[17] This means that it is up to States to decide (rather than the Commission), amongst other things, whether or not a land or maritime dispute exists. Thus, where a State indicates that a land or maritime dispute exists and the State invokes directly or indirectly the relevant provision of the Rules of Procedure (Annex I, paragraph 5(a)), the Commission is without jurisdiction to proceed with a submission since the Commission is not competent to evaluate whether and to what extent a dispute exists as this is a political matter for the States involved.[18]

The following is a list of documents presented to the Commission in 2009, official comments made concerning the documents, and other related legislative changes.

- Malaysia and Vietnam made a Joint Submission to the Commission respecting the outer limit of the continental margin beyond 200-n. miles in the southern part of the South China Sea.[19] In the Joint Submission, Malaysia and Vietnam identified 200-n. mile limits and an area of continental shelf (referred to as the "defined area") adjacent to these limits that might, in the future, be subject to Malaysian-Vietnam negotiation and a bilateral maritime boundary agreement.
- Vietnam made a submission to the Commission respecting its proposed outer limit of the shelf in the northern part of the South China Sea.[20]
- The People's Republic of China responded to each of the above submissions with nearly identical *notes verbales* claiming that Malaysia and Vietnam had "seriously infringed" on its "sovereignty, sovereign rights and jurisdiction" in the South China Sea.[21] Attached to both of People's Republic of China's *notes* was a map (the U-shaped dotted line map).
  - The People's Republic of China notified the Commission of its intention to submit information respecting an outer limit of the continental shelf adjacent to its 200-n. mile limit in the East China Sea and reserved its right to also make a submission respecting "other sea areas."[22]
- The Republic of China responded to the submissions by Vietnam and Malaysia in very similar terms to that of the People's Republic of China asserting that the island groups and their surrounding waters including the seabed are part of the its territory.[23] One variation is that no reference was made to the dotted lines map or to any identification of the area that the Republic of China claims in the South China Sea.[24] In May 2009, the Republic of China issued the "Declaration of the Republic of China on the Outer Limits of Its Continental Shelf" in lieu of the presenting of a

submission or a preliminary information to the CLCS to which it does not have legal access.[25]

- The Philippines also responded to the Joint Submission of Malaysia/Vietnam and the Submission of Vietnam with nearly identical *notes verbales* noting that the areas covered in the submissions "overlap" with areas claimed by the Philippines.[26]
  – In March 2009, the Philippines adopted a new law on baselines for the archipelago.[27] Although the Philippine archipelagic baselines prescribed in the law seem not to extend to the insular features claimed by the Philippines in the South China Sea, the Philippines indicated that they continue to claim sovereignty over "their" insular features in the South China Sea, including the Kalayaan Island Group and the Bajo de Masinloc, also known as Scarborough Shoal. The Republic of China, the People's Republic of China and Vietnam objected to the new Philippine law on the grounds that the law interfered with their claims over islands in the South China Sea.[28]
  – The Philippines submitted information to the Commission in 2009, but the continental shelf area in question was adjacent to the east coast of the Philippines and not within the South China Sea.[29] In the submission the Philippines made it clear that it reserved its rights as regards the outer limits of the continental shelf in other areas adjacent to the Philippines.[30]
- Brunei notified the Commission of its intention to submit information respecting an outer limit of the continental shelf adjacent to its 200-n. mile limit,[31] but made no comment respecting the Joint Submission of Malaysia – Vietnam.
  – Brunei and Malaysia, through a March 2009 Exchange of Letters, have agreed on a maritime boundary for the territorial sea, continental shelf and exclusive economic zone.[32] The precise details of the delimitation have not yet been made public.

A Brief Analysis

It is to be noted that the May 2009 *notes verbales* from the People's Republic of China regarding the Malaysia/Vietnam Joint Submission and Vietnam's Submission regarding the northern South China Sea makes specific reference to Annex I, paragraph 5(a) of the Rules of Procedure of the Commission and states: "the Chinese Government seriously requests the Commission not to consider" the Joint Submission or the Submission of Vietnam.[33] The August 2009 *notes verbales* from the Philippines similarly requests the Commission "to refrain from considering" the two submissions.[34] It can be safely predicted that the Commission will not proceed with a consideration of either submission unless new communications are received.

One of the enduring legal questions about the South China Sea is that of islands versus rocks. Not all insular formations are equally capable of generating a full set of maritime zones. The 1982 LOS Convention draws a distinction between islands that can legally generate a 12-n. mile territorial sea, 200-n. mile EEZ and, where possible, a continental shelf area beyond 200-n. miles, and islands that are rocks that can legally generate only a 12-n. mile territorial sea and a 12-n. mile contiguous zone.[35] While some direction is provided in the LOS Convention regarding how to differentiate between an island and a rock, this is an area of uncertainty and debate.[36]

Malaysia and Vietnam did not use any of the insular features in the Spratly Islands in the construction of their 200-n. mile zones shown in the Joint Submission. The identified 200-n. mile limits are based on baselines along the coasts of each State. A peculiarity is that there are a number of Vietnam occupied islets that are within the depicted Malaysian 200-n. mile limit. Presumably, Vietnam's position would be that these claimed islands vis-à-vis Malaysia would be enclaved with territorial seas within Malaysian waters. As regards the northern South China Sea, in Vietnam's Submission the depicted 200-n. miles line is delineated based on the mainland coast and not relying on any insular formations. The northern end point of the Vietnam 200-n. mile limit is described as being "the equidistance line between the territorial sea baselines of Vietnam and the territorial sea baselines of the People's Republic of China."[37] While the Submission indicates that Vietnam has sovereignty over the Paracel's archipelago,[38] no effect is given to the islets of the archipelago in the determination of Vietnam's 200-n. mile limit. Also worth noting is that the Vietnamese Submission does not indicate any significant ocean area adjacent to the Scarborough Shoal/Reef or Lincoln Island and Bombay Reef, the latter two located between the Paracel archipelago and Scarborough Shoal/Reef.

The Philippine situation in terms of its determination of the baselines for the Kalayaan Island Group and the Scarborough Shoal is less certain, as the 2009 Archipelagic Baselines Law indicates in Section 2 that:

> The baselines in the following areas over which the Philippines likewise exercises sovereignty and jurisdiction shall be determined as "Regime of Islands" under the Republic of the Philippines consistent with Article 121 of the United Nations Convention on the Law of the Sea (UNCLOS): (a) The Kalayaan Island Group as constituted under Presidential Decree No. 1596; and (b) Bajo de Masinloc, also known as Scarborough Shoal.[39]

The implication is that while the Philippines claims to exercise its sovereignty and jurisdiction over the Kalayaan Island Group and the Scarborough Shoal, the baselines or baseline systems of the Kalayaan Island Group and the Scarborough Shoal may be different from the archipelagic baselines prescribed for the Philippine archipelagos and that the legal status of the insular features of the Kalayaan Island Group and the Scarborough Shoal may be determined in accordance with the "Regime of Islands" article of the LOS Convention. The latter further implies that some of the insular features may be rocks, rather than islands, that will not generate a 200-n. mile EEZ and/or continental shelf. However, it was the sovereignty and jurisdiction claims in the Philippine Archipelagic Baselines Law over the Kalayaan Island Group and the Scarborough Shoal that invited protests from both Chinas and Vietnam.

Malaysia, the Philippines and Vietnam appear to have accepted that the LOS Convention and the definition of rock/islands applies to the insular features of the South China Sea, with Malaysia and Vietnam clearly of the view that many of the insular features are rocks and thus, at most, entitled to a 12-n. mile territorial sea.

This leaves the two Chinas (both the Republic of China and the People's Republic of China) and the U-shaped dotted line. While the U-shaped dotted line map has been known about for years, as it goes back to at least the late 1940s when the government of the Republic of China for the first time publicized a "South Sea Islands Location Map" with 11 discontinuous U-shaped lines to depict the localities of the four island groups within the lines,[40] the attachment by the People's Republic of China of the map to its 2009 *notes verbales* to the United Nations is the first time in an official and diplomatic matter publicly that the People's Republic of China has asserted the line contained on the map.

Post 2009

The South China Sea as a "Core Interest" for the PRC

Much has been made of the report that in March 2010 unnamed senior officials of the People's Republic of China told U.S. officials that Beijing considered South China Sea to be a "core interest" of its sovereignty and territorial integrity, wording usually reserved for the non-negotiability of Taiwan, Tibet and Xinjiang.[41] Exactly what was said, by whom[42] and what was meant has attracted much attention mainly due to the perceived escalation of the South China Sea disputes by Beijing with much being made of a "new" position or policy. In official communications, Beijing has apparently avoided explicitly commenting on the matter or repeating the language, nor has it denied it. Hence, a year later a *New York Times* headline stated "China Hedges Over Whether South China Sea is a 'Core Interest' Worth War."[43]

While detailed analysis by foreign commentators reveals confusion about the meaning and use of "core interest",[44] Chinese government officials, military professionals, scholars, and columnists seem to agree that downplaying or obfuscating the linkage of "core interests" with the South China Sea issues is in the national interest, at least for the time being. For example, Chinese State Councillor Dai Bingguo (戴秉國) in 2009 broadened the usage of the term by saying that China had three core interests: maintaining its political system, defending its sovereignty claims and promoting its economic development.[45] An international relations professor at Peking University thought that "It's not Chinese policy to declare the South China Sea as a core interest, [b]ut the problem is that a public denial will be some sort of chicken action on the part of Chinese leaders. So the government also doesn't want to inflame the Chinese people."[46] A Chinese columnist doubted whether it was wise to elevate "South China Sea" to a core interest since it would upset and enrage the United States which had enjoyed preeminence and hegemony over the region, could strike a nerve with China's neighboring countries, and would be superfluous when China had always claimed indisputable sovereignty over the islands in the South China Sea.[47] Thus, a plausible interpretation for the term "core interest" and its application to the South China Sea is that the Chinese government considers that sovereignty and territorial integrity of all the insular features within the U-shaped lines are important as a core national interest, however, it would be premature for it to publicly declare as such when, as Han Xudong (韓旭東), a PRC army colonel and a professor at PLA's National Defense University put it, "China's comprehensive national strength, especially in military capabilities, is not yet enough to safeguard all of the core national interests. In this case, it's not a good idea to reveal the core national interests."[48]

The rhetorical claim of "core interest" for the South China Sea needs to be understood from the Chinese perspective. The Kuala Lumpur Security Review (KLS Review)[49] once reported that a "Southeast Asian Spratly Group" was "shaping up," meaning that the ASEAN countries were forming a coalition against China to increase their bargaining power.[50] Although a senior PRC diplomatic official dismissed the existence of such coalition,[51] a signed article released by a Hong Kong-based news media group argued that the greatest problem for Beijing was not the existence of a "Spratly Group;" rather it was the activities of certain countries: "double speed-up" (雙加快) (speed-up of actual occupation加快事實佔領 and speed-up of unilateral exploitation加快獨自開發) along with three "becomings" (化) – "military stationing becoming normal practice, military fortification becoming perpetuated, and military position becoming deepening" (駐軍常態化、工事永久化、陣地縱深化).[52] Besides the strengthening of military control over the islets and rocks in the South China Sea, especially in the Spratly Islands, by intra-regional States, the maneuvering of American forces in the region along with the "return of the U.S. to Asia," all contribute to the rhetorical and practical reaction of the PRC.

The United States

Over the last few decades, the United States had been seen as maintaining a "hands-off" policy respecting the South China based on the May 1995 U.S. Statement on the South China Sea.[53] The 1995 Statement expressed concern about increasing tensions in the region, noted that the United States had no position on the merits of the sovereignty disputes, indicated that the United States was willing to assist in seeking a resolution and that the "United States would, however, view with serious concern any maritime claim or restriction on maritime activity in the South China Sea that was not consistent with international law...."[54]

This has changed in July 2010 as a result of Secretary of State Hilary Clinton's comments at the ASEAN Regional Forum. Clinton indicated in her remarks that

> we have a national interest in *freedom of navigation, open access to Asia's maritime domain*, the maintenance of peace and stability, and respect for international law in the South China Sea. . . . The United States supports *a collaborative diplomatic process by all claimants* for resolving the various disputes in the South China Sea. . . . (emphasis added)

She stressed that "we do not take a position on the competing territorial claims over land features in the South China Sea. We believe all parties should pursue their territorial claims and accompanying rights to maritime space in accordance with international law, including as reflected in the 1982 Law of the Sea Convention."[55]

The U.S. posture at the meeting has been reported in the press as being a "sharp rebuke" to Beijing and that the United States "would step into the tangled dispute" in the South China Sea.[56]

Clinton reportedly suggested that a formal legal process be established to resolve the outstanding issues.[57] At a 23 July 2010 press briefing, Clinton reiterated the long-standing U.S. position that it "does not take sides on the competing territorial disputes over the land features in the South China Sea," noting however, that the United States "is prepared to facilitate initiatives and confidence building measures" in order to "help create the conditions for resolution of the disputes and a lowering of regional tensions."[58] While a close reading of the comments of Secretary Clinton indicates a significant congruence with the 1995 Statement, nevertheless, Clinton's comments are said to reflect a renewed focus by the United States on the South China Sea situation arising, according to one writer, as a result of "... China's turn in 2009 toward an assertive, even aggressive approach – especially in its efforts to control U.S. naval activities in the South China Sea ..."[59] Clinton's comments have also been tied to the above noted reported comments of senior Chinese officials that the South China Sea was a "core interest" for Beijing.[60]

While Beijing responded negatively to Clinton's remarks,[61] reportedly the South China Sea has not been a significant issue in subsequent U.S.-People's Republic of China dialogue.[62]

A January 2012 headline in the *Washington Post*, "U.S. seeks to expand presence in Philippines: Nations discussing a bigger footprint to help counter China,"[63] describes the delicate interaction between the Philippines and the United States in bolstering their military partnership with a common goal of encountering the rising power of the People's Republic of China in the South China Sea. The article says:

> The number of port visits by U.S. Navy ships has soared in recent years. The Philippines recently acquired a cutter from the U.S. Coast Guard and is seeking two more of the ships to boost its naval forces. It also wants to buy F-16 fighter jets from Washington. In interviews, neither Philippine nor Obama administration officials would rule out a return by U.S. ships or forces to Subic Bay. . . . But even a small, visiting U.S. force in the Philippines would send a strong signal to Beijing. Although Washington has said it is not trying to contain China's rise as an economic and military superpower, Obama announced a new military strategy this month under which the Pentagon will 'rebalance' the armed forces toward the Asia-Pacific region in the aftermath of the wars in Iraq and Afghanistan.

The same article also reports that U.S. Senator James Webb, chair of the Senate Foreign Relations Subcommittee on East Asia and Pacific Affairs considers that: "The presence of the United States has become the essential ingredient for stability." This perceived "essential ingredient for stability" is accented by a U.S. Navy vessel's visit in August 2011 to the Vietnamese naval base at Cam Ranh Bay, the first such visit in 38 years.[64]

What is stated by the United States to be a "rebalance" of its armed forces in the Asia-Pacific region together with a perceived developing partnership of the United States with some ASEAN States on South China Sea issues can be viewed by the People's Republic of China as a move towards joint containment.

Implementing the 2002 Declaration on Conduct

Two of the key contents of the 2002 Declaration on Conduct are:

- the parties undertake to resolve their territorial and jurisdiction disputes using peaceful means;[65] and
- self restraint is to be exercised by the parties in conducting activities that might complicate or escalate the existing disputes including refraining from occupying uninhabited features.[66]

Overall, the thrust of the 2002 Declaration is one of enhancing cooperation and building trust and confidence as regards the South China Sea. While it might have been hoped by some ASEAN States that a treaty-like document with internationally legally binding status might have been adopted,[67] the 2002 Declaration is a political rather than a legal document. It has been assessed that the Declaration is a "formal ... framework for understanding and cooperation" and as "safety valve to prevent ... further unilateral actions ... in the disputed waters and area."[68] The most common narrative of the 2002

Declaration is that it was a beginning of a step-by-step process with the end goal being, not a direct resolution of the disputes, but a legally binding code of conduct.[69]

As a follow-up to the 2002 Declaration, the ASEAN – People's Republic of China Joint Working Group on the Implementation of the Declaration was established.[70] In 2006 the Working Group identified six projects dealing with, among other things, search and rescue and regional oceanographic exchanges,[71] which could be seen as attempts to encourage regional ocean cooperation. While the working group continued to meet, there was little progress on the establishment of these or similar type projects.[72] A positive cooperative endeavor that might be attributable to the 2002 Declaration was a bilateral joint marine seismic undertaking agreement and a tripartite joint marine scientific research agreement in the region. The bilateral Agreement for Joint Marine Seismic Undertaking in Certain Areas in the South China Sea by and between China National Offshore Oil Corporation and Philippine National Oil Company was signed in Beijing on 1 September 2004 and was for a term of three years.[73] In its preamble, the Agreement stated that: "the Parties' respective governments have expressed the commitment to pursue efforts to transform the South China Sea into an area of cooperation," noting, however, that "the signing of this Agreement by herein Parties shall not undermine the basic position held by the Government of each Party on the South China Sea issue."[74] The Tripartite Agreement for Joint Marine Scientific Research in Certain Areas in the South China Sea by and among China National Offshore Oil Corporation, Vietnam Oil and Gas Corporation and Philippine National Oil Company was signed on 14 March 2005 in Manila for a term of three years.[75] Again, in its preamble, this tripartite Agreement states that "the Parties' respective governments have expressed their commitment to pursue peaceful efforts to transform the South China Sea into an area of peace, stability, cooperation and development; . . . the Parties shall abide by their respective government's commitment to fully implement the United Nations Convention on the Law of the Sea (UNCLOS) and the ASEAN-China Declaration on the Conduct of Parties in the South China Sea (DOC); . . . for a joint marine seismic undertaking within the Agreement Area; . . ." while "the Parties recognize that the signing of this Agreement shall not undermine the basic position held by the Government of each Party on the South China Sea issue."[76] Along with the Tripartite Agreement, the three State-owned oil companies issued a Joint Statement, which it states that:

> The three parties affirm that the signing of the Tripartite Agreement will not undermine the basic positions held by their respective Governments on the South China Sea issue and will contribute to the transformation of the South China Sea into an area of peace, stability, cooperation, and development in accordance with the 1982 United Nations Convention on the Law of the Sea and the 2002 ASEAN-China Declaration on the Conduct of Parties in the South China Sea.[77]

From the perspective of a Vietnamese Foreign Ministry spokesman, this Agreement "highlights the principles of equality and consensus among relevant Parties during the joint research process."[78]

While Philippine President Gloria Arroyo spoke of the historic significance of the tripartite Agreement,[79] the Agreement and the previous one were smeared by domestic allegations in the Philippines that the signing of the agreements were made in exchange for official development assistance from the PRC to fund government projects. Critics also raised the issue of treason against the Arroyo government for the alleged "sellout" of Philippine territory since the agreements covered 24,000 square kilometers of undisputed Philippine territory and encroached on some 80 percent of the Kalayaan group of islands claimed by the Philippines.[80] These ill-fated agreements fell well short of achieving the goals hoped for by the parties to them.

New life may have been given to the 2002 Declaration when the Foreign Ministers of ASEAN and the People's Republic of China reached agreement in July 2011 on Guidelines for the Implementation of the Declaration of Conduct.[81] The Guidelines, which are little more than a statement of good intentions, endorse the promotion of dialogue and consultations and a step-by-step approach to confidence building measures. In the face of a number of incidents involving the People's Republic of China and both Vietnam and the Philippines and a perceived rising of tensions in the South China Sea, the timing of a recommitment to the Declaration on Conduct is important. As the People's Republic of China noted:

> In the current circumstances, the parties recognized that completing the consultations on the guidelines as quickly as possible, actively implementing the "Declaration" and promoting pragmatic cooperation is a necessary requirement to maintain peace and stability in the South China Sea ...[82]

Moreover, the People's Republic of China proposed a series of cooperative initiatives including holding a workshop on freedom of navigation in the South China Sea, and committed to continuing with the cooperative projects already being led by Beijing.[83]

In a statement delivered by Premier Wen Jiabao at the 14th China-ASEAN Summit as a Commemorative Summit to Celebrate the 20th Anniversary of China-ASEAN Relations on 18 November 2011 in Bali, Indonesia, expansion of practical maritime cooperation was highlighted as one of the six fields of cooperation between Beijing and ASEAN.[84] The Premier also stated:

> The disputes over the South China Sea between the relevant countries in the region have existed for many years. They should be settled through friendly consultation and negotiation between the sovereign states directly concerned. *Outside forces should not get involved under any excuse.* In 2002, China and ASEAN countries signed the Declaration on the Conduct of Parties in the South China Sea and agreed to advance practical cooperation and work for the final conclusion of a code of conduct. This is the common desire of ASEAN countries and China. We stand ready to work actively with ASEAN countries to fully implement the Declaration on the Conduct of Parties in the South China Sea, enhance practical cooperation and begin discussions on a code of conduct in the South China Sea. (emphasis added)[85]

It is apparent that the PRC's approach to the South China Sea disputes has not changed: it favors bilateral solutions, or intra-regional solutions at most, and opposes extra-regional involvement, especially the involvement of the United States under the guise of "freedom of navigation" in order to pursue its foreign policy "shift in emphasis to Asia" based on its view that US presence in the region is an "essential ingredient for stability."

Communications to the Commission

Further to the 2009 Joint Submission made by Malaysia and Vietnam and the Submission by Vietnam respecting the Northern Area to the Commission and the diplomatic missives that ensued in 2009, Indonesia (on 8 July 2010),[86] the Philippines (on 5 April 2011),[87] the People's Republic of China (on 14 April 2011),[88] and Vietnam (on 3 May 2011)[89] have provided *notes verbales* to the Commission.

The Indonesian communication zeroes in on the map appended to the People's Republic of China's 2009 *notes* and comments: "Thus far, there is no clear explanation as to the legal basis, the method of drawing, and the status of those separated dotted-lines."[90] Indonesia states that if the lines on the map are based upon maritime zones from the various small features in the South China Sea then "the so-called 'nine-dotted-lines map' ... clearly lacks international legal basis."[91] The Indonesian communication refers to several statements made by Chinese delegates in 2009 that small island features, i.e., rocks, are not entitled to zones beyond 12-n. miles and that Indonesia is in agreement with these observations.[92]

The Philippines April 2011 *note* asserts sovereignty over the Kalayaan Island Group and the jurisdiction permitted under the LOS Convention adjacent to the islands mindful of Article 121 (respecting islands and rocks) of the Convention.[93] The Philippine *note* also indicates that there is "no basis under international law, specifically UNCLOS" for the People's Republic of China's claim to "relevant waters as well as the seabed and subsoil thereof" captured by the U-shaped line.[94]

The April 2011 response of the People's Republic of China to the Philippines asserts "indisputable sovereignty over the islands ... and adjacent waters as well as the seabed and subsoil thereof" and that "China's sovereignty and related rights and jurisdiction in the South China Sea are supported by abundant historical and legal evidence."[95] The 2011 *note* indicates that since the 1930s that "the Chinese Government has given publicity several times to the geographical scope of China's Nansha Islands and the names of its components."[96] The *note* continues: "In addition, under the relevant provisions of the 1982 United Nations Convention on the Law of the Sea" as well as national law, "China's Nansha Islands is fully entitled to Territorial Sea, Exclusive Economic Zone (EEZ) and Continental Shelf."[97] As has been observed: "This sentence ... states publicly for the first time the Chinese official position on the status of the Nansha Islands" that they "meet the requirements of Article 121 to have their own EEZ and continental shelf" and is "an indirect response" to Indonesia's *note*.[98] While there is no explicit reference in the April *note* to the U-shaped line, it is not necessarily the case that Beijing has abandoned it. The tying of historical and legal evidence to "China's sovereignty and related rights" can be said to keep the ambiguity of the U-shaped line alive.

Conclusion

While the disputes and maneuvers among the South China Sea littoral governments has long been the focus of regional and multilateral attention, there is no question that 2009, with its flurry of official communications, has increased local sensitivities and global awareness of the issues. There has been a degree of clarity of what is being claimed and the basis for the claims that is hopefully helpful, particularly, if there is coalescence around shared principles or approaches such as those in the LOS Convention. While the lens of this contribution (and this collection) has been primarily one of international law and marine policy, there is no doubting that the fluctuating temperature of the South China Sea disputes is a matter of the political choices of the governments of the region with the most important actor being the government in Beijing. The fizzle of the "core interest" hubbub and the adoption of the Guidelines for the Implementation of the Declaration on the Conduct of the Parties in the South China Sea in 2011 can be viewed as calming events. Even the April 2011 communication from the People's Republic China clarifying its view of the legal status of the insular features of the South China Sea can be seen as a positive. There is no denying, however, that to the consternation of its neighbors and even the United States, the People's Republic of China has actively, and in the eyes of some aggressively, pursued its position respecting the waters of the South China Sea, which has included increased patrols and surveillance activities in large parts of the South China Sea largely coincident with the ambiguous U-shaped line.[99] Who knows whether the 2011 calming events are just "the calm before the storm"?

ANNEX

Guidelines for the Implementation of the DOC

[Adopted on 20 July 2011 by Senior Officials of the People's Republic of China and the ASEAN States in Bali, Indonesia.]

Reaffirming that the DOC is a milestone document signed between the ASEAN Member States and China, embodying their collective commitment to promoting peace, stability and mutual trust and to ensuring the peaceful resolution of disputes in the South China Sea;

Recognizing also that the full and effective implementation of the DOC will contribute to the deepening of the ASEAN-China Strategic Partnership for Peace and Prosperity;

These Guidelines are to guide the implementation of possible joint cooperative activities, measures and projects as provided for in the DOC.

1. The implementation of the DOC should be carried out in a step-by-step approach in line with the provisions of the DOC.

2. The Parties to the DOC will continue to promote dialogue and consultations in accordance with the spirit of the DOC.

3. The implementation of activities or projects as provided for in the DOC should be clearly identified.

4. The participation in the activities or projects should be carried out on a voluntary basis.

5. Initial activities to be undertaken under the ambit of the DOC should be confidence-building measures.

6. The decision to implement concrete measures or activities of the DOC should be based on consensus among parties concerned, and lead to the eventual realization of a Code of Conduct.

7. In the implementation of the agreed projects under the DOC, the services of the Experts and Eminent Persons, if deemed necessary, will be sought to provide specific inputs on the projects concerned.

8. Progress of the implementation of the agreed activities and projects under the DOC shall be reported annually to the ASEAN-China Ministerial Meeting (PMC).

Notes

1. For a good overview, see: Mark J. Valencia, Jon M. Van Dyke and Noel A. Ludwig, *Sharing the Resources of the South China Sea* (The Hague: Martinus Nijhoff, 1997), at pp. 17–38.

2. See, amongst many others: *ibid.*; Nguyen Hong Thao and Ramses Amer, "A New Legal Arrangement for the South China Sea?" (2009), 40 *Ocean Development and International Law* 333–349; and Sam Bateman and Ralf Emmers, eds., *Security and International Politics in the South China Sea* (London: Routledge, 2009). For a rich analysis of events in 2010, see: Carlyle A. Thayer, "Recent Developments in the South China Sea: Grounds for Cautious Optimism," 14 December 2010, RSIS Working Paper No. 220 (S. Rajaratnam Scool of International Studies, Singapore) and regarding the actions by the People's Republic of China, see: Zou Keyuan, "China's U-Shaped Line in the South China Sea Revisited" (2012), 43 *Ocean Development and International Law* 18–34.

3. Declaration on the Conduct of Parties in the South China Sea, 4 November 2002, available on the website of ASEAN at <www.aseansec.org/13163.htm> (accessed 19 July 2009) and as an appendix to Nguyen Hong Thao, "The 2002 Declaration on the Conduct of Parties in the South China Sea: A Note" (2003), 34 *Ocean Development and International Law* 279, at pp. 282–285.

4. For a detail review of the 2002 Declaration, see: Thao, "The 2002 Declaration: A Note," *supra* note 3, at pp. 279–282; Nguyen Hong Thao, "The Declaration on the Conduct of Parties in the South China Sea: A Vietnamese Perspective, 2002–2007" in Bateman and Emmers, *supra* note 2, at pp. 210–211; Ralf Emmers, *Geopolitics and Maritime Territorial Disputes in East Asia* (London: Routledge, 2010), at pp. 118–120; Aileen S.P. Baviera, "The South China Sea Disputes after the 2002 Declaration: Beyond Confidence Building" in Saw Swee-Hock (蘇瑞福), Sheng Lijun (盛立軍) and Chin Kin Wah (陳建華), eds., *ASEAN – China Relations: Realities and Prospects* (Singapore: Institute of Southeast Asian Studies, 2005), pp. 348–350; and Tran Truong Thuy, "Recent Development in the South China Sea: From Declaration to Code of Conduct," 15 July 2011, on the website of the Program for East Asia (South China Sea) Studies, Diplomatic Academy of Vietnam, at www.nghiencuubiendong.vn.en (accessed 12 September 2011).

5. See: Thao, "The 2002 Declaration: A Vietnamese Perspective," *supra* note 4, at pp. 211–215; Emmers, *supra* note 4, at pp. 74–76; and note: Gao Zhigou, "South China Sea: Turning Suspicion into Mutual Understanding and Cooperation" in Saw, Sheng and Chin, *supra* note 4, at p. 340.

6. See: Nien-Tsu Alfred Hu, "South China Sea: Troubled Waters of a Sea of Opportunity?" (2010), 41 *Ocean Development and International Law* 203–213, at 206–207 (in this collection) and Valencia, et al., *supra* note 1, at pp. 29–30.

7. See: Nien-Tsu Alfred Hu, "Semi-enclosed Troubled Waters: A New Thinking on the Application of the 1982 UNCLOS Article 123 to the South China Sea" (2010), 41 *Ocean Development and International Law* 281–314, at 301; Yann-huei Song, "The South China Sea Workshop Process and Taiwan's Participation" (2010), 41 *Ocean Development and International*

Law 253–269; and Kuan-Hsiung Wang, "The ROC's Maritime Claims and Practices with Special Reference to the South China Sea" (2010), 41 *Ocean Development and International Law* 237–252 (all of which are in this collection).

8. Lui Fu-Kuo (劉復國) and Wu Shicun (吳士存), eds., *2010 South Sea Region Situation Assessment Report* (*2010 年南海地區形勢評估報告*, in Chinese) was jointly published in July 2011 by the Institute of International Relations of the National Chengchi University (國立政治大學國際關係研究中心) in Taipei, Taiwan and the National Institute for South China Sea Studies (中國南海研究院) in Haikou City, Hai-Nan Province, mainland China. There are seven chapters in the Report along with an annex of major events. It is worth noting that each chapter was co-written by one scholar from Taiwan and another from mainland China and the final presentation was made after group discussions. The report reflects the academic view of both sides of Taiwan Strait on the current situation in South China Sea.

9. See: U.N. Convention on the Law of the Sea, done at Montego Bay, Jamaica, 10 December 1982, entered into force 16 November 1994, 1833 *U.N.T.S.* 397, Article 76(8) and Annex II. See the website of the Commission of the Limits of the Continental Shelf, available at www.un.org/Depts/los/clcs_new/clcs_home.htm.

10. *Ibid.*, Article 76(8).

11. *Ibid.*, Annex II, Article 4

12. Eleventh Meeting of the State Parties, "Decision regarding the date of commencement of the ten-year period for making submissions to the Commission on the Limits of the Continental Shelf set out in article 4 of Annex II to the United Nations Convention on the Law of the Sea," Doc. SPLOS/72, 29 May 2001, available on website of the U.N. Division on Oceans and the Law of the Sea (DOALOS), at www.un.org/Depts/los.

13. It is worth noting that a recent International Tribunal for the Law of the Sea (ITLOS) judgment delivered on 14 March 2012 on the "Dispute concerning Delimitation of the Maritime Boundary between Bangladesh and Myanmar in the Bay of Bengal", or the Case No. 16: Bangladesh/Myanmar, the first case of the ITLOS relating to the delimitation of maritime boundaries, states that the continental shelf rights are inherent and unaffected by the procedural aspects of the CLCS which deals only with the outer limits (in particular, paragraphs 407 to 409) and the same Judgment considers that the activities of ITLOS and the CLCS are complementary to each other so as to ensure coherent and efficient implementation of the Convention (paragraphs 373, 376, 377, and 379). See: the ITLOS press release at www.itlos.org/fileadmin/itlos/documents/press_releases_english/pr_175_engf_02.pdf, and the full text of the ITLOS judgment at www.itlos.org/fileadmin/itlos/documents/cases/case_no_16/1C16_Judgment_14_02_2012.pdf (accessed 10 April 2012).

14. Eighteenth Meeting of the States Parties, "Decision regarding the Workload of the Commission and the Ability of States to fulfil the Requirements of Article 4 of Annex II," Doc. SPLOS/183, 20 June 2008, paragraph 1, available on the DOALOS website, *supra* note 12.

15. LOS Convention, *supra* note 9, Article 76(10) and Annex II, Article 9 and Rules of Procedure of the Commission, Doc. CLCS/40/Rev.1, 17 April 2008, Rule 46(2) and Annex I, paragraphs 3 and 5(b), on the website of the Commission, *supra* note 9.

16. Rules of Procedure of the Commission, *supra* note 15, Annex I, paragraph 5(a).

17. *Ibid.*, Annex I, paragraph 1.

18. See generally: T.L. McDorman, "The Commission on the Limits of the Continental Shelf (CLCS): The Nature of its Existence and Role in the Establishment of the Outer Limits of the Continental Shelf" (paper presented at the "Colloquium on the Outer Limits of the Continental Shelf and Consideration of Submissions," Kuala Lumpur, Malaysia, May 2010). See also: Alex G. Oude Elferink, "The options to deal with a deadlock in the consideration of a submission by the Commission on the Limits of the Continental Shelf," presented at the same Colloquium.

19. Malaysia – Vietnam Joint Submission to the Commission on the Limits of the Continental Shelf pursuant to Article 76, paragraph 8 of the United Nations Convention on the Law of the Sea 1982 in respect of the Southern Part of the South China Sea, Executive Summary, May 2009, on the website of the Commission, *supra* note 9.

20. Vietnam Submission to the Commission on the Limits of the Continental Shelf pursuant to Article 76, paragraph 8 of the United Nations Convention on the Law of the Sea 1982, Partial Submission in respect of Vietnam's Extended Continental Shelf: North Area (VNM-N), Executive Summary, April 2009, on the website of the Commission, *supra* note 9.

21. People's Republic of China, *Note Verbale* to Secretary-General of the United Nations, doc. CML/17/2009, New York, 7 May 2009 and *Note Verbale* to Secretary-General of the United Nations, doc. CML/18/2009, New York, 7 May 2009, both on the website of the Commission, *supra* note 9.

22. People's Republic of China, Preliminary Information Indicative of the Outer Limits of the Continental Shelf beyond 200 nautical miles, May 2009, paragraph 10, on the website of the Commission, *supra* note 9.

23. See: Republic of China, Ministry of Foreign Affairs, "Statement concerning a Joint Submission presented by Malaysia and Vietnam to the UN Commission on the Limits of the Continental Shelf," 11 May 2009, available on the website of the Ministry at www.mofa.gov.tw/webapp/fp.asp?xItem=38047&ctnode=1901 (accessed 19 July 2009) and "The Ministry of Foreign Affairs of the Republic of China solemnly declares statement on the governments of Malaysia and Vietnam filed a Joint Submission to the Commission on the Limits of the Continental Shelf of the United Nations, extending the outer limits of their respective continental shelf 200 nautical miles beyond their shorelines," 11 May 2009, available on the website of the Ministry at www.mofa.gov.tw/EnOfficial/ArticleDetail/DetailDefault/890fb320-603c-49b2-a2cc-7842923e66c8?arfid=0b12b1ae-64ff-4e4b-b6bd-e20fbf2c7a13&opno=49be2475-017b-4647-8ac1-9a0ec20d892c#print (accessed 7 February 2012).

24. See, however, Republic of China, "Policy Guidelines for the South China Sea," March 1993, attached as Appendix I to Kuan-Ming Sun, "Policy of the Republic of China towards the South China Sea" (1995), 19 *Marine Policy* 401, at p. 408.

25. Republic of China, Ministry of Foreign Affairs, "Declaration of the Republic of China on the Outer Limits of Its Continental Shelf," 12 May 2009, English text is available on the website of the Taipei Economic and Cultural Representative Office in the United States, available at www.taiwanembassy.org/us/ct.asp?xItem=91327&ctNode=2300&mp=12 (accessed 7 February 2012).

26. The Philippines, *Note Verbale* to Secretary-General of the United Nations, doc. No. 000818, New York, 4 August 2009 and *Note Verbale* to Secretary-General of the United Nations, doc. 000819, New York, 4 August 2009, on the website of the Commission, *supra* note 9.

27. The Philippines, Republic Act No. 9522, An Act to Amend Certain Provisions of Republic Act No. 3046, as amended by Republic Act No. 5466, to Define the Archipelagic Baselines of the Philippines, and for Other Purposes, approved 10 March 2009, available on the website of the Philippine Law and Jurisprudence Database at www.lawphil.net/statutes/repacts/ra2009/ra_9522_2009.html. See generally: Rodolfo C. Severino, *Where in the World is the Philippines?* (Singapore: Institute of Southeast Asian Studies, 2011), at pp. 35–37 and 73–74.

28. Republic of China, Ministry of Foreign Affairs, "MOFA reiterates this Country's sovereignty over Nan-Sha islands and surrounding waters," 13 March 2009, available on the website of the Ministry at www.mofa.gov.tw/official/Home/Detail/649168df-4a62-495e-9267-fdd7a92e04b9?arfid=7f013c3f-f130-44a9-905f-84cbaba2eca6&opno=907477b5-1d95-4205-a89d-320ed4806d4b# print, in Chinese, (accessed 7 February 2012); People's Republic of China, *Note Verbale* to Secretary-General of the United Nations, doc. CML/12/2009, New York, 13 April 2009, available on the DOALOS website, *supra* note 12 and Vietnam, Permanent Mission to the United Nations, "Vietnam's Response to Philippine President's signing of Baseline Act," 13 March 2009, available at www.vietnam-un.org/en/news.php?id=77&act=print.

29. The Philippines, A Partial Submission of Data and Information on the Outer Limits of the Continental Shelf of the Republic of the Philippines pursuant to Article 76(8) of the United Nations Convention on the Law of the Sea, Executive Summary, May 2009, on the website of the Commission, *supra* note 9.

30. *Ibid.*, at pp. 1 and 12. The Philippines noted, at p. 12, that they opted only to submit information respecting its eastern coast "in order to avoid creating or provoking maritime boundary

disputes where there are none, or exacerbating them where they may exist … This is to build confidence and promote international cooperation in the peaceful and amicable resolution of maritime boundary disputes."

31. Brunei Darussalam, Preliminary Submission concerning the Outer Limits of its Continental Shelf, May 2009, on the website of the Commission, *supra* note 9.

32. Malaysia, Ministry of Foreign Affairs, "Press Release," 3 May 2010, available on the website of Ministry of Foreign Affairs. More generally, see: Severino, *supra* note 27, at pp. 80–82 and Johan Saravanamuttu, "Malaysia's Approach to Cooperation in the South China Sea," paper presented at the May 2010 International Conference, Cooperation on Dealing with Non-Traditional Security Issues in the South China Sea: Seeking More Effective Means, held in Haikou.

33. PRC *Note Verbale*, CML/17/2009 and *Note Verbale*, CML/18/2009, *supra* note 21, paragraph 3.

34. The Philippines *Note Verbale*, No. 000818 and *Note Verbale*, No. 000819, *supra* note 26, paragraph 4.

35. LOS Convention, *supra* note 9, Article 121.

36. See generally: Jon M. Van Dyke and Robert A. Brooks, "Uninhabited Islands: Their Impact on the Ownership of the Oceans' Resources" (1983), 12 *Ocean Development and International Law* 265–284; Marius Gjetnes, "The Spratlys: Are They Rocks or Islands?" (2001), 32 *Ocean Development and International Law* 191–204; and Victor Prescott and Clive Schofield, *The Maritime Political Boundaries of the World* (2nd ed.) (Leiden: Martinus Nijhoff, 2005), at pp. 57–91.

In the *Case Concerning Maritime Boundary Delimitation in the Black Sea (Romania v. Ukraine)*, 3 February 2009, available on the website of the International Court of Justice, www.icj-cij.org, the issue was raised whether Serpents Island constituted a rock. The International Court, at paragraph 187, decided that it did not need to answer the question.

37. Vietnam Submission, *supra* note 20, paragraph 6.

38. *Ibid.*, paragraph 1.

39. The Philippines, 2009 Archipelagic Baselines Law, *supra* note 27.

40. See: Wang, *supra* note 7; Zou, *supra* note 2; Hu, "South China Sea," supra note 6, at pp. 206–207; and Li Jinming and Li Dexia, "The Dotted Line on the Chinese Map of the South China Sea: A Note" (2003), 34 *Ocean Development and International Law* 287–296.

41. Edward Wong, "Chinese Military Seeks to Extend Its Naval Power," *New York Times*, 23 April 2010, available at www.nytimes.com/2010/04/24/world/asia/24navy.html?pagewanted=all and see further Thayer, supra note 2, at pp. 2–3.

42. For the names of Chinese and American governmental officials involved in the alleged dialogue from which the "core interest" came, Zeenews, an Indian news agency, reported that, according to a Japanese source, Kyodo News Agency, "China has officially conveyed its new state policy to the US that it considers the South China Sea part of its 'core interests'". It further reported that "China conveyed the new policy to visiting US Deputy Secretary of State James Steinberg and Jeffrey Bader, senior director for Asian Affairs on the National Security Council, in early March, Kyodo quoted the sources as saying. The two US officials met Chinese State Councillor Dai Bingguo (戴秉國), Foreign Minister Yang Jiechi (楊潔篪) and Vice Foreign Minister Cui Tiankai (崔天凱) in Beijing, and Dai is believed to have relayed the policy to the US side given that he provides overall management in foreign affairs, the Japanese news agency reported." See Zeenews.com, "China adds South China Sea to 'core interest' in new policy," 4 July 2010, available at zeenews.india.com/news/world/china-adds-south-china-sea-to-core-interest-in-new-policy_638592.html (accessed 11 February 2012).

43. Edward Wong, "China Hedges Over Whether South China Sea Is a 'Core Interest' Worth War," *New York Times*, 30 March 2011, available at www.nytimes.com/2011/03/31/world/asia/31beijing.html (accessed 11 February 2012).

44. Thayer, *supra* note 2, at pp. 2–6 and see: Michael D. Swaine, "China's Assertive Behavior: Part One – On 'Core Interests'," February 2011, *China Leadership Monitor*, No. 34 (Hoover Institution, Stanford University).

45. Wong, "China Hedges Over Whether South China Sea Is a 'Core Interest' Worth War," *supra* note 43.

46. *Ibid.*

47. Li Hongmei, "Unwise to elevate 'South China Sea' to be core interest?" *People's Daily Online*, 27 August 2010, available at english.peopledaily.com.cn/90002/96417/7119874.html (accessed 11 February 2012).

48. Wong, "China Hedges Over Whether South China Sea Is a 'Core Interest' Worth War," *supra* note 43.

49. Kuala Lumpur Security Review is an online military news portal cum media center registered in Malaysia. See its website at www.klsreview.com (accessed 3 May 2010).

50. See: Kuala Lumpur Security Review, "Southeast Asian Spratly Group is Probably Taking Shape Now", 28 July 2009, at www.klsreview.com/HTML/2009Jul_Dec/20090728_01.html (accessed 3 May 2010).

51. See: *ibid.*, "Special Representative of PRC Foreign Minister Dismissed the Existence of 'Southeast Asian Spratly Group'", in Chinese, at www.klsreview.com/HTML/2009Jul_Dec/20090728_02.html (accessed 3 May 2010).

52. See: "China Must Curb the Relevant Activities of Occupation on Islets by Nan-Hai Countries: Hong Kong Media Says" (港媒稱中國須遏制南海諸國侵佔島礁相關活動), in Chinese, at mil.news.sina.com.cn/2009-07-14/1218558823.html (accessed 12 December 2009).

53. United States, Department of State, "Daily Press Briefing," 10 May 1995, available at dosfan.lib.uic.edu/ERC/briefing/daily_briefings/1995/9505/950510db.html (accessed 9 October 2011).

54. *Ibid.*

55. For the full text of the Press Statement of Hillary Rodham Clinton, see: "The South China Sea", 22 July 2011, U.S. Department of State – Diplomacy in Action, available at www.state.gov/secretary/rm/2011/07/168989.htm (accessed 21 December 2011).

56. Mark Landler, "Offering to Aid Talks, U.S. Challenges China on Disputed Islands," *New York Times*, 23 July 2010, available at www.nytimes.com/2010/07/24/world/asia/24diplo.html (accessed 21 December 2011).

57. Jay Solomon, "U.S. Takes on Maritime Spats," *Wall Street Journal*, 24 July 2010, available at online.wsj.com/article/SB10001424052748703294904575384561458251130.html (accessed 21 December 2011).

58. United States, Department of State, Secretary of State Hilary Clinton, "Remarks at Press Availability," 23 July 2010, Hanoi, available at www.state.gov./secretary/rm/2010/07/145095.htm (accessed 9 October 2011).

59. Peter Dutton, "Three Disputes and Three Objectives: China and the South China Sea" (2011), 64 No. 4 *Naval War College Review* 42, at p. 44.

60. See: Landler, *supra* note 56.

61. See: People's Republic of China, Ministry of Foreign Affairs, "Foreign Minister Yang Jiechi Refutes Fallacies on the South China Sea Issue," 26 July 2010, available at www.mfa.gov.cn/eng/zxxx/t719460.htm (accessed 9 October 2010) and Andrew Jacobs, "China Warns U.S. to Stay Out of Islands Dispute," *New York Times*, 26 July 2010, available at www.nytimes.com/2010/07/27/world/asia/27china.html (accessed 21 December 2011). See also: Thayer, *supra* note 2, at pp. 13–16

62. Thom Shanker, "U.S. and China Soften Tone Over Disputed Seas," *New York Times*, 12 October 2010, available at www.nytimes.com/2010/10/13/world/asia/13gates.html?_r=1 (accessed 21 December 2011).

63. Craig Whitlock, " U.S. seeks to expand presence in Philippines: Nations discussing a bigger footprint to help counter China," *The Washington Post*, 26 January 2012, p. A1 and A12, available at www.washingtonpost.com/rw/WashingtonPost/Content/Epaper/2012-01-26/Ax1.pdf and www.washingtonpost.com/rw/WashingtonPost/Content/Epaper/2012-01-26/Ax12.pdf (accessed 29 January 2012). The same article was released again as Updated: Sunday, January 29 under the title "Philippines may allow greater U.S. military presence in reaction to China's rise," *The Washington Post*, available at www.washingtonpost.com/world/national-security/philippines-may-

allow-greater-us-presence-in-latest-reaction-to-chinas-rise/2012/01/24/gIQARRk9RQ_print.html (accessed 29 January 2012).

64. *Ibid.*
65. Declaration on the Conduct of Parties in the South China Sea, *supra* note 3, paragraph 4.
66. *Ibid.*, paragraph 5.
67. Emmers, *supra* note 4, at p. 133.
68. Gao Zhigou, supra note 5, at p. 340.
69. Thao, "The 2002 Declaration: A Vietnamese Perspective," *supra* note 4, at pp. 218–219 and Thao and Amer, *supra* note 2, at p. 337. Gao Zhigou, *supra* note 5, at p. 341 sees the Declaration as part of a positive trend and takes the view that: "The long-standing jurisdictional claims and territorial disputes in the SCS [South China Sea] have yielded to the concept of comprehensive security in the region."
70. Terms of Reference of the ASEAN – China Joint Working Group on the Implementation of the Declaration on the Conduct of the Parties in the South China Sea, text available on the ASEAN website at www.aseansec.org/16886.htm (accessed 19 July 2009).
71. See: Thao, "The 2002 Declaration: A Vietnamese Perspective," *supra* note 4, at p. 215 and Thao and Amer, *supra* note 2, at p. 338.
72. Thao and Amer, *supra* note 2, at p. 339. The Joint Oceanographic Marine Scientific Expedition in the South China Sea (JOMSRE-SCS), which predates the 2002 Declaration, has seen a renewal of cooperation post the 2002 Declaration. See: Thao, "The 2002 Declaration: A Vietnamese Perspective," *supra* note 4, at pp. 216–217 and Thao and Amer, *supra* note 2, at p. 338.
73. The English text of the bilateral Agreement can be found at pcij.org/blog/wp-docs/RP_China_Agreement_on_Joint_Marine_Seismic_Undertaking.pdf (accessed 27 February 2012).
74. *Ibid.*
75. The English text of the tripartite Agreement can be found at nghiencuubiendong.vn/trung-tam-du-lieu-bien-dong/doc_details/138-a-tripartite-agreement-for-joint-marine-scientific-research-in-certain-areas-in-the-south-china-sea (accessed 28 February 2012).
76. *Ibid.*
77. See: People's Republic of China, Foreign Ministry, "Oil companies of China, the Philippines and Vietnam signed Agreement on South China Sea Cooperation", 15 March 2005, , on the Ministry's website at www.fmprc.gov.cn/eng/wjb/zwjg/zwbd/t187333.htm (accessed 28 February 2012).
78. See: Answer to correspondent by Mr. Le Dzung, the Spokesman of the Vietnamese Ministry of Foreign Affairs on 14th March 2005, at www.mofa.gov.vn/en/tt_baochi_pbnfn/ns050314164241 (accessed 27 February 2012).
79. See: Oil companies of China, the Philippines and Vietnam signed Agreement on South China Sea Cooperation, *supra* note 77.
80. See: "Stirrings over Spratlys," dated 10 March 2008, at pcij.org/blog/2008/03/10/stirrings-over-spratlys (accessed 27 February 2012). The PCIJ, or the Philippine Center for Investigative Journalism, is an independent, nonprofit media agency that specializes in investigative reporting. It was founded in 1989 by nine Filipino journalists. PCIJ also publishes www.pcij.org/blog, a daily institutional news blog. See PCIJ official website, at pcij.org/about/ (access 29 February 2012). As a side note, Mr. Eduardo V. Manalac, then President and CEO of the Philippine National Oil Company, who was the representative of the Philippines signing the two Agreements, was later charged with "grave misconduct and conduct grossly disadvantageous to the interest of government service" for violation of the Anti-Graft and Corrupt Practices Act or Republic Act No. 3019 by a Philippine Order issued on 3 February 2006. See: "PNOC Corruption – Anti Graft – Eduardo Manalc" at sukhin-energy.net/PNOC_CORRUPTION.html (accessed 28 February 2012).
81. "Guidelines for the Implementation of the DOC," available at www.asean.org/documents/20185-DOC.pdf (accessed 8 October 2011) and are reproduced as an Annex to this contribution.
82. People's Republic of China, Ministry of Foreign Affairs, "The Senior Official's Meeting for the Implementation of 'the Declaration on Conduct of Parties in the South China Sea' Reaches

an Agreement on the Guideline," 20 July 2011, available at www.fmprc.gov.cn/eng/wjdt/wshd/t841727.htm (accessed 8 October 2011).

83. *Ibid.*

84. Premier Wen, Statement at the 14th China-ASEAN Summit, available on People's Republic of China's Official web portal at english.gov.cn/2011-11/18/content_1997716.htm (accessed 28 February 2012).

85. *Ibid.*

86. Indonesia, *Note Verbale* to the Secretary-General of the United Nations, doc. 480/POL-703/VII/10, 8 July 2010, on the website of the Commission, *supra* note 9.

87. The Philippines, *Note Verbale* to the Secretary-General of the United Nations, doc. No. 000228, 5 April 2011, on the website of the Commission, *supra* note 9.

88. People's Republic of China, *Note Verbale* to the Secretary-General of the United Nations, doc. No. CML/8/2011, 14 April 2011, on the website of the Commission, *supra* note 9.

89. Vietnam, *Note Verbale* to the Secretary-General of the United Nations, doc. No. 77/HC-2011, 3 May 2011, on the website of the Commission, *supra* note 9.

90. Indonesian *Note Verbale*, *supra* note 86, paragraph 2.

91. *Ibid.*, paragraphs 2 and 4.

92. *Ibid.*, paragraph 3.

93. The Philippines 2011 *Note Verbale*, *supra* note 87, paragraphs 3 and 5.

94. *Ibid.*, paragraph 6. For a detailed analysis of the Philippine communication, see: Nguyen-Dang Thang and Nguyen Hong Thao, "China's Nine-Dotted Lines in the South China Sea: The 2011 Exchange of Diplomatic Notes of the Philippines and China" (2012), 43 *Ocean Development and International Law* 35–56.

95. PRC 2011 *Note Verbale*, *supra* note 88, paragraph 2.

96. *Ibid.*, paragraph 4. The "Nansha Islands" (南沙群岛) in Chinese is the Spratly Islands in English.

97. *Ibid.*

98. Thang and Thao, *supra* note 94, at p. 45.

99. See generally: Zou Keyuan, *supra* note 2, at pp. 20–21.

Index

Page numbers in *Italics* represent tables.
Page numbers in **Bold** represent figures.
Page numbers followed by 'a' represent appendix.

Aden, Gulf of: PRC's anti-piracy deployment 34a
Alatas, A. 76–7
Anambas Expedition (2002) 74
Archipelagic Baselines Act (2009) 71, 159
Arroyo, Gloria (President of Philippines) 163–4
Asia-Pacific Fishery Commission (APFIC) 141–2
Association of Southeast Asian Nations (ASEAN) 32a, 41, 71, 97; China-ASEAN Summit 164; Declaration on the Conduct of Parties in the South China Sea 163, 164; Declaration on Heritage Parks 97; Regional Forum comments by Hilary Clinton 161–2; territorial negotiation with PRC 73
Australia: navel modernization 42

Barcelona Convention (1976) 127–8; environmental effectiveness 135; Land-Based Sources Protocol (pollution) 136; MAP Phase II 128–9; Meetings of the Contracting Parties (MoCP) 128; Protocols 129
Bateman, S. 47
Beckman, R. 117
Benham Rise 24
biodiversity research 117
Blair, D. (Commander US Pacific Fleet) 45
boundary delimitations (Smith on) 25–6

Caribbean Environment Programme (CEP) 133, 136–7
Caribbean Regional Fisheries Mechanism (CRFM) 129–31, **131**
Caribbean Sea **130**
Caribbean Sea region (Article 123 LOS): adoption of framework convention and protocol 133; management of marine living resources 129–31; marine environment protection 131–4

CARICOM Fisheries Resources Assessment and Management Programme (CFRAMP) 129
Cartagena Convention (1986) 133–4; Contracting Parties 133; convention area **134**; land-based pollution 137; oil spill protocol 137
Center for Marine Policy Studies (CMPS) 2
Chakalall, B.: *et al* 140
Chang, K.H. 111
Chang Wei-I 139–40
Chen Shui-bian (President of Taiwan) 78, 79
China *see* Peoples Republic of China (PRC)
Chircop, A. 8–9
Chungsha Islands *see* Macclesfield Islands
Clark, L. 135
Clinton, H.: ASEAN Regional Forum comments 161–2
Cloma, T. 24, 60
Coast Guard Administration (ROC) 116
coast guards 41
Commission on the Limits of the Continental Shelf (CLCS) 1–2, 9, 12, 39, 56, 147; Brunei's Preliminary Information submission 15–17; exchange of letters (Brunei and Malaysia) 17; Malaysia and Vietnam joint submission 2, 64, 72, 157; Philippine legislation 4; PRC submission 2, 21–2, 165; PRC submission map 2–4, **3**; ROC on outer limits of 64; ROC ratification 57–8; ROC statement on Malaysia and Vietnam's submission 4; submissions to 2–4, 21–2, *21*, 156–8; Vietnam's submission 22
common ecosystem heritage 9
confidence-building activities 116
conflict management *see* Workshop on Managing Potential Conflicts in the South China Sea (SCS Workshop)
conservation *see* marine environmental protection
Convention on Biological Diversity (CBD) 88, 90, 113

INDEX

Convention on Conservation of Migratory Species of Wild Animals 95, 96, 102
Convention on International Trade in Endangered Species of Wild Fauna and Flora (CITES) 90, 95
Cooperation Afloat Readiness and Training (CARAT) 81
Coordinating Body of the Seas of East Asia (COBSEA) 96, 144
Coral Triangle Initiative 88, 114–15

Dai Bingguo 160
Declaration on Conduct of Parties in South China Sea 1, 73, 92, 102, 155; ASEAN-PRC joint implementation working group 163, 164; guidelines for implementation 166–7a; implementation 162–4
defence spending: PRC and India 39; Southeast Asian States 38
Djalal, Dr H. 73, 77
Dutton, P. 72
Dyke, J.M., van: Ludwig, N.A. and Valencia, Mark J. 115; and Valencia, Mark J. 115

East Asia Seas 142; Action Plan 143–4; Programme (EAP) 96, 142, **143**
Economic Commission for Latin America (ECLA) 131
El Niño 113
Emory Report 57
Energy Futures in Asia (Booz, Allen and Hamilton) 40
exclusive economic zone (EEZ) 14, 32a, 33a; international accepted regime 25; marine scientific research 47; military operations 44–9; overlap ROC and Philippines 57; PRC law 72; ROC 200-nautical-mile zone 56; ROC claim 58–9; territorial sea rights 46; waters as high seas 45
ExxonMobil 71

fish stocks 96, 142
fisheries management organizations 125; Asia-Pacific Fishery Commission (APFIC) 141–2; Caribbean Regional Fisheries Mechanism (CRFM) 129–31, **131**; CARICOM Fisheries Resources Assessment and Management Programme (CFRAMP) 129; General Fisheries Commission for the Mediterranean (GFCM) 124–5; regional fisheries management organization (RFMO) 97, 131, 139; Western and Central Pacific Fisheries Commission (WCPFC) 142; Wider Caribbean **140**
food production 89
freedom of navigation 31a

Freedomland 60
Fu Chün 139

gas: and oil deposits 15
General Fisheries Commission for the Mediterranean (GFCM) 124–5
Gibraltar, Strait 123
Global International Waters Assessment (GIWA) 99, 113

Hague Conference on Codification of International Law (1930) 55
Hainan Island: US electronic intelligence-gathering aircraft 45; Yulin naval base 43
Han Xudong (Major General) 160
Hodgson, R.D. 19; and Smith, R.W. 19, 20
Hu Nien-Tsu 8
Hulm, P. 135
Huangyan Dao 63
hydrocarbon resources 15, 39, 57, 115

Impeccable, USNS 33a, 46, 47, 48, 72
Indonesian Department of Foreign Affairs: SCS Workshops 70
Intergovernmental Meetings 127, 131
Intergovernmental Panel on Climate Change (IPCC) 87–8
International Conference on Issues in the South China Sea (20090 2
International Convention for Prevention of Pollution from Ships (MARPOL) 9, 100–1, 137
International Court of Justice (ICJ) 13
International Hydrographic Organization (IHO) 36
International Maritime Organization (IMO) 89
International Union for the Conservation of Nature (IUCN) 113, 115
Itu Aba Island 1, 20, 60, 111, 156; airstrip construction by ROC 63; migratory birds 112; peace park 79; terrestrial vegetation 111

Japan Coast Guard 49
John S McCain, USS 48

Kalayaan claim line 22, **23**, 24
Kalayaan Island Group 4, 159, 164, 165
Kuala Lumpur Security Review 160
Kuangtung Provincial Government 5

land territories (surrounding SCS) 13
Large Marine Ecosystem (LME) 9, 88, 114
Law of the Sea (LOS Convention, 1982) 12, 15, 17–18, *17*, 32a, 33a, 123–4; Article (8) 65; Article (58) 45; Article (76) 30a, 31a; Article (121) 18–20, 20–1, 66; Article (123)

INDEX

see semi-enclosed seas (Article 122 and 123 LOS); Article (301) 47; cannot sustain human habitation or economic life 19, 20; fish stocks 96; Informal Single Negotiating Text 19; International Law Commission Draft Articles (1956) 57; and island sovereignty disputes 18; man-made structures 21; Meeting of State Parties (2009) 20; military intelligence-gathering activities 47; military operations in EEZ 44; party nations 24; peaceful uses of the seas 46; rock as a form of an island 19–20, 158, 165; Rules of Procedure 157; Third United Nations Conference 24, 73; U.S. protest 24
Leifer, M. 35–6
L'Esperance Rock 20
Li Zhang (General) 72
lighthouse (habitation and economic life) 19
Lin Szu-yin: McManus, J.W. and Shao Kwang-Tsao 7
Los Angeles Times 14
Ludwig, N.A.: Valencia, M.J. and van Dyke, J.M. 115

Ma Ying-jeou (President of Taiwan) 79, 116
Macclesfield Islands 4, 30a
McDorman, Ted L. 74–6
McManus, J.W. 112, 116; Shao Kwang-Tsao and Lin Szu-yin 7
Malacca Strait 37, 38
Malaysia 22; continental shelf claim 24–5
Man and the Biosphere (MAB) Programme 95
Map of the Location of the South China Sea Islands 60, **61**, 64–5, 141
Marciel, S. (Ambassador) 26; Senate Foreign Relations Committee 31–4a
marine environmental protection: assessment 101–3; Caribbean Sea region 131–4; conservation framework and actions 90–9; global framework 90–6; losses to costal and marine ecosystems 88; marine ecosystems and related knowledge 89–90; Mediterranean Sea region 125–9; pollution from land-based activities 89–90; regional framework 96–7; regional Memorandum of Understanding (MOU) 102; SCS costal state ratification or accession *91*
marine jurisdiction (of a country) 20
Marine Protected Areas (MPAs) 9, 88; additional international protection 100–1; ecosystem-based management 99; establishing 7; national action 97–9; practice in Philippines 98; Spratly Islands 113–14; World Database 97, *98*, 99
maritime boundary: defined by treaty 15

maritime delimitation: allocation lines 22–4; archipelagic straight baselines **23**; geographical scope 13–17; solutions 5
Maro Reef 20
media reporting 12
Mediterranean Marine Protected Areas **136**
Mediterranean Sea **124**
Mediterranean Sea region (Article 123 LOS): draft legal instruments 126–7; integrated development 126; management of marine living resources 123–5; marine environment protection 125–9; marine pollution problems 125–6; Plenipotentiary Conference 127, 128
merchant fleet tonnage 37
Military Maritime Consultative Agreement (1998) 48
military operations: exclusive economic zone (EEZ) 44–9
Millennium Development Goals 88
Miller, M.A.L. 137, 147
Mischief Reef 40

Nansha Islands *see* Spratly Islands
National Oceanic and Atmospheric Administration (NOAA) 114
naval modernization: aircraft carriers 42; amphibious ships 42; antiship cruise missiles 42; Australia 42; characteristics 41–4; drivers 39–41; helicopter carriers 42; land-attack cruise missiles (LACMs) 42; PRC 42–3; submarines 3, 41–2, 43
navigation rights 48
Negroponte, J. (Deputy Secretary of State) 32a
New York Times 160
newspaper headlines 12
Ng, P.K.L.: and Tan, K.S. 90
North Sea Continental Shelf Cases (ICJ) 13
Oceans and Seas, Limits of (IHO) 36

oil 37; and gas deposits 15; spill protocol (Cartagena Convention) 137; supplies (PRC) 40
oil companies 15; state-owned 163
Okinotorishima Atoll (Japan) 20, 21
Operation Enduring Freedom 38

Pagasa Island: Philippines' attempt to populate 14
Paracel Islands 4, 13, 22, 26, 30a, 159; tourist tours to Phu Lam Island 72, 73
Paris Treaty (1898) 17, **23**, 24
Particularly Sensitive Sea Areas (PSSAs) 9, 100; designated sites to date 101; strategic designation 101
Partnership in Environmental Management for Seas of East Asia (PEMSEA) 144

INDEX

Peace Treaty: between ROC and Japan (1952) 60
peaceful settlement (assessment) 5–9
People's Liberation Army (PLA) 40; Navy submarines 43; Zhanjiang naval base 43
People's Republic of China (PRC): aircraft carriers 43; assertiveness at sea 47; China-ASEAN Summit 164; China-Vietnam maritime boundary **16**; cooperative initiative 164; Core Interest 160–1, 166; Defence Ministry 46; geopolitical competition 49; historic claim line 22; jurisdiction claim of most of SCS 48; LOS Article 121 paragraph (3) 21; naval modernization 42–3; oil supplies 40; response to US military operations 44–9; South Sea Fleet's 9th Destroyer Flotilla 43; sovereignty over islands 2; string of pearls 40; submission to CLCS map 2–4, **3**; territorial negotiation with ASEAN 73; territorial waters 46; *Yuzheng 311* (fishery patrol ship) 71
Philippines 22–4; Congress 18; MPA practice 98; Republic Act No. 9522 (archipelagic baselines) 4, 17, 56; territorial sea law 24; treaty limits 22, **23**
Philippines-Vietnam joint research program 114
Pratas Islands 4, 30a; Taiwanese National Marine Park 112

Raffles Bulletin of Zoology 113
Rahman, C.: and Tsamenyi, M. 8
Ramsar: Convention 92; sites of SCS states 93–4
Red Sea Marine Peace Park 115
regional fisheries management organization (RFMO) 97, 131, 139
regional joint programs 114–15
Regional Seas Action Plan 135
Regional Seas Programmes (RSPs) 126; common elements Mediterranean and Caribbean Sea regions 134–5; organizational chart 138, **138**
Republic of China (ROC): claims and state practice 60–4; Coast Guard Administration 116; continental shelf claim 57–8; Department of Navy 54–5; diplomatic channel problem 7; diplomatic relations 55; Dongsha Marine National Park 100; Executive Yuan 55, 56, 57–8, 60, 62, 65, 77; fishing fleet protection 59; government's territorial claims 5; Law on Territorial Sea and Contiguous Zone 60; maritime zone laws and regulations 59–60; Ministry of Foreign Affairs (MOFA) 62, 63–4; National Security Council 78; Nationalist Party (KMT) 80; outer limits of its continental shelf declaration (2009) 30–1a; Policy Guidelines for South China Sea 62, 77–8; policy and participation in SCS Workshops 77–80; Presidential Decree (1979) 56–7; statement to CLCS on Malaysia and Vietnam's submission 4; Taiwan Fisheries Research Institute 113; Taiwan Strait 4; territorial sea claim 54–7; U-shaped lines and policy implications 64–6
Republic of the Philippines *see* Philippines
rivalry (religion and ethnic factors) 41
Rockall 20

St Peter and St Paul's Rocks 20
sea lines of communication (SLOC) 8, 35, 37–8
sea-lanes 37–8; East Asian 40
seaborne trade route 36
seafood 39, *see also* fish stocks
security and naval issues 35–53; choke points 36–7; strategic geography 36–8
semi-enclosed seas (Article 122 and 123 LOS) 8, 91–2; application to SCS 139–41; definition and requirements 122–3; future cooperation 144–7; intraregional mechanisms 122–3; lessons from Mediterranean and Caribbean Sea regions 134–9; management of marine living resources 141–2; marine environment protection 142–4; marine space perspective 122; regional cooperation mechanisms 144, *145*, *146*; *see also* Caribbean Sea region (Article 123 LOS); Mediterranean Sea region (Article 123 LOS)
Senate Foreign Relations Committee: Scott Marciel (Ambassador) 31–4a
Senkaku Islands 33a
Shantung Province: Japanese fishing boats 55, 59
Shao Kwang-Tsao: Lin Szu-yin and McManus, J.W. 7
Sheehy, B. 137–8
Shisha Islands *see* Paracel Islands
Smith, R.W. 5; and Hodgson, R.D. 19, 20
South China Sea Coastal States 17
South East Asia Network for Education and Training (SEA-NET) 71, 80
South East Asia Ocean Network for Education (SEAONE) 79
Spratly Initiative 78
Spratly Islands 13, 21, 22, 30a, 39, 159; average annual temperature 111; double speed-up 161; ecological research 117; ecological significance 111–13; geographical features and legal aspects 110–11; international Marine Peace Park 7,

INDEX

79, 115–17; Malaysian occupation and ROC's protest 62–3; retroceded to ROC (1946) 60; ROC claim 62, 78; ROC's role in peace park plan 116–17; sovereignty disputes 4, 18, 72, 74; Swallow Reef 63, 71; threats (types and severity) 113
Strait of Gibraltar 123
Strategic Action programme for South China Sea (SAP) 96
submarine fleets 41–2, 43; China 43; Malaysia 42; Singapore 42; Vietnam 42

Tai-Ping *see* Itu Aba Island
Taiwan *see* Republic of China (ROC)
Taiwan Fisheries Research Institute 113
Taiwan Strait 4
Tan, K.S.: and Ng, P.K.L. 90
territorial waters: breadth 55, 56, 65, 159; claims 32a; ROC 59
Thitu Island 20
Tiao-Yu-Tai Islands 58
tidal datum 13
Tonkin, Gulf 25, 36; delimited zone 15
Townsend-Gault, I. 74, 77
Truman Proclamations (1945) 55, 57
Tsamenyi, M.: and Rahman, C. 8
Tungsha Islands *see* Pratas Islands

U-shaped lines 5–7, **6**, 141; and improved cross-strait relations 4–5; median line principle 65; and policy implications ROC 64–6
UNESCO 95
United Nations (UN) *see* Commission on the Limits of the Continental Shelf (CLCS); Law of the Sea (LOS Convention)
United Nations Environmental Programme (UNEP) 89, 113, 114, 131; Regional Seas Programme 134–9, **143**
United States of America (USA): Department of State's map of SCS 13–14, **14**; Director of National Intelligence 47; hands-off policy 161–2; incidents-at-sea agreement 48; interest and views (SCS) 26; Senate Committee of Foreign Relations hearing (Dutton) 72; Treaty of Amity and Cooperation in Southeast Asia 81
US Armed Forces 31a; military operations and China's response 44–9; Operation Enduring Freedom 38

US Navy 49; electronic intelligence-gathering aircraft 45; *Impeccable,* USNS 33a, 46, 47, 48, 72; *John S. McCain*, USS 48; *Victorious*, USNS 47
US Pacific Command 38

Valencia, M.J. 76; and van Dyke, J.M. 115; van Dyke, J.M. and Ludwig, N.A. 115
Vietnam: naval base at Cam Ranh Bay 162

Wang Kuan-Hsiung 7
Washington Post 162
Waterton-Glacier International Peace Park 115
Webb, J. (Senator) 162
Wen Jiabao (Premier of China) 164
Western and Central Pacific Fisheries Commission (WCPFC) 142
wildlife conservations 95–6
Workshop on Managing Potential Conflicts in South China Sea (SCS Workshops) 7, 114; basic objectives 73; Canadian funds 74; Indonesian Department of Foreign Affairs 70; informal basis of meetings 74; meetings held / activities *75–6*; One-China principle 79, 80; process and its achievements 73–7; rising tensions 71–3; ROC's policy and participation 77–80; Taiwanese and Chinese participants 80; Technical Working Group (TWG) 71
World Conservation Union (IUCN) 90
World Heritage Convention 92–5
World Heritage List 95
World Parks Congress, Fifth (2003) 88
Wu Zhuang 71
Wyrtki, K. 112

Yu Kuan-Tss 139
Yulin naval base (Hainan Island) 43
Yuzheng 311 (Chinese fishery patrol ship) 71

Zhang Zhaozhong (Rear Admiral) 43–4